Richar

Bonne Chance!

Building a Life in Rural France

by the author of Bon Courage!

BONNE CHANCE!

Summersdale Publishers Ltd
46 West Street
Chichester
West Sussex
PO19 1RP
UK

www.summersdale.com

Printed and bound in Great Britain

Dedicated to my children for the missed years

Contents

Acknowledgements

Special thanks to Summersdale Publishing for giving me the opportunity to write this sequel to *Bon Courage!* and for Jennifer Barclay's invaluable guidance in honing the text. Heartfelt thanks are due to Bernard Morestin for introducing me to the charming world of llamas, and to my brother Phill and sister-in-law Stephanie, always there to bail me out and dust me off. Fond thoughts for their friendship go out to Jill and Jean-Michel, David and Dennie, Claude and Martine, Harry and Sue, Keith and Peta, David, Lynda and Dawn, the inimitable Patrick, and not forgetting the ebullient Jazz. Many thanks to Zsuzsa Szentes for scanning my illustrations. *Merci bien* to all the French characters I have encountered, for their invaluable advice and inspiration. You have all provided the rich fodder for this tale. My gratitude is also due to Al for her insistence that I should tell it like it is. Posthumous thanks to the Montgolfier brothers for inventing the hot-air balloon; without you my feet would ever have been rooted to the ground!

'Un clou chasse l'autre'
One nail chases the other

Talisman plots his escape

Prologue

First catch your llama

The llama regarded me with a certain degree of unwarranted suspicion from the corner of the corral into which I had managed to cajole him. The placid, mirror-like orbs of his big chestnut eyes, framed by long, curling and sensuous lashes, were unblinking. But I knew that this particular *petite camelide* was plotting his escape route already. Talisman's downy felt nose twitched as he sniffed the fresh morning air. His pouting upper lip parted down the centre to reveal a pair of long, yellowish incisors that protruded from his lower jaw, and the bony gum of his upper jaw. His long, banana-shaped ears were cocked forwards as he listened intently to my inane cooing '*bon lama, bon lama*'. But the animal's body language told me that he was poised to spring off at a moment's notice. My attempts to capture the beast had so far been thwarted by his nimbleness and he had wrong-footed me several times. Undeterred, I crept forward, arms outstretched, a head collar in my right hand attached to a lead rope, the other end of which I grasped in my left hand.

'You 'ave to show 'im who ees boss, Richard,' I recalled the wise advice of my llama mentor, Bernard Morestin, who had coached me in the fine art of capturing a llama in an open field. The Frenchman had made it look so easy. The reality was another kettle of fish. 'Remember, you are the leader of the 'erd.' Bernard had intoned his mantra. 'Once you get the lead rope around 'is neck, the llama 'e will become submissive and you can slip the halter on 'im, *pas de problème*.'

My wife Al stood behind me, arms outstretched, ready to deflect my adversary, should he daintily nip to one side again and evade me. I had to admit that Al certainly looked the part. Clad in jeans with deep turn-ups, cuban-heeled cowboy boots, checked shirt, neckerchief and Stetson, she was every bit the wrangler. By contrast, my knee-length khaki shorts, white T-shirt bearing the faded logo of the Hastings Half-Marathon, circa 1995, flip-flops and back-to-front baseball cap were perhaps less practical attire for rounding up livestock. However, the fleeting thought crossed my mind as to why my wife had of late taken to dressing as a cowpoke.

Snapped from my idle reverie to the stark reality of catching a llama, I wondered what the animal's gripe could be, anyway. Why was he so mistrusting? Thousands of years of selective breeding by enterprising Incas had produced the 'domesticated' species of llama, after all, and to me the word domesticated was synonymous with 'tame'. So why was this mutinous mammal so keen to remain at large? All I wanted to do was slip the halter on, tie him to the fence and try my hand at grooming his lustrous fibre. Llama fleece can be woven into wonderfully soft items of clothing, or used to stuff pillows, and I harboured romantic notions of gathering sufficient fibre to spin into sumptuous skeins of lanolin-free wool and knitting fetching south American-style hats, mittens and scarves: just the job when the winter winds of France's Limousin region bite the skin.

Jazz, our young boxer pup, was crouched on the other side of the corral fence, backside and docked tail pointing skywards. Jowls splayed out on the grass, he peered through the chicken wire beneath the lower rail with restrained interest. He knew better than to enter the corral.

'Llamas detest *les chiens*,' Swami Bernard had forewarned. 'If they catch 'im, they will 'ave 'is guts for the gaiter!' Young llamas such as these would be just starting to grow their fighting teeth, the sharp fangs which were used for the rather unsavoury act of castrating rival males. In Jazz's youthful exuberance he had initially attempted to cavort with the two gentle-looking creatures, but he had been singularly dissuaded from this foolhardy action on being chased at breakneck speed around the paddock, with a pair of rampant llamas snapping at his youthfully exposed genitals. A few well-landed back kicks had finally convinced the playful pup that keeping his distance was perhaps his wisest move.

Somewhere behind me across the lane that fronted our property, a door creaked open. I glanced around to see the rotund figure of Madame Véronique Desveaux, our next-door neighbour, emerge in her doorway. The elderly lady, grey hair cut short and shaved at the nape of the neck like a man's, as usual wore her rather grubby blue and white checked housecoat. Thick, varicose vein-compressing stockings hung wrinkled around her calves. Her face was bathed in beads of perspiration due to the fact that, even during the hottest weather, she was apt to swelter in her kitchen, windows firmly closed, with the wood-burning *cuisinière* smouldering at her back. Véronique began to cough loudly in her time-honoured way of announcing her presence. She removed her big, horn-rimmed spectacles and polished the perennially smeary lenses, then popped them back on her nose. Folding her arms over her matronly bosom, she propped herself up on the gnarled tree branch she used as a walking stick and prepared to watch the circus animals perform.

'*Bon courage*, Monsieur Richard!' she croaked.

'Great,' I thought. 'All I need is an audience!'

Just then another llama's head appeared at the opening to the stable, where the second of my pair of newly-acquired llamas had been rolling in the bedding, judging by the many strands of straw that clung to his dark brown fleece. The beast looked a mess. If ever a llama needed grooming to remove the tangle of brambles that clung to its coat, this was a prime candidate. But my attentions were on what I regarded as easier pickings. The loutish Thursday, runt of the litter, who had arrived at the farm as Talisman's companion, trotted daintily into the corral, his head bobbing backwards and forwards with each stride. The cantankerous animal had decided that if attention was being doled out, he would certainly have some. The crunchy sheep pellets that filled the pockets of my shorts, no doubt discerned by his finely-tuned nostrils, could have been a contributing factor. Llamas are greedy for these tasty treats, which – Bernard had advised me – are best kept as training incentives. However, Talisman, who seemed graced with higher intelligence, had steadfastly refused to accept any.

'Sod off, Thursday,' I muttered out of the corner of my mouth. But the scruffy beast strode purposefully towards his companion, ears flattened back against his head. I edged closer and, while Talisman's attention was momentarily distracted by Thursday's approach, reached forward and slipped the halter around the base of his long neck, then grasped it in my other hand. Success! I had caught my first llama. And, true to Bernard's words, the beast had immediately become placid and submissive. He emitted a low, throaty *hmmm* and his big ears flattened back against his head. I was flushed with pride and turned briefly and nodded to my admiring onlookers.

'*Bravo*, Monsieur Richard!' called Véronique from the doorway.

'Well done, Rich!' encouraged Al. I shrugged gallicly. It was, after all, a mere bagatelle!

Carefully, I encircled Talisman's neck with my arm, close to the base of his skull and raised the halter, then slipped the noseband over his long snout. I was in the process of buckling up the crown of the halter behind the llama's ears when the beastly Thursday stretched out his sinewy neck and launched a great gobbet of spit and partially chewed cud squarely into the face of his companion. Not unnaturally, my captive took exception to this insult and promptly spat back.

'The llama, 'e never spit at a person,' wise old Bernard had once told me. But, as I discovered, the hapless human could easily be hit in the crossfire. In the next few moments there followed a rapid-fire spit-fest in which I became the unintentional victim. I felt like a medieval miscreant pelted with rotten eggs and over-ripe vegetables by the populace, while pinioned in the stocks. Llamas tend to spit at each other when trying to establish a pecking order within the herd or, as females, to fend off unwanted male attention. Two llamas did not constitute much of a herd, it's true, but in Thursday's case, he wanted to discourage any sign of perceived favouritism from his human keeper, while at the same shunning capture himself. My initial attempts at capturing a llama had begun earlier that morning with this smaller animal, but he had evaded me with ease, stomping his feet madly like a child in a tantrum then bucking off across the corral. I rather wished he'd buck off right now.

While Talisman – a sturdy two-year-old – was stockier and at five feet to the withers, a foot taller than the scrawny, eighteen-month-old Thursday, he had a somewhat laid-back demeanour. This character trait did him no favours in a herd mentality. It made him a prime target for the bullying tactics of his stable-mate. As spumes of saliva exploded around me, I could sense that poor, downtrodden Talisman was clearly no match for the violently gobbing Thursday. He soon felt that enough was quite enough. Momentarily considering the options of 'fight or flight', the animal chose the latter and immediately began bounding across the corral, while I clung onto his neck for dear life. Despite being tossed around like a rag doll, I was not going to give up my catch that easily. I suddenly found myself flung onto the animal's bony back like a cowboy in a rodeo. My flip-flops flipped off. One does not ride a llama: they are not built to carry a mount. Now I knew why.

'Yee-haa!' I heard Al call out, rather inappropriately, I felt. 'Ride him cowboy!' Talisman performed an outrageous buck, which dislodged me from my perch. Still clinging on to his halter, I slithered to the underside of his long neck, my bare feet dragging along the ground between his front legs. My legs became entangled in the lead rope, but still I maintained my grip on his neck.

The excitement proved too much for a rowdy boxer and Jazz slithered under the gate and began to chase after the llama, barking loudly. Now Thursday joined in the fun, tearing around the corral and launching well-aimed back-kicks at the dog. The corral became like a greyhound racetrack as both llamas hared around the perimeter in hot pursuit of the floppy-eared canine. Jazz realised the error of his involvement in the *mêlée* and shot under the gate again. He now tore back and forth along the fence line, barking madly and goading the llamas. Both llamas started to screech loudly in competition. It was a blood-curdling sound reminiscent of the extra-terrestrial predator *Alien*, which sprang from the warped mind of surrealist HR Giger and the stomach of poor John Hurt in the film of the same name.

Thanks to some deft footwork, llamas are skilled in the art of vertical take off. This dainty 'sproinging' action, which Bernard preferred to poetically describe as a 'leap dance', was utterly charming to behold on a warm summer evening as the creatures frolicked in their field. But to me – locked in an ill-advised embrace around Talisman's neck – it was more like the gut-in-the-mouth sensation of a bungee-jump. Suddenly, my tenuous grip was lost and I found myself dumped unceremoniously within the midden that was the llamas' communal toilet. Llama dung is, under normal circumstances, composed of small, firm, round pellets that exude a not unpleasant aroma. But, although my friend the Frenchman had boasted about the animals' versatility and love of travel, and his claim of cramming a fully-grown llama into a Renault Five without difficulty, I sensed that the animals had not travelled well in the tiny, rattling tin trailer during the hour-long drive from his farm south of Limoges. Since their arrival on the occasion of my fiftieth birthday party the previous week, the llamas had been stricken with a severe bout of traveller's tummy. I clambered to my feet, dripping with foul-smelling green filth. The slime was oozing between my bare toes most unpleasantly. My shirt and shorts were so spattered with shite that they resembled jungle camouflage fatigues. Jazz, who had developed a gourmet taste for llama dung, crept into the corral again and promptly rolled in the dreadful excrement, no doubt copying my actions as his father figure.

The llamas, having ceased sproinging, simply gazed at me for a few moments with rather superior expressions on their long faces, then, quite unperturbed lowered their long necks and recommenced munching the juicy green grass. The cud-chewers had won the first round.

Véronique, who had shambled over to the fence for a closer look at the action, murmured a consoling '*Ooh, la la la la…*' Watching in safety from the perimeter of the communal dung heap, Al could hardly suppress her mirth at my misfortune.

Clearly, raising llamas was not going to be a doddle.

Milliaire, St. Léger Magnazeix

Chapter One

Cops and robbers

How I became a budding llama farmer in the rural backwater deep within the agricultural heartland of central France's Limousin region is probably due to an impulsive urge that has ruled, or should I say dogged my existence. It is true to say that Al and I had been wholly unprepared for our relocation from England to the tiny hamlet of Le Mas Mauvis in the Haute-Vienne *département*. With the same dash of romanticism that had been responsible for us purchasing the run-down, thirteen-acre farm some five years previously, we had carefully weighed our options and decided to go with what would be regarded in most camps as the least practical one. Although Al shared some of my madder aspirations, we had chosen to purchase a property in France for many of the same reasons that thousands of like-minded Britons swarm into this huge, beautiful and welcoming country each year. We wanted to grab a large, juicy portion of what we perceived to be a better quality of life than we could achieve in our homeland. Despite some furious back-pedalling I was incontrovertibly approaching my half-century on earth and was intent on cranking down several gears and concentrating on *la vie* rather than merely *l'existence*.

Research had revealed to us that France offered a plethora of properties at affordable prices. The country, then, became our route to a new and fascinating life. The pair of us, finding ourselves in the middle of France on what was intended to be a purely investigative, fact-finding mission, had been immediately smitten by the dubious charms of a ramshackle collection of farm buildings, a pair of tumble-down, uninhabitable cottages and thirteen acres of exhausted pasture and choked woodland. Centrepiece of the complex, the massive *grange*, a stone-built barn with a vast, church-like interior and a vaulted oak ceiling six metres high, was to be an open-plan living space streaming with light and fresh air, commanding magnificent views over open countryside. If we could envisage the pitfalls of such a spontaneous purchase, we chose to ignore them. The farm, we reasoned, would become our oasis. Surrounding our oasis were fields of maize, sunflowers and *blé noir*, source of the Sarrasin flour from which savoury *galettes* and cakes are made. In green pastures roamed flocks of sheep or herds of tan limousine cattle, and the countryside was dotted with quaint hamlets, placid lakes, historical remnants from prehistory, charming neighbours and exciting new horizons.

At that time the number of British television programmes charting the adventures and misadventures of Britons choosing to move abroad had begun to reach saturation point. These programmes and the many niche magazines that espoused the joys of French life had begun to tout Limousin as the next major destination in France for those wishing to buy a holiday or a retirement home. Budget airlines made it simple, quick and cheap for thousands to flock to the country in search of bargain properties. Limousin was lucky enough to be served by an international airport at Limoges, its adminstrative capital. This modest single runway offered daily flights from London, Southampton, the East Midlands and Liverpool, in addition to other major European cities and connections to Paris. Airports at Poitiers and La Rochelle on the western coast – both in the neighbouring Poitou-Charentes region – made Limousin even more accessible. Even Bergerac airport in Aquitaine was only a few hours' drive from Limousin's southern border.

The Limousin region is made up of three *départements*, the Creuse in the north-east, the Haute-Vienne in the north-west and the Corrèze in the south. It borders the northern Centre region, the eastern Auvergne, the western Poitou-Charentes and Aquitaine, with the Midi-Pyrénées in the south. It is largely an unspoilt haven, a land of lush, low-lying pastures and table lands on which cattle and sheep contentedly graze. One of the most spectacular is the *Plateau de Millevaches* in the Corrèze. Not as one might imagine from its name, home to one thousand cows – the name is a derivation of 'melo', meaning a high place, and 'vacua', empty – the plateau is a vast, undulating upland with stunning views. Set at an altitude of nine hundred metres on the northern edge of the Massif Centrale mountains, the landscape is sparsely populated. Houses, where they exist, are austere, stone buildings. This is a land of beech and chestnut woodland and *étangs*, ponds fringed with reeds.

The region is criss-crossed with many rivers that are well stocked with fish, making it a lure for rodsmen, particularly from fishing-crazy England. Carp fishing, watersports and boat trips are catered for on the numerous man-made lakes that are spread around the region. Grandest of these is Lac de Vassivière, constructed in the 1950s and covering an area of more than one thousand hectares. One of the largest lakes in Europe, it is also a site for art buffs, since its island features a centre for contemporary art, designed by the Italian architect Aldo Rossi.

The Limousin is also a land beloved of walkers and nature lovers, while cyclists adore its frequently poker-straight and largely traffic-free network of roads. Mountain-bikers thrill to its many challenging off-road trails. Within the region, the terrain of the Haute-Vienne is predominantly quite flat, although in places gently rolling and dotted with many beautiful lakes and thousands of trees, mainly majestic oaks. But to my mind there was little infrastructure in place to support a burgeoning tourism industry. The *département* had not generally been regarded as the destination for masses of holidaymakers simply because it was predominantly agricultural land. Restaurants and bars might well offer regional, well-cooked and often inexpensive dishes but their interiors were frequently plain and drab or, where some effort has been made to add a touch of character, appeared unattractively kitsch. All this was fine for Al and me, for we looked forward to the prospect of becoming hermits together, content with each other's company in our own home. We relished the thought of entertaining our friends with home-cooked meals rather than painting the town red.

It is the choice of many Britons who *déménagent* to France to create for themselves a buffer of ex-pat enclaves, in which thoroughly British foods such as Heinz baked beans, Chicken Tikka Masala and Marmite are imported and consumed with relish, where British satellite television is viewed, and where English is the predominantly spoken tongue. This was not my choice. The thought of creating a 'little Britain' in France was abhorrent to me. As a lover of some of these typically English delicacies, nevertheless, I could well appreciate how many folk might suffer the deprivation of such produce. But on balance I knew that I could survive without it. Provided, of course, that I had an ample supply of strong, flavoursome Yorkshire Tea (for I found the teas commonly available in France to be weak and insipid). A case of double standards, perhaps, but there were just some luxuries that even I was not prepared to forgo!

In broader terms, for Al and me the move to France also gave us an opportunity to immerse ourselves in the richness of a foreign culture and the complexities and subtleties of its florid language. The French generally love foreigners to make a stab at their notoriously difficult language but it is sad that many Britons do not make any attempt whatsoever to learn even a modicum of the lingo. Many seem to be of the opinion that simply shouting in English will make the poor French girl on the supermarket till understand; others speak slowly and deliberately as if talking to a child. While Al was reasonably fluent in French, I had only begun to study the language on purchasing the property, having never learned even the basics at school. My single-minded perseverance with tutorial and tape – along with staunch support from my wife – had given me a good grasp of the language and I was soon able to converse with the natives, although falteringly, and discovered that I had a talent for reading and writing French with a good degree of accuracy.

It was hard, nonetheless, to face the prospect of turning our backs on certain ties in the UK. We were concerned that Al's elderly parents, who had recently suffered the premature loss of their eldest daughter, would now lose the proximity of their youngest child. The Doctor and his wife, however, were entirely supportive, virtually insisting that we leave the country. Both of my teenage children had sadly estranged themselves from me since their mother and I had divorced five years previously. I felt that my life was on hold, hoping that they would restore contact. But until that day arrived – if it ever did – there was, frankly, little left for me in England. Both of my parents were deceased, while my elder brother Phill (unofficially anointed with the title the Count) and his wife Stephanie also owned a property in the neighbouring Creuse *département*. They had every intention of moving permanently to France in the near future. It would be the first time in many years that my sibling and I would live close by, a prospect we both relished.

The repercussions of a bitter divorce, followed by an unexpected redundancy, had left me hard up and living in rented property with little opportunity to clamber back up the rungs of the UK house-owning ladder: if I worked hard and saved for several years I could, perhaps, buy a poky two-up, two-down house elbow-to-elbow with my neighbours on a cramped estate. The thought horrified me.

Al and I knew from bitter experience that despite the summers in Limousin being generally long, languid and at times extremely hot, the winters – although frequently short – were likely to be intensely cold. There was no way, we had solemnly promised each other, that we would ever endure an entire winter there while the uninsulated barn remained so exposed to the elements. This had been one of the main reasons why we had not planned to move definitively to France for another year. But we had not bargained for the intervention of unscrupulous thieves to sway our minds otherwise. We would even have cause to express our deep-felt thanks to those same *voleurs* for jump-starting our new life in our adopted country. We had arrived for a short spring holiday to discover the chain securing a downstairs shutter forced and the window beyond it smashed.

The thieves had, after forcing entry, free rein to rummage through our belongings undisturbed, opening the trunks in which we stored clothes, linen and personal effects. The hamlet was small and our property located in a quiet nook with only Véronique as our immediate neighbour. As the dear lady unfortunately suffered from poor health and had spent several periods in hospital since our last visit, the thieves could take their time without risk of discovery. They had obviously come with a clear idea of what items to search for, helping themselves to virtually all of our valuable tools – saws, hammers, power tools, chisels, screwdrivers – but leaving behind equipment they considered inferior quality, our stereo system, CD collection and electrical kitchen appliances. Perhaps it was the English plugs still attached to many of these appliances that had dissuaded them. 9/203767/.

'There's nothing a thief hates more than to have to change a plug before fencing his spoils,' I explained to my wife. Most of these items would no doubt find their way to the frequent

vide grenier bric-a-brac sales that were hosted by many of the communes in the region.

Before departing with their booty, the thieves had cheekily made themselves comfortable by lighting the wood-burning stove, drawing forward a few cosy armchairs and putting their feet up. Disturbingly, the imprints of their bodies in the dustsheets covering the chairs still remained. At first I was concerned that the stove's copper boiler had been fractured due to the fire and a lack of water in the system. I had drained down the plumbing system after our previous visit in preparation for the winter, when we would be back in England. But on closer investigation, we had been lucky in that respect; there appeared to be no damage.

It was not until I embarked upon the task of refilling the plumbing system and hot water cylinder – when I required certain spanners and other tools – that I was able to ascertain the full extent of the thievery. We immediately telephoned the local *gendarmerie* and explained our predicament. We were asked to touch nothing until officers arrived to investigate the crime. While awaiting their arrival, Al and I sauntered in despondent mood down the little leafy path that leads to the *étang*, the spring-fed pond we had lovingly dubbed the Ugly-Bugly five years earlier when we bought the property because of its resemblance to a rough quarry. Broom, brambles and self-seeded saplings had softened the overall effect in the intervening years and we agreed that it was no longer unsightly but a rather tranquil spot. However, there was a noticeable lack of the mounds of large, craggy, granite rocks that had previously surrounded the high banks of the pond. It appeared that not only had our house been robbed but also that someone had trespassed on our land with the sheer audacity to pilfer tonnes of our stone! Tractor and trailer tyre tracks in the sandy earth revealed the means by which the rocks must have been appropriated.

The *gendarmes* had arrived swiftly after our telephone call, their blue van with flashing light drawing several curious residents from their homes to witness this unusual event. Out of the van slid the tall, suave uniformed figure of officer Battisou and his shorter, stouter partner, officer Bezaud. Thorough to a fault, the officers carefully examined the scene of the break-in and even took photographs of the broken chain that once secured the shutter: it was first necessary for us to pose the chain and its padlock in its former position especially for the picture. There was much rubbing of lantern jaw lines as the inspectors inspected the broken window pane and fractured frame, conferring in rapid, indecipherable French before the short, stocky *gendarme* deduced proudly: 'Monsieur Wheels, we think the thieves entered here and that a *pied-de-biche* may well have been used to force entry to this window!' No kidding. These guys were hot! The telltale gouges on the wooden frame must have been a clue that a crowbar had been employed by the thieves.

Battisou retrieved a large, polished wooden suitcase from the van and opened it to reveal an impressive fingerprinting kit that contained cork-stoppered bottles of various fluids and jars of powders, brushes, rolls of adhesive tape and other diagnostic implements. He seemed overjoyed by the presence of literally hundreds of perfectly formed fingerprints that peppered the surface of the broken pane.

'Ah, Monsieur Wheels, I see the thieves have been careless here! Normally they would wear gloves and we would get nothing!' he announced. I felt honour bound to set the record straight by revealing that the 'dabs' in question were undoubtedly mine: glazing the window frame had been my last task during our previous visit and I had not yet had the opportunity to clean the glass after pressing the pane into its rebate. I was certain that my putty-smeared fingers were responsible for the prints. Unperturbed, the policeman shrugged in true gallic fashion before continuing with his mission, dusting the prints with powder applied by a long-bristled brush, then applying pieces of sticky tape to the whorls, peeling off the impressions and sticking them to a special sheet of paper attached to a clipboard. He then painstakingly labelled the prints in spidery handwriting.

In my downstairs workshop, the duo took photographs of the empty places where tools had once resided (I found myself wondering whether there were bulging, dusty albums full of such snapshots stored for posterity in the basement of the *gendarmerie*) and then followed us upstairs, where we showed them the stove and the revealing pile of ashes on the hearth. I indicated the dust-sheeted armchairs with perfectly formed bum-prints (would it be possible to catch a criminal by the distinctive shape of his *derrière*, I pondered?) and the various trunks which had been ransacked. The efficient Battisou used a huge magnifying glass to examine the candlesticks that had been arranged on top of one of the trunks, which he felt certain the thieves must have touched in order to gain access to the trunk. He inspected a particularly dusty coffee table top that was simply littered with fingerprints. Al and I were too embarrassed about our lack of a housekeeping regime to reveal that the table in question had been that way for some months, if not years. It wasn't easy to keep such a big room clean, we reasoned, particularly due to the constant renovation work. So we tended not to bother. Again, the dabs were probably ours.

Nevertheless, Battisou meticulously made impressions of what he regarded as a fine clutch of evidence.

When their work in the house had been completed we accompanied the officers along the path to show them where the missing stone had once been, and indicated the tyre tracks in the earth. The pair shook their heads and frowned.

'This is undoubtedly the work of different *voleurs*,' announced Battisou finally. 'I think you will find that a neighbour has helped himself to your stone in your absence, Monsieur and Madame Wheels.' Al and I exchanged shocked glances. A neighbour? Surely not! 'We will make some enquiries,' said the officer.

The *gendarmes*, having completed their investigation, departed, asking us to prepare for them a comprehensive list of all the items stolen, their make and their value, and to deliver it to the police station the following day. We would also be called upon to fill out an official statement. We were assured that rigorous investigations into the *cambriolage*, the break-in, would follow. Having compiled our list, we duly reported to the *gendarmerie* the following day to complete our statement. While waiting for our interview with Battisou, we studied the walls of the station's waiting room, which were hung with wanted posters depicting ruthless-looking, unshaven villains, which included a head-and-shoulders portrait of a particularly nasty-looking character: he was an extremely hirsute individual with mad, staring eyes and a pair of vicious-looking orange teeth. The coypu was thought to be responsible for damage to local riverbanks. I was convinced that I recognised this swarthy individual as being a resident of our own Ugly Bugly, but had to admit that perhaps one coypu looked much like another.

Battisou appeared and showed us into the rear office, where he seated us next to his computer and ran through the process of filling out a *Dépôt de Plainte*, or register of complaint against an *auteur inconnu*, or unknown person. Our copy of the official document assured us that, should any relevant evidence come to light in the course of investigations about our break-in, we would be informed immediately.

'We shall do our best, Madame, Monsieur,' said the officer, shaking our hands on showing us out of the office. 'Although in all honesty, I think it unlikely we will recover your possessions. As for the stone, I think there is nothing we can do, other than make enquiries. Perhaps, after all, it was a mistake... a neighbour who thought your land was communal?'

We had considered this possibility. Perhaps the stone theft had been a genuine error. Physical boundaries between rural properties are frequently quite indistinct, or even non-existent, with divisions nothing more than a ragged tree-line or even the rotting stumps of felled trees. Most of the fields and woodland that we owned were fenced with rickety, rotten posts and a few strands of rusty barbed wire, where any fencing still existed. In some places a fence had been swallowed entirely by a wayward line of hawthorn hedge that had not been maintained for a decade or more. The *chemin* that led past our barn had for generations been used by village women, in an era before the introduction of household appliances, to access the communal pond where they would wash their clothes. The large, flat stones against which they would beat their *lavage* still remained, although nowadays the pond was so clogged with malodorous silt from many years of fallen leaves that any clothes dunked in the green water would emerge filthier than when they went in. In days when the water was clearer, however, the pond had been the scene of vicious in-fighting between neighbours: formerly respectable wives, mothers and grandmothers removed their aprons and engaged in a frenzied and undignified bout of hair-pulling, should another person have the audacity to commandeer their washing stone. It was tough in the days before the top-loader.

The rough grassy pathway that led past this historic site of what could be described as *rage-à-lavage* was now flanked pond-side by a line of self-seeded saplings and on our side by an unruly tangle of brambles; it eventually merged imperceptibly into our land. Only the *cadastre*, the land registry maintained by the mayor's office – and the photocopied extract attached to the deeds of our property – revealed the precise legal division of the many odd-shaped and often minuscule *parcelles* that comprised our total acreage. According to Mâitre Marsolet, the lady notary who originally dealt with our purchase of the farm, breach of a person's *bornage* – the setting of boundaries – is one of the most common and serious causes of bitter dispute between neighbours.

In olden days *bornes* were not only markers used to define boundaries, but also served as important milestones along the thoroughfares that criss-crossed the country. They were generally carved stones and many boasted surprising longevity. A treasured *milliaire*, or milestone within our own commune had been discovered in St. Léger Magnazeix in 1847, when an ancient cemetery was removed during road building. The blue granite stone was thought to have once supported a cross – a common sight to this day on the sides of roads, marking routes once trudged by pilgrims – but had been broken at each end. All that remained was a cylindrical section about seventy centimetres long and sixty centimetres in diameter, which bore a perplexing, roughly carved inscription:

IMP. CAES
PIO. ESVV
TETRICO. PIO
AVG. CLL

Reconstruction by experts revealed that the words on the stone once read 'With the emperor Caesar (Caius) Pius Esuvius Treticus Pius (Felix) Auguste, City of Lémovices, Miles X'. The milestone had been created during the rule of the Roman Emperor Tétricus, between 268 and 273 AD at a period when the road between Argeton and Bordeaux passed to the east of St. Léger. Tétricus had been the governor of Aquitaine between 254 and 267 AD, and was later elected emperor of the region. The fourth line of the inscription is difficult to decipher but experts believe that it could reveal that the stone originally marked another, long-lost road between Limoges, Confolens and Bordeaux.

As illustrated by the aged milestone, *bornes* were made to endure. Nowadays, however, domestic boundary markers are commonly made of concrete, or take the form of metal or plastic pegs; rather like giant wall plugs, they are driven into the ground and incorporate wings that splay out and grip the earth, preventing their easy removal. Wilful removal of a *borne*, the position of which can only be set by a qualified *géomètre*, or surveyor, carries a hefty fine in France.

However, we reasoned, even if one of our neighbours had been innocently oblivious of our boundaries, would they have had the right to help themselves to what might have been regarded as communal stone?

Véronique, having returned to the fold from a brief spell in hospital, was truly distressed when we relayed to her the news of the break-in later that morning, sipping strong black coffee in the stifling heat of her kitchen. The three of us sat around her long table, sweating copiously. It was a warm day, but still our neighbour had insisted on lighting her wood-burning *cuisinière* and sitting closely adjacent to it. Shaking her grey head solemnly, she removed her spectacles and wiped the mist from the lenses onto a handkerchief. 'Oh, how terrible!' she moaned. 'And in our little village, too! The world is a terrible place! How dreadful for you!'

She was, however, unfazed by the revelation that tonnes of granite had been swiped from our land.

'Oh that!' she exclaimed. 'But I know who took your stone.'

'You know who took it?' reaffirmed Al. We leaned forward on our chairs, intrigued by this information.

'*Bien sûr!* Do I not sit here all day at my window? *Ecoutez*, I don't have many callers, as you know, apart from Madame Bussiere that is. So, naturally I see who comes and goes.'

'Who was it then?' I asked.

'Four trips they made.'

'But who was it?'

'Four full trailer loads of stone.'

'Yes, but who?'

'Your stone,' she stressed.

'Who?'

'Oh, Monsieur Richard, I couldn't say. I don't want to gossip.'

Véronique did not need to reveal the identity of the scurrilous stone thieves, as once the news of our burglary got out the hamlet became rife with speculation, accusations and counter-accusations. Not a lot happened in the little community, so any unusual event was likely to be inflated into a major scandal.

The *gendarmes* returned to the hamlet and systematically interviewed all the residents in the search for vital clues. They paid a special visit to the home of our neighbour, Monsieur Bruno Bussiere, a retired member of the *gendarmerie* himself: from our vantage point across the communal green, we had noticed Bruno making his own enquiries into the incident, notebook and pencil in hand. No doubt he had important information to impart to his colleagues. The fact that Bruno had been a cook in the police force rather than an investigating officer did not seem to matter.

Most of our neighbours expressed their sympathy at the break-in and the horrible feeling of defilement we must have felt. But the theft of our stone was somehow considered to be more intriguing. Bruno and his Polish-born wife Jolanta reckoned the culprits were a passing band of *romanichelles*, travelling folk out to make a quick centime. Others even pointed fingers at their fellow villagers (some of whom had been involved with building works on their property, where a bit of stone would come in quite handy). Other neighbours made light of the matter, saying that we must have been mistaken about the amount of stone we had: no one would bother to steal a load of old rocks; it wasn't worth anything. In truth, the stone might not have been worth much, but the fact was that it was ours and someone had pinched it! Furthermore, I had earmarked some of the huge boulders as decorative features in our future garden, while the smaller rocks would have made excellent garden walling material, or failing that, hardcore as a sub-base for concrete laying.

While all this gossip-mongering was sweeping like wildfire through the hamlet, Al and I – once we had recovered from the initial shock of the burglary – decided to simply sit back and watch. The probable identity of the stone thieves had been revealed to us by several sources but we had no intention of flinging accusations hither and thither without any concrete proof. They knew that we knew. We knew that they knew that we knew. And that was enough for us.

What the theft did bring to light, however, was a problem concerned with the fact that the property was a holiday home, and not our principal residence. This worrying fact was revealed to us by Madame Isabelle Rairat, the representative of our insurance company, when she came to survey the scene of the crime.

'You will no doubt have noticed that most homes have their windows and doors shuttered?' said Madame Rairat. This was true, for it was one of the main reasons that many of the villages in the vicinity appeared devoid of human life. 'But this is not merely because we French are intensely protective of our privacy,' continued Madame Rairat. 'This much is certainly true, madame and monsieur. But the reason is mainly because insurance companies insist that a property left unoccupied for more than sixty days a year is fitted with shutters bearing three-point security of a specific quality. You have no such security…'

'What does this mean for us, then?' queried Al. We could sense bad news was forthcoming.

'Madame, monsieur, it could be argued by the cynical that a shuttered house represents an open invitation to a prospective burglar. It generally means that the householder is absent. *Mais, tristement*, I am sorry but if a property is considered to be one's *résidence principale*, then shutters are not even a requirement and if you chose to fit them, are not obliged ever to shut them. But if it is your *résidence secondaire…*'

'We're not insured, are we?' I said, stating the obvious.

'*Non, monsieur*, I am afraid you are not. Not against your stolen goods.'

Although our barn boasted rustic oak shutters on the front façade, they bore no security locks, while the windows on the rear elevation had no shutters at all. As a holiday home, our property was wholly unprotected by insurance. As our main residence it would be fully covered. Al and I pondered our options and came to the momentous conclusion that we could not afford to leave the *grange* and its outbuildings so woefully unprotected any longer. Our only realistic option was to bring forward our plans, up sticks and move lock, stock and barrel to France.

As the lease on our Kent cottage still had some months to run, we agreed that Al would initially remain in the UK, while I would commute back and forth from France. The arrangement would mean that we would be forced to spend tracts of time apart. However, we had already coped with the prolonged periods of separation during stages of the renovation, and felt that we could survive until Al could join me at Le Mas Mauvis.

Al worked in the licensing department of an international company in the hectic music industry. She had been suffering a bout of ill health and when she was finally diagnosed as having a suspected ulcer – to all appearances provoked by an unreasonable overload of work and stressful working conditions – she was instructed by her doctor to take some time off. Her period of recuperation reinforced our wish to rid ourselves of such pointless yet harmful stresses and Al handed in her notice to quit, also citing our eventual relocation overseas. Once this decision had been made, her health began immediately to improve and I could see how happy she was in her unaccustomed role as homemaker. As the child of a 'horsey' family and herself a former professional equestrian, Al had toiled long and hard since her early teens, never really knowing a time when she did not have stables to muck out, horses to exercise, manes to plait, tack to clean and competitions to prepare for. Forsaking the highly competitive show jumping arena for the cut and thrust of the music industry, she had merely swapped one set of stresses for another. It was time to take a breather.

'Why don't you take a sabbatical,' I suggested spontaneously on one of my return trips to Kent, discovering Al happily weeding our little garden (although to my wife 'weeding' generally meant pulling up the perennial plants by the roots and leaving the weeds behind; this was, I felt, only a teething problem in her horticultural education). The idea of the sabbatical had not been an entirely selfless suggestion on my part, because the previous year Al had valiantly brought home the bacon for a period of six months, during which I took time off from bread-and-butter earning in order to write this tome's predecessor, *Bon Courage!*, the chronicles of our first years renovating the barn. It was only fair that I should support my wife now and allow her free time to enjoy her forthcoming new life in France.

After five years of roughing it in a tent pitched on the wooden upper floor of the huge stone-built *grange*, we had exported the bulk of our furniture to France in a temperamental horsebox masquerading as a removal van, leaving behind some scant possessions that would make Al's solitary existence more comfortable. With sad thoughts that an era of bold adventure had passed, we had packed the tent away for the final time, reminiscing about the numerous adhesive tape patches in the ground sheet that made good the gnawed holes, and the heady whiff of rodent droppings that clung to the grubby fabric. I was able to languish at night in a real bed, although woken frequently by dusty cobwebs plummeting from the dizzy six-metre-high, vaulted, oak-beamed ceiling onto my head.

My ability to relocate relied upon the fact that as a freelance writer and magazine editor I could, with the aid of a computer and an Internet connection, work from virtually anywhere. At that time I was involved with developing new magazines for the international market and the publisher for whom I worked could see no reason why my tentative suggestion of working on the same projects from France would be any different to the existing arrangement, whereby I worked from home in the Kent cottage we rented. Although involved in publishing, I rarely had the need to touch actual pieces of paper: all my work was in electronic form and once I had tweaked and fiddled with the on-screen magazine layouts, would simply zap them off down the telephone line. On the rare occasions I would need to attend meetings in London, I could fly back at my own expense in just a few hours. On alternate months my production schedules demanded that I arrange and supervise four-day photographic sessions in the central London studio owned by the publisher. As a result of the frequently cheap flights offered by the budget airline that ran daily flights to and from London and Limoges or Poitiers airports, I was able to depart from the *grange* at a reasonable hour in the morning and – leaving my car in the free airport car park (which, at Poitiers, was generally the skirt of the football pitch adjacent to the terminal) – fly to the UK, arriving in the studio at lunchtime. This was indeed fortuitous, since the long, liquid lunches I spent with my photographer friend, Mike Leale, had become legendary.

Attack of the lizard people

Chapter Two

Fire and rain

Wandhen I, as the advance party, arrived *définitivement* in our new home, France was simmering at the start of an unseasonably warm spring that was to come rapidly to a ferocious boil as one of the country's hottest summers since the 1950s. Even in April – a month that normally receives some ninety centimetres of rain – the grass pastures of the Haute-Vienne were already dry and yellowing as a drought took hold. Hosepipe restrictions were immediately put into place, with the *Mairie* – the mayor's office – in each commune posting advisory leaflets. Regular low-level flights by military aircraft pinpointed properties that boasted abnormally green lawns and illicit swimming pools, and suspected flouters of the water ban were then paid a visit by officials from the water authority.

The region's abundant and majestic oak trees, recently returned to foliage after the autumn leaf-fall, seemed pale and wan. Our hamlet's communal pond drained entirely of water and the little stream that led from it across our land, usually a gushing torrent, had dried up. By the month of June the entire country – along with the rest of Europe – was sweltering under a heatwave that sent temperatures soaring to over forty degrees Celsius.

Setting up my office was not as plain sailing as I had expected. The intense heat that was starting to bake the countryside to a crisp caused me – bathed in perspiration and dressed only in a pair of shorts – to wilt over my keyboard, while my poor computer was apt to lapse into the occasional coma. After the machine had crashed several times, losing vital tracts of my work, I purchased a small electric fan, plugged it in and aimed it at the computer. However, all it did was to waft warm air over the desk.

Without insulation on the underside of the vast roof of the barn, the tiles became baking hot and exuded their heat downwards. The upper floor, while it was akin to a freezer cabinet in the winter, became like an pizza oven in the summer, despite the six double casement windows that we had installed, piercing ventilation holes in the front and back elevations of the building. Its one-metre-thick stone walls, built with only mud joints, prevented the considerable heat from escaping.

Keeping cool became my priority. Frequent cold showers helped in this respect but as domestic water in France is metered, I decided that this was likely to prove a costly indulgence. One afternoon, after a long day's work at the keyboard, I called on my friend David Wrightham, a sassy Yorkshireman in his mid-fifties who lived across the village's communal green patch, to see if he wanted to join me for a well-earned dip in the cool waters of the nearby swimming lake, Lac du Mondon. I found my friend perched atop a large sit-on mower, chugging around the sea of yellowing lawn in front of the property. Treating my arrival as a welcome respite from his labours, David pulled the mower to a halt and proffered a sweaty forearm for me to shake.

'Too bloody hot to work, David. Fancy taking a dip at Mondon?' I said as the mower's engine sputtered then was silent.

'Eeh lad, now that'd be grand!' sighed the Yorkshireman with a knowing wink. He drew heavily on the cigarette that invariably dangled from his lips. He was wearing a straw hat with a crumpled brim, a pair of disreputable, sweat-stained khaki shorts and leather sandals, complete with socks. Scraping the hat off his head, he wafted it in front of his face. I noticed that his forehead was white, a distinct line between this and the nut-brown tone of his face. His shoulders and back were brown, while the front of his torso was white. This two-tone effect was due to the fact that he had spent much of the summer bent double laying a patio. For the last five years David had been living in his brother Victor's house, renovating the property while his elder sibling and his wife Anne lived and worked in England. One of David's ongoing responsibilities as seasoned retainer was to maintain the spacious formal gardens that surrounded the property, which he had helped to create from the rough field that had previously existed. During summer this onerous task included twice-weekly mowing of bowling-green smooth lawns, which were marred only by a perennial mole problem. The Yorkshireman clambered down from the mower and stretched his legs. 'Just gimme a minute to get me trunks and we'll head for't water... grand idea, lad!' Heading off for the house, the dapper Yorkshireman gave a delighted little skip in the air.

The area that served as a car park adjoining the lake, visitor centre and café was packed with vehicles, arranged haphazardly under the shade of the well-trimmed trees. David and I parked up, then tucked our towels under our arms and headed for the grassy expanse that led down to the lake. I was surprised that, although there were numerous groups of people lying around on the grass – mainly mothers with gaggles of children – no one was swimming. David and I selected a slender sapling that might offer a modicum of shade, laid out our towels and stripped down to our swimming shorts. Without any more ado, the nimble Yorkshireman gave another delightful little skip again and sprinted off towards the little sandy beach. 'C'mon lad, last one in's a namby pamby!' he hollered.

When he reached the water's edge he waded quickly into the shallows until he was thigh deep, shrieking loudly as the cold liquid enveloped his skin. Suddenly, he launched himself headfirst into the water and promptly disappeared from view beneath the surface. He emerged a considerable distance away, beyond the string of buoys that marked the limit of the swimming area. Then he was off again, crawling strongly out towards the centre of the lake, spluttering and splashing.

Not to be left behind, I tip-toed swiftly across the hot grass to the little sandy beach, then paddled into the shallows. The heatwave had done little to warm up the water appreciably, although its level had receded dramatically. I noticed, however, that the water was a cloudy green colour: standing up to my knees in the water, I could not even see my toes beneath the surface. Undeterred, I scooped handfuls of the cool liquid onto my chest and rubbed it into my upper arms. Its coolness was delightful. I was just about to plunge headlong into the water when I was tapped on the shoulder with something hard.

I looked round. The young lifeguard normally stationed in the little cabin adjacent to the beach had poked me with an oar. He stood a respectable distance away on dry land. 'Monsieur, you and your friend did not see ze red flag, no?' he asked in heavily accented English. How on earth did he know I was English anyway?

'Red flag? Oh, *je suis désolé*…' I looked at the flagpole beyond me, where the little pennant was hanging limply from the top. I had to admit that, in my eagerness to cool off, I had not even thought to look. No wonder no one else was swimming.

'Ze water, she is dangerous…'

'Dangerous?'

'Dangerous, monsieur.' I gazed down. My feet were still invisible in the green murk.

'Eet is ze algae… to bathe is forbidden…'

'Algae? What will it do to us?' I asked, wading out of the water. My legs were covered in a thick, green slime.

The lifeguard backed away from me cautiously. 'Eet make you very very sick… eet give you irritation of ze skin, eet give you – 'ow you say? – ze sheets.'

'The sheets?'

'Yes, ze sheets of ze backside. Not very nice, I think, *non*?'

'No…' I was beginning to feel distinctly unwell.

'Maybe even eet kill you.' With that, the impudent youth turned, flipped the oar onto his shoulder, narrowly missing cracking me across the head with the paddle, and retreated to the safety of his little cabin. 'And please tell your crazy friend to get out of ze water, monsieur. I cannot be responsible for 'is 'ealth...' he said, rather offhandedly. I turned to gaze at the distant figure of the Yorkshireman, whose head was just visible. I raised an arm and beckoned him back to shore. In misguided response the fool merely elevated a green arm from the depths and waved frantically back at me. 'Coo-eee Rich! Come in! Water's loovely!' he shrieked. Eventually, however, he seemed to realise there must be a reason for my reluctance to enter the water and I could see him begin to crawl back to shore. I, meanwhile, headed for the outside shower – running the gauntlet of families who regarded me with some distaste, holding on to their offspring lest they should stray too close – and rinsed off my green legs and chest as thoroughly as I could.

David arrived at the shower panting, shivering and dripping wet. 'What's up, lad?' he asked.

'Ooh, nothing...' I said, glancing at my friend's rather green-tinged body.

'Eeh, bloody 'ell! It's lovely in't water... you're not going in, kid?'

'No, I think I'll give it a miss today, actually...'

'It were your idea in't first place, lad... well, it's up to you! You don't know what you're missing!'

'I don't feel terribly well, actually...' I feigned an excuse.

'Come to think of it, lad,' said the Yorkshireman, squinting at me through the cleansing spray of the shower. 'You do look a bit green in't gills.'

Suitably rinsed off we headed for our towels and flopped down in the sun to dry off. However, we were immediately assailed by masses of tiny flies, which swarmed around us, biting our scalp, ears and other areas of exposed skin.

Swatting madly at the insects, I noticed that other people huddled under the neighbouring trees seemed to be free of the irritation. Unable to withstand the attack for long, we patted ourselves dry, dressed and headed for home feeling more hot and bothered than we had when we arrived for our ill-advised dip.

I read later in the local newspaper that the intense heat had caused a proliferation of the dangerous blue-green algae in the water of Mondon. The presence of this noxious cyanobacteria in the water had forced the authorities to close the lake to bathing. This was a blow to the many caravanners and campers who had flocked to the site adjacent to the lake for their annual holidays. Many of the other lakes in the region had suffered the same fate, while the waters remained tantalisingly calm, cool and utterly tempting. Immersion in this biological breeding ground, however, could be severely detrimental to the health. The report warned of the presence in the water of hepatotoxins, which affect the liver and other organs, and neurotoxins, which affect the nervous system. Over the next few weeks I was convinced that I had developed an uncontrollable twitch above the left eye and a dull ache in the small of my back, and was apt to scrutinise my friend the Yorkshireman for signs of affliction, fully expecting us to be stricken with some terrible malady. As time wore on it appeared that we had been spared this cruel fate by the lifeguard's quick action.

In July, a series of ferocious storms afflicted France, bringing a deluge of rain to the drought-stricken land. The ground – baked to a crisp, dry shell – was unable absorb the mass of water, resulting in serious flood damage as torrents washed through villages and towns, carrying with them abandoned cars, uprooted trees, the roofs of damaged houses and other detritus. At Le Mas Mauvis, while I cowered within the vastness of the barn, hailstones the size of Brussels sprouts clattered down on the roof tiles and battered the flimsy panes of my single-glazed windows. On passing, the fields were left white with frozen slush, which lingered the whole day. The violent thunderstorms that rattled across the Massif Centrale were responsible for the frequent total shutdown of the electrical grid and the telephone system. This meant that my working day was at best spasmodic and at worst even curtailed for hours. Tuning in to Radio France between power cuts I learned that the foul weather was indeed causing chaos countrywide. Driving conditions had become lethal and the populace were advised to stay at home. Many, like me, would resort to huddling around a candle to sit the storms out, and it was reported on one news bulletin that power had been cut to over 300,000 homes.

Winds travelling at speeds of up to one hundred and fifty kilometres per hour swept in from the Pyrénées, causing devastation to many areas in their wake. In the relatively sparsely populated Limousin many ancient oak trees were lost, pulling down power cables as they fell. Further south and in western France – popular tourist destinations – several holidaymaking campers had tragically lost their lives. Previously protected from the intense heat of the sun by a canopy of leafy boughs, many campsites had been simply flattened by uprooted trunks, which fell like ninepins. Thousands of tourists, left exposed to the elements, were obliged to throw themselves upon the mercy of local communes, who made available public buildings as makeshift shelter.

In stark contrast, parts of southern France mercifully not afflicted by the storms, had received no rain for over two months and the pastures were burnt to a crisp. Farmers were obliged to feed their cattle with their winter's supply of hay. There was to be no respite. After the storms had subsided, the crippling heatwave returned with a vengeance in an attempt to beat the country into a sweltering submission.

Perhaps the heat was starting to coddle my brain, for I found that I had developed a rather grumpy demeanour and a general lack of patience. Too much time spent alone, I guessed. This irritability was particularly pronounced when the phone started to ring incessantly, usually in the early evening after I had just knocked off work. They were mainly cold calls trying to sell me double glazing or central heating, neither of which I wanted to consider when sweltering twenty-four hours a day. One evening, however, I picked up the phone to a different kind of call.

'*Oui, allô?*' I said.

'*Allô?*' came the voice of a woman I did not recognise.

'*Allô ?*' I repeated, a little more grumpily.

'Monsieur Trompey.'

'*Non*, you have the wrong number,' I snapped. 'Sorry.' I plonked the receiver back in its cradle. A minute later the phone rang again.

'*Oui, allô?*' I said. There was a pause.

'Oh, *encore* Monsieur Trompey!' said the caller. It was the same woman as before.

'*Non*, look, I am afraid that you have dialled the wrong number…' I explained again in my best formal French. 'What number did you dial?'

'Monsieur Trompey,' insisted the caller. Then the phone went dead as my mystery caller hung up. Rude bitch, I grumbled.

I thought nothing more of the matter until about a week later I again answered the phone. '*Oui, allô?*' There was a pause, then a man's voice crackled into the earpiece.

'Monsieur Trompey.' Oh bugger, I thought. The mysterious Monsieur Trompey. Not him again.

'Look,' I said. 'I'm afraid that you have the wrong number.'

'*Oui,*' said the caller. 'I know.'

'You know? OK. It's just that you're the second person to phone for Monsieur Trompey. But he doesn't live here. Sorry.'

'Monsieur Trompey?'

'Yes, Monsieur Trompey. He doesn't live here.'

'Who is Monsieur Trompey?' asked the caller.

'I haven't a clue. You're the one who's phoning to speak to him...'

'No I'm not, monsieur. I'm calling to speak to my cousin Maude.'

'Your cousin Maude? Then why did you ask to speak to Monsieur Trompey,' I queried. This was beginning to get a mite tiresome. Just then peels of hysterical laughter crackled from the receiver as my caller appeared to be wetting himself on the other end. 'And what's so funny?' I asked, disgruntled.

'Nothing monsieur,' giggled the caller, having switched to perfect English. 'I do not wish to be rude. But...' he broke off to guffaw heartily. '... I did not ask for Monsieur Trompey. You must have misheard. I simply said *je me suis trompé* – I made a mistake in dialling the wrong number. Sorry monsieur... *au revoir.*' Amid more hysterical laughter, the man hung up, leaving me feeling highly embarrassed and convinced that perhaps the French language would ever evade my comprehension. Or maybe the intense heat had melted the wax in my ears and rendered me hard of hearing?

By the month of August, along with most other European countries, France was forced to endure stifling temperatures. There were a staggering number of deaths – mainly elderly people unable to defend themselves against the effects of the heat – directly attributable to the climatic conditions. It was estimated by the Health Ministry that, even in the first half of the month, almost 11,500 people died. The organisation *Pompes Funèbres Générales*, which represented a quarter of France's funeral services, claimed that the figure was more like 13,000 dead. Mortuaries and funeral parlours were desperately strained by the sheer number of bodies, and hospitals struggled to care for those victims who were still clinging on to life. As the heatwave endured and the death count continued to rise, the government was heavily criticised by doctors and the left-wing opposition for what was regarded as its mishandling of the crisis. Government ministers promised the initiation of a long-term plan to protect the elderly, but warned that it would come with a high price tag.

I was beginning to question the sagacity of my move to Limousin. So far my existence had been far from the idyll I had expected. If intense heat, violent storms and immersion in the poisonous waters of a lake had not been omen enough, the unusually warm weather patterns brought about an invasion of the *grange* by millions of tiny flies. One of the penalties of living in a farming community, cheek by jowl with the herd of cows that was led back and forth from the fields to our neighbour's barn for milking, and the inevitable trail of stinking waste they left spattered in their wake. The flies would appear miraculously from apparently nowhere in a matter of minutes, swarming over the window panes in a black mist. Why did they do that, in any case? Were they trying to get out? What was their purpose in the scale of things? No matter. They had to go. Once doused liberally with noxious spray they would drop dead onto the sill only to be replaced immediately by reinforcements. I strung up sticky ribbons of flypaper but caught my hair in the goo more times than I care to remember, which was extremely painful to extricate myself from. If I attempted to toil during the evenings due to the disruption of my working day, the hordes of flies – joined then by fluttering moths – shunning the flypapers, would be attracted to the glowing computer screen, making it difficult to read my documents.

Reading in bed at night was a far cry from the relaxing activity it was intended to be. My bedside light was like a beacon that attracted legions of flying insects – shield bugs (which smelled of vanilla), stag beetles, moths – and small bats intent on their nightly prey. While the insects buzzing around my head and inevitably taking a dip in my whiskey night-cap were an annoyance, I found the bats to be enchanting. The little *chauve-souris*, or 'bald mice' would streak silently through an open window, perform a sequence of high-speed aerial manoeuvres around the network of beams in the roof space, then cling momentarily onto the rough stone walls as if taking a breather, before continuing their dance. Frequently they would swoop low over the bed and I could detect a light rush of air caused by their flapping wings.

While I could have banned some of the more irritating creatures of the night from entering the *grenier* by simply shutting the windows, I relished the delicate breeze that wafted through the room. None of my French neighbours could rationalise my decision not to close and shutter the windows, for each evening they would shut out the world and live in their own enclosed environment. However, when the first mosquitoes of the season started to buzz in my ears and I awoke in the mornings with my skin dotted with itchy bites, I invested in a mail-order mosquito net. Inserting lengths of stout wooden dowel through the loops at the top of the flimsy fabric, I strung the netting over the bed, suspended from the ceiling beams on virtually invisible high-tension fishing line. Proud of my ingenuity, I had to admit that the net assumed a somewhat ethereal quality, appearing to hover over the bed without any obvious means of support. If I should inadvertently tweak the valance when clambering onto the bed, however, the entire highly-strung contraption would twang upwards like a stage magician's *coup de grâce*.

The mosquito net was a boon at night, but while I worked at my computer by day I would often be assailed by monstrous *frelons*, bad-tempered hornets that could sometimes reach almost five centimetres in length: no insect should be permitted to grow to that size. It's just not normal, in my opinion. These overblown stripy insects, which bore a distinctly nasty stinging ovipositor and make English wasps look like midges with attitude, had an unpleasant habit of buzzing around in the roof of the *grange*, searching for whatever it is that hornets search for, before plummeting down like kamikaze aeroplanes with the effect of scaring the living daylights out of me. To get rid of these monsters I bought a giant-sized aerosol canister of killing solution, which the label boasted was capable of squirting a powerful jet some ten metres. The user would thereby be able to douse the hornet's nest from a respectably safe distance. Launching an attack on ingressors high up in the apex of the *grange* roof, I was amazed at the distance the jet reached. Aiming at that altitude was nevertheless rather hit-and-miss and on most occasions I merely aggravated the insects, which then proceeded to chase me around the room as the killing solution slowly descended like fine snow, settling on me and my furniture, but leaving them unscathed.

Had I been a more sensitive type, prone to heed sinister omens, I might have imagined that the forces of nature were pitted squarely against me, or perhaps out for revenge for a perceived transgression. It seemed that all manner of creatures were attempting to make life intolerable for me, or even to oust me from my new home. I knew, for instance, that the sturdy walls of the barn had once housed armies of rats and their beady-eyed spawn. During our first months in occupancy I had – with help from my stocky English builder friend Big John (Jean le Grand in Véronique's parlance) – hoicked the beastly rodents from the network of tunnels they had carved, or else entombed them within the structure during repairs. While the rats had made themselves scarce, their place had been taken by families of small lizards. Unlike the disease-carrying rodents, the lizards were certainly no direct threat to my health (and I had held a life-long fascination for reptiles). Typically shying away from close proximity to humans, these particular lizards nevertheless displayed no such compunctions. Whether relaxing after work or when preparing a paltry meal for myself I would find myself pelted with small pebbles and puffs of dust. For days I could not locate the origin of the attack. On scouring the walls through a pair of binoculars, I would catch sight of a scaly tail disappearing into one of the many tiny holes in the wall or found myself scrutinised by a pair of blinking reptilian eyes and a flickering tongue. A few wine bottle corks deftly bunged in the holes seemed to convey the message and the attack of the lizards eventually subsided. As usual, however, the dainty creatures would invariably be found sunning themselves on the walls outside, or scurrying along the window sills.

I also fought a running battle with other pests, which were responsible for attempting to devour my desk as I worked. Before we had ferried over the remaining remnants of our furniture from England, I had been forced to make do with a temporary desk constructed from an old laminated chipboard kitchen unit. Admittedly this arrangement was not terribly high-tech or even professional in its tawdry appearance (and might have made my publisher reappraise my ability to function from a barn in the middle of rural France, had she seen it). But it was in line with the attitude of temporariness that had caused me to label Al and me the Make-Do Family. The unit had no worktop, so I fashioned a desk surface out of a panel of laminated plywood found amongst furniture we were storing for the Yorkshireman, who was in the process of buying a house for he and his lady friend, Dennie, in a nearby village.

'You can use any of't stuff you like, Rich,' he had kindly offered. 'Just 'elp yourself, lad.' So I had. But retrospectively, I wished I had not.

Perched princess-and-pea fashion on a rickety old, high-backed dining chair piled high with cushions – make-do office seating – I had noticed how a scattering of pale brown dust would tend to form on the surface of the make-do desk and on the floor around its base. When wiped off, the dust would reappear the very next morning. On sliding open the drawers beneath the top I would again be confronted by more dust, which began to form in little piles at a quite alarming rate. The desktop seemed to be disintegrating before my very eyes, its collapse exacerbated by the hefty weight of the computer. After about a week of this inconvenience I decided to investigate matters further, only to discover that the culprits were part of a veritable legion of wood-boring insects intent on chomping their way through my work station. In a frenzied panic I removed my computer and flung the plywood top out of the window, for by now it was riddled with sizeable bore holes and crawling with crunchy brown beetles and wriggling little grubs that oozed horrid gunk when squashed. Without reporting the incident to the Yorkshireman, I quickly burned the infested wood, hoping that the voracious insects – presumably prior natives of Sheffield, having hitched a ride across the channel concealed in David's household effects – had not been so lured by the exotic flavour of French oak that they had taken up residence in the structure of our barn.

Bug emergency behind me, I replaced the woodworm-eaten panel with planks of tongued-and-grooved floorboard that I had been using to patch the floor of the *grange* and settled back intent on concentrating on my work. This was not going to be easy.

The grange, Le Mas Mauvis

Chapter Three

Knee jerk reaction

F inding myself alone in France I had ample time to explore and familiarise myself with the countryside on foot. I loved the open spaces: in particular I loved to run. When in England, rain or shine, I would slip into my trainers and take off for hours at a time, trudging the highways and byways of rural Kent and Sussex, exploring my environment at grass-roots level. However, after many years, I had started to feel stale running the same routes. A competent club runner, I had participated in many local races, the courses of which had become over-familiar. Now ensconced in the midst of France, I sought new challenges and unexpected vistas. Armed with a small-scale map of the region, equipped with a water bottle, and suitably clothed in Daglo Lycra, I would trot out from the hamlet in the relative coolness of the morning or early evening, with only a scant notion of where I was headed. I would often not return home for three or more hours, having discovered delightful, scarcely frequented, tree-lined *chemins*, pathways winding their way to placid ponds, or narrow, virtually deserted roads to neighbouring hamlets.

On my travels *à pied* I would rarely encounter a soul or be passed by a car, although whenever I did I would invariably be greeted with a friendly wave or a *'Bonjour monsieur! Bon courage!'* It was always a mite risky, on the other hand, running past some of the more remote farmsteads along the way. These properties were frequently patrolled by fierce dogs unused to anyone passing by in a car, let alone running. On numerous occasions I was forced to put on a spurt of speed, pursued by snapping jaws at my heels. A squirt in the face from the water bottle I carried for hydration purposes would usually discourage a persistent dog, although sometimes I had to resort to lobbing a stone.

Some animals, however, did not give up so easily. A favourite run took me along the leafy VTT (*Vélo Tout-Terrain*) off-road bicycle trails that snake out into woodland from the cemetery in St. Léger-Magnazeix, the nearest village to our hamlet. The three trails, a popular venue for annual bike races and hordes of visiting cyclists during the summer, are indicated by pennants colour coded yellow, blue or red according to the ten, twenty or thirty kilometre distances they covered. I had just enjoyed an exhilarating run of some eight kilometres, although plagued by a dull ache in my left knee, and was glad that I had reached the final four-kilometre stretch along the road that led from the village to my home.

As I was passing the war memorial at the edge of the empty square, a blurred shape materialised from my peripheral vision and circled around me as I ran. Momentarily startled as one is when inadvertently colliding with a bollard or lamppost when looking the other way, I smiled when I saw that this was nothing more scary than a little fluffy white pompom of indeterminate canine pedigree. The little animal was racing around me wildly and making pathetic little leaps in the air, which reached no further than about a foot off the ground. The dog was about the size of an overweight guinea pig and its bark a series of irritating hiccups. The animal had no discernible features apart from two raisins for eyes, which appeared whenever its fringe flipped up with every leap. Wrong-footed by the troublesome mutt as it wove between my legs, I tried to leap out of the way lest I was tripped. Suddenly my attacker sank a set of razor-sharp teeth into my right calf and refused to let go, even when I had reached down and grabbed it by its scrawny neck in an attempt to dislodge it. I began to prance around, swatting at the deadly candyfloss clamped to my leg, but the little sod would not let go. I reached down and closed my hand around what I assumed to be its scraggy throat and squeezed hard. The beast relinquished its vice-like grip and I took the opportunity to give it a tremendous boot up the rear end, sending it sprawling across the gravel with a whelp. But no sooner had the dog regained its feet than it was on the attack again. Performing an admirable version of Riverdance, I lashed out with my feet in a vain attempt to keep the savage beast at bay.

A high-pitched whistle stopped the dog in its tracks, and the fluffy menace slunk away in the direction of the memorial. A man sat on the stone bench beneath the cross. He was a rather scruffy, unshaven individual wearing mud-spattered, baggy jeans, a tweed jacket two sizes too small for him, and an ill-fitting peaked cap. The dog leaped onto the man's lap and nuzzled into his filthy jacket. The man appeared not to have noticed me and was staring ahead blankly, unblinking.

Bending down to examine the back of my leg, I could clearly make out the dog's teeth marks on my grazed skin. Blood was oozing from the puncture marks. I looked back at the man, who was absently stroking the mutt. 'Monsieur, your dog has just bitten me,' I said in French, limping towards him. The dog growled at my approach but the man did not move or appear to have heard me. 'Monsieur, I said your dog has bitten me…' This time the man turned his head towards me but still did not respond. 'You have nothing to say, monsieur? No apology?' I was furious now by the man's silence and the wound on my calf was throbbing madly. Foolishly I had not brought with me any tissues or other means of mopping up the trickle of blood that was running down my leg. '*D'accord*, so I will call the police, monsieur. And your bastard dog will be put down! You understand? What's the matter with you, monsieur? Are you *fou*?'

'Mister, eet will do no good,' came a voice from behind me, in heavily accented English. I turned to see an elderly, white-haired gentleman standing by proffering a wad of paper tissues. 'Please, Mister, come over to my house…' The man gestured towards the building a few metres away across the square. A lady I assumed to be his wife was peering from over the stone garden wall. I hobbled to the wall. Taking the tissues from the gentleman, I mopped up the blood from my leg. His wife handed him something over the garden wall, which he passed on to me: an aerosol container. 'This ees antiseptic, Mister…' Thanking him, I took the bottle and sprayed the site of the wound. The liquid stung on contact. I winced. Holding some clean tissues against the puncture marks, I applied pressure to staunch the flow of blood.

'Do you know that man?' I asked the elderly couple, indicating the motionless figure still seated under the memorial cross, apparently oblivious to the attack.

'*Oui, monsieur,*' said my helper's wife, a rosy-cheeked lady with a pink hair rinse and wearing a blue and white checked housecoat. 'He lives here in the village.' She elaborated in French. Her husband pointed to his own temple and made little circles with his forefinger in the universal sign language that said 'he's loopy'.

'Oh…' I felt momentarily embarrassed. I felt ashamed to have shouted at him. 'Oh, I am sorry. He has a mental problem?'

The man shook his head, then held the thumb and forefinger of his closed fist up to his nose and revolved it twice. 'Not at all. A problem wiz drink…'

'Ah, I see. He did not seem to care that his dog had bitten me.'

'He does not. He cares about nothing. He is always very very drunk. But ze dog ees this man's only companion… he has no one else. He live alone with this dog…'

'That's very sad, monsieur,' I said, suddenly feeling sorry for the dog owner. I dabbed at my leg. The blood had stopped flowing.

'Not at all, Mister. Ze dog ees a menace and should be put down. You must inform the police. They will come and take eet away to the *veterinaire*.' He sliced his extended hand across his throat, his meaning clear. 'Ze man, unfortunately, cannot be put down…' He shrugged. '*Tant pis.*' Too bad.

'You would like to call someone to collect you, monsieur?' said the man's wife. I re-examined my leg. Although the wound was throbbing, it was not serious enough to warrant a lift home. I reckoned that I could continue with my run. I thanked my helpers and bade them farewell, pausing before I set off to enquire: 'How did you know I was English anyway?'

The man flashed me an extravagant wink and grinned broadly. 'Monsieur! Who but the English would be running around here dressed like that?' When I reached home, I cleaned and dressed my wound and contemplated what action to take.

'But it is *obligatoire*, Riche!' insisted Daniel, proprietor of the travelling grocery shop that visited the hamlet each week. When he had arrived that afternoon I had limped out to show him the bite and he had become highly agitated. 'In France it is a matter of law to inform the *gendarmes* if a dog attacks a person. The animal must be destroyed.'

Véronique, standing by the counter with a bulging basket of produce, nodded her agreement with Daniel. She peered down at my exposed calf. 'That's going to go septic,' she affirmed.

'My tetanus jabs are up to date,' I revealed.

'Tetanus protection will do you no good if this animal carries *la rage*!' insisted Daniel, glowering down from the counter of his van like a preacher delivering a stern sermon from the pulpit. 'You would suffer a long and painful death from *la rage*!'

'Long and painful,' concurred Véronique, nodding solemnly. 'A horrible death.'

La rage. Rabies. The very word filled me with fear and trepidation. I began to feel a little hot under the collar. What if I had been infected with the disease by the rabid pompom? Clearly it was my duty to inform the authorities – and to visit a doctor. Although mildly embarrassed to be accusing the miniature mutt of a serious and unprovoked attack, I performed my civil duty and contacted the *gendarmerie*. I was relieved that my attacker and I would be spared the horror of death when I was informed that investigations revealed that the animal had – despite its owner's constant inebriation – well documented health records and vaccinations and was subsequently declared free of rabies.

I had been lucky. France, in fact, had only recently been declared officially free of the disease after a six-month period during which the Institut de Vielle Sanitaire (INVS), the national health protection body, searched for evidence of rabies transmission in the south-west of the country. It transpired that a four-month old bitch had been illegally imported into the European Union from Morocco, through Spain and into France. The owner of the infectious pet, flaunting the rules imposed by the Pet Travel Scheme, had brazenly taken his rabid pet for walkies around the city centre of Bordeaux, where he resided, and pleasant strolls amongst members of the public enjoying the riverside and botanical gardens. Several people were known to have been bitten, and the dog had consorted with other animals. The reckless dog-owner had also visited various areas in the Gironde, in addition to neighbouring *départements* of Dordogne and Lot et Garonne. After no secondary cases of rabies had been detected, the area was again declared rabies free.

Attacks by potentially rabid dogs notwithstanding, my running excursions would predominantly be free from dangers and were typically a time for me to relax and appreciate my surroundings. On my travels I would make a mental note of interesting architecture, intriguing gardens and other features that I could later show to Al. Each evening I would catalogue the routes I had run on a computer spreadsheet and the times each would take to complete. Not only was this a valuable training log but also provided a detailed snapshot of my environment. Soon my database offered me the choice of twenty routes between three and forty kilometres in length.

In coming to live in France, Al and I had been keen not to hide inside one of the enclaves of English that we knew to exist in the region. We tried to live a French life, but this did not mean that we needed to shun contact with other English people. As in the UK, there were some neighbours who we just did not have anything in common with, while there were others whose company we enjoyed. One such couple were Harry and Sue Amey, who lived in a neighbouring hamlet with their four children: three boys and a girl, all under ten years old. Although we lived close by we had not met for over three years, both parties not wishing to inflict themselves on the other, when such contact might be unwelcome. Once circumstance had thrown us together, however, we soon became fond friends. The children attended the village school and were rapidly becoming bilingual. George, the eldest boy, spent his free time tending a small flock of sheep under guidance of French farmer friend. The younger kids mixed with the local children, chattering incessantly in French then trying out dubious swear words on their parents. This was one English family who had become wholly absorbed in the local culture and community.

Like me, Harry adored running, not only for his health, but also as pure escapism from the exuberant noise and chaos that generally reigned supreme within the Amey household. Although we both generally preferred to run alone, we enjoyed infrequent *sorties* together, during which we could chat idly about shared interests, or dabble in some intriguing gossip about our other neighbours. Harry, a London policeman, lived a strange half-life: every three weeks he would fly back to the UK, where he would endure eight gruelling days of twelve-hour night shifts, patrolling the streets in his squad car and helping to keep the city safe for the slumbering inhabitants. Arriving back in his French bolt-hole after a week in the bustling metropolis, he would take to his bed for many hours of exhausted sleep, temporarily undisturbed by the chaos of family life, in order to unwind again and reintroduce himself to his alter ego. Running became part of this unravelling. This type of commuting was by no means a rarity among British policemen; one enterprising copper even made the commute between London and his family home in New Zealand.

Perennially jovial and quick-witted, with a teasing, cheeky sense of humour, the Laughing Policeman also ran like the clappers. Slim-framed, extremely fit and flexible of limb, Harry was the Hare to my Tortoise. Mismatched in this way, he would stretch the boundaries of my running by making me maintain a faster pace than was perhaps sensible for a man of my delicate age, while I would drag him moaning around a particularly long course, albeit at a slower velocity.

'You used to race regularly in the UK, didn't you, Rich? Ever thought of racing now you're in France?' asked Harry during one of our jaunts. He seemed to find verbal communication easy even when running up a steep incline. In fact, he hadn't stopped yakking since we had set off an hour earlier.

We had driven in Harry's disreputable car to tackle one of his favourite runs, which I had not been familiar with.

Starting in the village of Dreux, near the picturesque town of Bellac, the clearly marked trail followed the route of the disused railway line. Strewn with chunks of granite and dangerous, ankle-turning potholes, the trail wended its way through leafy woodland before leaving the embankment to follow a torturously steep and muddy pathway leading to a higher plateau of pastures. There it joined a narrow tar road before branching off into woodland again. It was a beautiful trail, although demanding concentration to negotiate, but I was feeling most uncomfortable; my legs were unusually stiff, my muscles taut and my breathing quite laboured.

'Thought about it… there are some great races… *Les Gendarmes et Voleurs de Temps* in Ambazac, near Limoges for one…' The renowned 'cops and robbers' race had appealed to me for a long time. 'I've always hankered after running a classic French road race like the Paris-Versailles… I want to enter for the Paris Marathon next April…' I wheezed, struggling along behind the nimble copper. I had scoured French running magazines and Internet websites for races in my new locale and had been tempted by several. The *'Gendarmes'* race in Ambazac, for example, was renowned for its tough fourteen-kilometre course and was said to attract some three thousand runners. Where the entrants all hung out I could only surmise. Such a big field suggested that running in France was an extremely popular pastime, but I had to admit that Harry had been the only other human being I had ever seen moving faster than a slow stroll since I had taken up residence. In such a vast country, running clubs were few and far between, particularly if one lived in the sticks, as we did. Distance in reaching a race venue had never been a concern of mine; in England I had driven many miles in order to participate in a race that attracted me. On days like today, when even jogging at what Harry claimed would be 'a leisurely pace' was proving uncommonly arduous, I scarcely dared think that my running days – let alone competing days – were on the wane.

Although I was by no means a hugely competitive athlete, I adored racing for the sheer thrill, spectacle and companionship of running with masses of other like-minded souls. Injuries notwithstanding, I was at my most content when hovering in a perpetual state of preparedness for tackling at least two or three marathons a year. In England my self-imposed daily training schedules had dictated that I run a minimum of thirty-five miles per week, culminating in a gruelling sixty or more miles per week towards the end of a fifteen-week approach to a marathon. Whilst I harboured no delusions of ever winning a race, I enjoyed pitting myself against runners of similar ability and improving my 'personal best' times.

Since coming to live in France I had started to hunger for a race. Unfortunately, after years of tromping the streets, my poor maltreated legs had begun to protest. In an attempt to forestall what I imagined was my fate I had reduced my hours running on hard, unyielding road surfaces in favour of off-road trails. However, I was more content on the roads, where I could enter a steady rhythm. During the 1970s, when I was a callow youth who had barely run a step in his life, I had been obliged to endure the removal of a diseased cartilage from my left knee. Doctors had advised that I should embark on a programme of regular exercise to strengthen my muscles and so prevent my articulated joints from grinding against one another and eventually seizing up. I don't think that my medical advisers had assumed I might take their words as a cue to prance around the streets on an almost daily basis for the next thirty years. But this is what I had done. During my

forties my knee – lacking its cushioning connective tissue
– had become prone to painful swelling and was apt to lock
in the bent position after, or more inconveniently during, a
long run.

Snapped back from my private thoughts to the painful
reality of my agonising run with Harry, I pulled up suddenly
as my left knee locked in a semi-bent position, sending me
sprawling across the rough forest track we were negotiating.
Harry ground to a halt and trotted back down the track. I
resisted his offer to help me to my feet, realising that I would
have to manipulate the knee back into a straight postion first.
'You'd better go on, Harry,' I said, disheartened. 'I'm not
going to be running anywhere for a while.' Limping back to
where we had left the car at the start of our run, I reflected on
just how I would fill the huge void that would remain, should
I be prevented from ever running again.

Back at home, after I had showered and prepared an icepack
for my swollen knee, I took up a comfortable position on
the sofa and telephoned Al in England to tell her of my
woes. Worryingly, in addition to a painful knee, I was also
experiencing excruciating pain in both of my shins.

'I think I have shin splints,' I told my wife, although I had
to confess that I had not the foggiest idea what shin splints
actually were, let alone what they felt like. The advice pages
in my running magazines always cited the ailment as a prime
reason for leg injuries such as this, but somehow I had not
absorbed the crucial information as to its cause and effect.

'What do your legs feel like, then?' Al asked just the question
I'd hoped she would not ask. 'I thought a splint was something
you put on a broken leg.'

'No, I just have severe pain in the shins…'

'So you'll just have to be a brave boy and hobble to the doctor,' said the ever-practical Al. Nothing much fazed my wife. But then there she was swaddled in cosy, familiar Kent, the Garden of England, with the technological advancements of the National Health Service ever on hand. Conversely, here I was exposed, alone and afraid in the backwaters of rural France, where I imagined medical science was still in its infancy. I was sure they must practise centuries-old medicine that involved the use of leeches, and performed surgery without anaesthetic.

'Err, we don't have a doctor,' I reminded Al as the sudden realisation hit me. A shiver ran down my spine. 'How do we go about getting a doctor here in France? I don't have a clue.' There was panic in my voice. 'Do we just turn up at the local surgery and ask to be taken on?'

'Don't worry,' said Al. 'It's all in hand. I've been worried about what would happen if you were taken ill or injured while you're there in France, so I've been doing my homework. I've contacted a local surgery in Magnac Laval. Doctor Boely says we can just turn up and give him our details and he'll treat us if necessary.'

As Al explained what she understood about the healthcare system in France, I became more relaxed and confident that, should I require it, help of a high standard was readily on hand. The French system was highly regarded and the World Health Organisation had even placed it top of the charts for provision of universal healthcare for its citizens. Compared to Britain's National Health Service, the system in France was enviable in many ways. The French invest almost twice as much money on healthcare as in the UK. The quality of care between private and public hospitals in France is broadly similar and waiting lists do not generally exist.

All medical treatments are charged according to a tariff, whether they are a routine visit to *un médecin généraliste*, a general practitioner, or a major surgical procedure. The majority of medical practitioners and hospitals or clinics adhering to the tariff are known as *conventionné*, while those that do not are *non-conventionné*.

The social security system, *sécurité sociale*, refunds seventy per cent of medical fees, including the doctor's twenty-euro consultation fee. For those subscribing to the French social security system, as an employee or employer, most general healthcare needs – medicines and drugs, for example – are partially reimbursed, at varying rates between thirty-five and sixty-five per cent. It is common, however, to additionally subscribe to a *mutuelle*, a medical insurance company that will provide a 'top-up' for expenses not covered by the state. Many *mutuelles* are specific to types of profession. Whereas people in generally good health might pay for their routine visits to the doctor out of their own pocket, reserving insurance cover only for the expense of hospitalisation, those on regular medication would choose a plan that covered this. One hundred per cent cover is available for those suffering serious conditions such as cancer.

Access to specialist treatment – for X-rays, laboratory examinations and physiotherapy – is generally through referral from a *médecin généraliste*, in order that costs can be refunded. Social security refunds are obtainable for consulting specialists such as psychiatrists, dentists, ophthalmologists and gynaecologists, but not for visits to osteopaths, chiropractors or psychoanalysts.

As an EU national resident in France I would be obliged to affiliate to the French health system, via the Caisse Primaire d'Assurance Maladie (CPAM). To do this I would require one of the so-called E-forms from the UK. Al and I were already in possession of the E111, which provides for emergency medical treatment while on temporary visits to France, or another EU state, but now that I was to become a permanent resident it was invalid and I would require an E106. Issued to those under state retirement age but not considered to be working in France, it would be valid for a maximum of two years, dependent upon the amount of National Insurance contributions paid in the previous two UK Income Tax years, the month of arrival in France, and whether the applicant was employed or self-employed. My actual status in this regard was something of a moot point, and one that Al had taken responsibility to clarify. So far she had received conflicting information from the UK and French tax authorities, both of who claimed that I should pay tax to them. Although self-employed and resident in France, all of my work was carried out for UK companies, and my income tax paid in the UK. Could I be said to be working in France, or working in the UK?

On a purely practical basis, however, it seemed that I would be able to visit a doctor, or a dentist for that matter, and apply for a reimbursement of my expenses to the local CPAM. The procedure, should I be given a prescription, was to peel off the detachable *vignettes*, or stamps, from the medicine containers and stick them on the *feuille de soins*, the claim form provided by the doctor, and send them to CPAM for a refund.

Running was just one of the enthusiasms that fired my imagination and my explorative urges. While I was temporarily disabled in my athletic passion, I was able to indulge myself in another area of interest. Maps and the geographical features they detail have long fascinated me and one of the best ways of feeding this enthusiasm is from the air, when the countryside is laid out beneath like a tapestry. In this regard, I am lucky enough to own a hot-air balloon, after having studied hard to gain my pilot's licence over a decade ago. Like many balloonists, I craved the space to fly without the restrictions that are typically applied to the sport in England. These are frequently caused by farmers unfriendly to the presence of balloons and exacerbated by the numerous commercial balloon companies who are seen to be making pots of money while trespassing in their fields. This ultimately results in a dearth of places to set down a basket. Having flown in Northern France during my year-long training, I knew that *la montgolfière* was considered with far higher regard in the country that was the birthplace of the hot-air balloon. It had been on 19 September, 1783 that the brothers Joseph and Jacques Montgolfier, paper mill owners from Annonay in the Ardèche *département* of the Rhône-Alpes region successfully launched a paper-lined silk balloon from Versailles, carrying a rooster, a sheep and a duck – the first air travellers. The balloon had flown for eight minutes to the rapturous applause of Marie Antoinette and the French court.

When trying to convince ourselves that buying a farm in France was foolhardy, the lure of a permanent, home-based take-off site for my balloon had been one of the main factors that clinched the deal for me. Although not a runner, Al adored what I regard as the next best thing, walking. As for flying, while she professed to enjoy floating around in an oversized laundry basket three-thousand feet up in the sky, she was in her element retrieving the balloon from ground level with car and trailer. Because the balloon is broadly at the mercy of the wind in terms of its direction of travel, returning to one's starting point is a rarity, although not impossible given certain atmospheric conditions. In chasing the balloon Al frequently found herself in parts of the countryside that would otherwise have been bypassed, obliged to follow little-used farm tracks in order to keep pace with the balloon. To all accounts this country had so much to offer a ballooning runner who also hankered after keeping llamas. Oh, yes. There was also the question of the llamas.

Flower borders, the grange

Chapter Four

Good breeding

Llamas, distant relations of the camel, had long fascinated me. But when I discovered that llamas were also excellent animals for helping to eradicate brambles, nettles and other *mauvaise herbes* from long-neglected fields, I was determined to enlist the aid of my own modest herd in maintaining our property. I was also intent on training the animals to accompany Al and me on trekking trips, whereby the beasts of burden would carry all our food, clothing and a tent. I had the idea that we could set off on foot, a pair of llamas in tow, exploring the network of pathways that interlaced the country, visiting rural villages and places of interest along the way. Stopping before nightfall we would pitch our tent and tether the beasts to a convenient tree, then perhaps enjoy a barbecued feast beneath a gin-clear night sky resplendent with stars and streaked by the Milky Way. The next day the trek would continue, following a circuitous route over several days that would return us to our starting point. This was not merely a passing fancy of my own, for llama trekking – either short walks lasting one or two hours, visiting local tourist sites, or longer hikes over several days – is an established and popular pursuit in many rural counties of England, and in America. In France, however, the sight of strings of llamas traversing the byways was a rarity, if non-existent.

We had befriended a local llama breeder, Bernard Morestin, after I had noticed his magazine advert proclaiming the benefits of *petites camelides* in clearing long neglected land. Bernard, a Frenchman by birth, had spent many years in England during the Seventies working as an air steward. He had married an Englishwoman and had started a family. After divorcing some years later, however, he had found himself back in his native France, a country, nevertheless, he professed to dislike.

'Why come back here then?' I had asked.

'There are too many cars in England,' had been his stark reply.

During his years in England, Bernard had adopted a vocabulary of colourful colloquial phrases and slang words, many of which had subsequently fallen into disuse by the natives – rightly, some would say. In Bernard, however, such linguistic gems as 'Crikey', 'Flippin'eck' and 'Blimey' lingered on, delivered in everyone's idea of a spoof French accent.

Our friend owned a herd of some fifty llamas, and bred them at his property in the Haute-Vienne, south of the city of Limoges. Although the Frenchman owned an adorably cute little house ripe for renovation, nestled in beautiful countryside, he chose instead to live in a poky caravan parked alongside during winter, and in a large, draughty barn during summer. The llama-exporting business had suffered during the UK's tragic epidemic of foot-and-mouth disease, so Bernard's bread-and-butter job was as an *agent immobilier*, an estate agent. Thus his days were spent selling houses to the burgeoning English settlers, while the rest of his time was devoted to caring for his beloved llamas.

I had planned to purchase three or four llamas from him, once Al and I had decamped to France permanently. One fine day in the early spring, when Al had come to France to spend a few weeks with me, we had travelled down to Bernard's farm with the express purpose of selecting a pair of llamas from his herd as the basis of my own modest herd. Our friend greeted us as we clambered out of the car: me with a firm handshake, Al with the inevitable kisses on both cheeks. He wore a washed-out red polo shirt and a pair of khaki utility pants, the pockets of which bulged with sheep pellets. His grey hair was in disarray, his cheeks ruddy. Bernard looked about fifty but we had been amazed to learn that he was actually more than ten years older than that.

'*Bienvenue, mes amies!*' he said in his sing-song voice. 'So I am soon to 'ave a llama-keeping neighbour, eh! This ees very nice. So Richard, I 'ave separated two chaps from the 'erd that you might like to look at,' said Bernard. 'I 'ave bunged them in this paddock 'ere... ' As we followed him towards the field I noticed that he was limping badly.

'What's the matter with your leg, Bernard? Thrown a shoe?' I asked.

'Rich!' said Al, clapping me on the back. 'Don't be so rude!'

'What?' I said.

'But it is true, I am lame! It ees this flippin' 'ip,' moaned Bernard, tapping his right flank. 'It ees worn out and I need a new one! But I 'ave to wait for the operation. Who knows when that will be?'

'I've got trouble with my knees,' I announced, fishing for the sympathy I never received from my wife. 'And I have shin splints, too.' Al raised her eyebrows in despair. Bernard looked at me quizzically.

'Well, what do you expect?' he said in his sing-song voice. 'Running marathons. What's that all about, eh? Nobody to blame but yourself!'

'Huh!' I grumbled.

'It ees OK for you, Richard! You just sit at a desk tip-tapping on a keyboard. I'm on my feet all day! It ees no good for me. I cannot catch the llamas and I need to prepare some guys for sale. You 'ave to get them used to 'andling, you see, but they don't want to be caught, the beggars!' We had reached the perimeter of the little orchard where the llamas were kept. ''Ere are these guys – Talisman ees the big one, and Thursday's Boy the smaller one. What do you think of them, Richard?'

Watching us curiously from behind the sagging wire mesh fence that enclosed a little orchard were two young llamas aged, I estimated, about two years old. The larger one, Talisman, had a stocky, upright frame, with a deep, broad chest and a long, thick neck. He stood about three-feet high to the withers, with his head held aloft on a neck that was another two feet long. Most of his body was covered in a thick, downy coat that was reddish brown in colour, revealing pale grey beneath as the light breeze parted it. His neck was clothed in long, fine white hair, which resembled a pointed neckerchief. His powerful forelegs were covered in the same white fibre, except for his knees, which were quite hairless and rather grubby. The animal's face was predominantly white, except for a black muzzle and a pair of black panda markings around his doleful eyes. His ears, perfectly curved like bananas – a requirement of the finest pedigree animals – were black and erect. His back was flat and broad and his torso graduated to a neat, slim waist from which a pair of powerful back legs emerged. His tail, a somewhat comical addition to the llamas' makeup, was a fluffy mop of brown fibre, which he twitched from side to side as he weighed us up. He was indeed an impressive creature.

Thursday's Boy was another matter entirely. Considerably smaller than Talisman, this llama was scrawny and extremely scruffy in appearance. His fleece was mainly dark brown in colour, while his legs were the colour of dark chocolate. Only his head, ears and a portion of his scraggy neck were white. He had a black muzzle and a black patch on the back of his bony head that looked like a skullcap. His eyes were surrounded by dark, angular streaks which, unlike Talisman's beguiling panda markings, gave this animal a rather mean look. His fleece was dirty, matted and covered with strands of straw.

The animals approached the fence and allowed us to stroke their long snouts. Talisman had a docile demeanour but his companion was cantankerous. If too much attention was paid to Talisman, Thursday's Boy would nip at the larger llama's ears.

'I like Talisman,' I said, weighing up the animals. 'He's a splendid chap! Sturdy, attractive markings and colouring.'

'Yes, he 'as a good straight back, strong, straight legs. Ideal for trekking, I think. And if you want to breed from 'im, just take a look at the back end… he 'as a good plump pair of balls! That's a very good sign, *non*!' Great, I thought, we've only been here five minutes and already Bernard has managed to drag the conversation around to the subject of genitalia. That must be something of a record, I reflected.

'Fine. I'll take your word for it.'

'Plenty of – what is the word? – sperm in there, I think…'

'OK. Thanks.'

'You could put 'im with a woman right now!'

'Oh, I'm sure you could…'

'But eet ees very important!' he stressed, suddenly reaching through the fence to grab the llama's mop tail. 'Just look at those!' he said hoicking up the tail to reveal a pair of plum-like testicles. Talisman's long neck twisted around to see what on earth was occurring at his *derrière*. He stamped his back legs in irritation and Bernard released the mop.

'Very nice. So, anyway, I think we've established that Talisman is a virile young man. But the other llama's a bit of a weed, don't you think?' Thursday's Boy seemed to glower menacingly at me from the other side of the fence.

'Oh, Richard! 'ow could you! 'e ees not that bad! 'e ees only two month younger than Talisman. 'e just needs to fill out a little bit. And his balls aren't too small, either.'

'Hmm. Fascinating. But haven't you got anything else that looks more like a llama than an emaciated sheep?'

'Rich!' said Al, giving me a playful push, which catching me unawares, sent me sprawling into the wire fence. At this kerfuffle both llamas turned on their heels and pelted off across the orchard. Bernard shrugged. 'Anyway, it's no problem. You can see the other young boys if you don't like Thursday,' said

Bernard. 'They are with their mothers in the back field. But I don't 'ave any that are ready right now… all the youngsters need 'andling first. And with this 'ip, I am stuffed.'

Bernard led us past his little caravan at the rear of the property. A huge, extremely woolly llama with a dense chocolate brown fleece stood tethered to a post, chewing on the nettles that surrounded the caravan. With its curly tresses, the animal looked rather like an overgrown poodle, although not unattractive. He looked up nonchalantly as we passed, then resumed his munching.

'Boris ees my unpaid gardener,' announced Bernard, patting the fluffy beast on its broad back. Clouds of dust wafted up. 'Tie 'im up somewhere and he'll happily eat everything within range of the rope. It beats pushing a lawnmower around, I can tell you!'

Bernard opened the makeshift gate that led into a large, rolling field dotted with patches of nettles. A little stream wound its way through the centre, passing through a reed-clogged pond before disappearing underground, only to emerge ten metres further on. Several small black-fleeced sheep with gnarled, curly horns had been contentedly nibbling at the grass. They scuttled out of our way as we passed, bleating hoarsely. Beyond, where the ground fell away to a lower level, a group of about thirty female llamas were calmly grazing with their offspring. The young llamas were shy, peering at us suspiciously from behind the protective cover of their mothers. Suddenly, curiosity getting the better of them, the entire herd raced up the incline and began to mill around us, eager to see if we had any tasty treats for them. Bernard delved into his pockets and administered handfuls of sheep pellets to the greedy, jostling throng. Here there were animals with fleeces in a myriad of colours and markings: dark browns, rusty tones, pure whites, greys, fawn hues. Each llama sports unique and divergent markings and colouration, which are impossible to predict in breeding. Few are plain in colour. Peeping from the rear of the herd I immediately noticed a small, chocolate brown llama with a pretty, dark brown – almost black – face. His fleece was extremely woolly, in contrast to many of the other llamas, which predominantly had straighter fibre. The little llama's ears were cocked forward in a display of curiosity but his overwhelming shyness caused him to hang back while the others pushed, shoved and spat at each other in an attempt to reach the sheep pellets.

'He's a nice looking chap,' I announced, pointing out the young animal. I took a few paces towards the little llama, but he immediately scuttled behind his mother, a large white llama, and regarded us suspiciously from beneath her belly.

'Oh, that's Uriel,' said Bernard. 'A very sweet boy. Only two month old. I've never been able to get close to 'im, though: he ees still feeding from his mother. And she's pretty protective. He's a cutey, though! But very, how you say, nervous. You can 'ave him but not for a few month more. I'd need to wean 'im off 'is mother and then I 'ave to catch the little bugger and get him in the halter.'

'There's no hurry,' I said. 'We have to fence off the fields first. Would he be OK to live with Talisman, then?'

'Blimey, why not? But you can't take just one llama, Richard. They don't like to be on their own. They need company. They are 'erd animal, remember. If you want this Uriel, why not take Talisman and Thursday first and when this little chap is ready, I bring him and take back Thursday?'

'Sounds like a good plan,' I said.

'OK. So it's a deal then! And now, to clinch things, how about some lunch?' Al and I both smiled and nodded our heads gleefully. Bernard's lunches were always a welcome way to while away several hours.

On the drive back to the hamlet that afternoon, I was satisfied that I had selected my first llamas well. Al, sitting in the passenger seat while I drove, came up with a suggestion.

'It's your birthday in a few months,' she announced. 'I'll buy you Talisman as my present, and you can buy Uriel yourself.' Turning momentarily away from the road, I glanced at my wife with a bright smile on my face, thrilled with her offer. The car swerved.

'Oops!' I said, controlling the vehicle. 'That's wonderful, darling!' I said. 'Thank you.' I blew her a kiss.

'It's a pleasure, Rich. Now keep your eyes on the road or you won't make your birthday!'

Before we could entertain the idea of providing a home for these South American cud-chewers, however, it would be necessary to erect suitably high fencing around our fields in order to contain the notoriously high-jumping animals. A fully-grown llama would think nothing of leaping over a mere sheep fence. With several acres to encircle, fencing was destined to be a major task and one for which we had no ready funds. Without the llamas to graze the fields, on the other hand, our land was rapidly becoming swamped by unrestrained growth. It was a paradox for which there was no ready solution.

Vélo-Rail, Bussière Galant

Chapter Five

On the right track

The summer's intense heat had drained me not only physically but also mentally. I was in a dangerous downward spiral towards depression because of my inability to run. The pain in my legs had not subsided or improved at all. In desperation I had been to consult Doctor Boely, who had referred me to a sports physiotherapist in Limoges.

'*Douleurs à l'intérieur du tibia inférieur,*' confirmed Christelle the physio on examining my legs. '*En anglais*, you 'ave ze sheen spleents. Naughty boy!' she admonished, wagging a stern finger at me. 'You 'ave been over-training, *ne c'est pas?*' I flopped down on the examination couch: Christelle had made me drop my trousers then hop on the spot until the shin pain kicked in, then repeat the torture for the other leg, while she stood back and watched, arms folded, smiling sardonically. I was sure that this had nothing to do with a serious examination, for I believed that the evil Christelle simply loved to humiliate her patients.

'Is that what's caused the problem?' I whined, massaging my shins. 'I've never experienced it before and I train quite heavily…'

'*Oui, mais* remember you're not ze spring chicken any more. How old are you? *Cinquante ans*? You should know better. A *décrépit* old body like yours takes longer to recover from stress, and you will insist on running marathons. You men are all alike. Too damn *machiste* for your own good. Then you get a little twinge, you come running to *les filles* for help.'

'That's grossly unfair!' I whinged. I did not regard myself as at all macho. Well, let me rephrase that: not overly macho.

'It's grossly true! *De tout façon*, your problem might be allied to a biomechanical *anormalité*: you do have an off-centre alignment of ze hip…'

'I do?'

'*Oui, c'est vrai*. You're all lopsided. Left leg is shorter than the right. But I still think it is *suractivité* in the muscles on the inside of the shin – the muscles that produce the outward turning movements of the ankle. They stabilise the rear foot as it pronates – rolls inwards – when the heel strikes the ground. *Donc* overpronation; *donc* damaged tibialis posterior muscle; *ainsi* shin pain; *ainsi* you pay me a lot of money to put it right.'

'So how *do* I put it right?'

'I can tape up your legs to immobilise the damaged muscles. But also you should do some gentle stretching. Stretch your gastrocnemius, the main calf, and the soleus, lower calf muscles.' She guided me through a set of exercises that I must follow rigorously, which amongst other tortures entailed describing the alphabet in mid-air with my toes. I was also banned from running, although cycling was permitted. This was not a good option for one who has a painful history of falling off bikes. Strips of elastic tape were stretched around the lower parts of my legs, preventing my stricken muscles from moving. It felt most awkward and meant that I could only waddle like a duck. If this was not enough, Christelle also demonstrated a ludicrous procedure which at first I took to be a joke, finding it hard to stifle a smirk.

'*Pendant les soirs*,' said my torturer in all seriousness, 'each night, you must tie your feet to your knees to prevent them from flopping forward under the weight of the duvet and hyper-extending the damaged muscles. *C'est clair*?' A sharp slap on the bare thigh soon stopped my inane giggling. 'As for your *genou*, your knee, basically it's *épuisé*. Worn out, not just because you run, but because of its medical history. Your knee is your Achilles heel…' She smiled smugly. I did not respond. 'Now get dressed and go home. No running until this is cleared up. *Entendu*?'

'I guess there's no chance that I might run in the Paris Marathon next April?' I chanced my hand. The physio merely peered at me, unblinking, over the top of her spectacles. I took her silent stare to mean a definite '*non*'.

'So you can't run, can you, 'Orrible Onc? Shame in't it!' sneered my impertinent niece Hollie over the telephone line one evening. She and her parents – my brother the Count and sister-in-law Stephanie – were over in France for a few weeks holiday.

'That is correct, nasty child,' I replied.

'What about cycling then, Onc?' she hollered in her Cheshire accent. The girl had, since she was a cute little thing in frilly dresses, always been loud, but now that she was pushing eighteen she had developed the dulcet tones of a junior league fishwife.

'Well, Niecey, your poor old uncle is allowed to cycle but, if you remember, he does tend to fall off quite regularly...' I reminded the girl. I winced as I recalled my last unfortunate tumble: clipping an unseen dip in the road with the front wheel of my mountain bike, I had plummeted face first into the tarmac, and was hauled off to hospital to have my upper lip agonisingly sewn up by an A&E doctor who had not long finished playing with dolls.

'Yeah, but you'd have a hard job falling off the type of bike we have in mind!' she bawled. 'Are you up for it, Onc?'

'So long as I don't have to share a tandem with you, I'm up for it.' I replied. In need of a diversion, I was indeed up for whatever plans my family had.

The following morning they collected me en route for Bussière-Galant. The village lies to the south-west of Limoges in the Périgord Limousin region, about ten kilometres from historic Châlus, the village where Richard Coeur de Lion was killed by a crossbow bolt and where his bowels are preserved in the chapel. As fascinating though this historic fact was, the Lionheart's innards would have to wait for another day. We had more exciting thrills to experience. We were heading, my niece enthusiastically explained, for an attraction called Vélo-Rail, which was based around a redundant railway embankment that meandered along the gentle rise of the Vallée de la Dronne. This was not a venue for miniature steam train buffs, or a hiking route for *randonneurs*, however. The six-kilometre trail was to be negotiated on rail-bikes.

We purchased our tickets from the *guichet*, the office housed within the carriages of an ancient mail train, which sat in a siding off the *chemin de fer*, the railway line. Ushered to the queue of rail-bikes lined up on the main track, along with our fellow travellers, we were given a well-rehearsed briefing on the rules of the rail. Next, we were given a rundown on our unique mode of transport. Metal-framed carts with four miniature train wheels, which fitted across the gauge of the railway track, the rail-bikes were to be propelled by pedal power. Two passengers could loll in comfort in the deck-chair seats strung between the cyclists.

'You two pedal first,' said Stephanie decisively, settling into a deckchair. Hollie leaped into the spare seat like a whippet, leaving Phill and me standing by like a pair of glum chauffeurs. My brother and I mounted our respective bikes and waited while the carts in front of us were given the word to move off along the track. Soon we were off, pedalling in unison to propel our cart along the track. The carts were sufficiently spaced apart to allow individual parties to proceed at their own pace, although some giggling riders were so inept at pedalling that they were obliged to dismount and lift their cart off the tracks entirely to allow the backlog to pass.

Once into our rhythm we could appreciate our sylvan surroundings on what was a beautifully warm, sunny day. We passed through delightful copses of chestnut trees, skirted green meadows grazed by cattle and sheep and crossed arched viaducts. Barely visible in amongst the trees were a number of *belles demeures*, beautiful dwellings with their façades clad in ivy. Families looked up from their gardens to wave pleasantly as the rail-bikes trundled past with a ta-tac-tatoum, ta-tac-tatoum rhythm. At certain points along the route, lanes intersected the railway line at level crossings. These were invariably watched over by characterful *maisons de passage à niveau*, level-crossing keepers' cottages that had, since the line's redundancy, become quaint, if rather tiny homes.

Sections of the track were quite steep and allowed us to freewheel downhill at a disconcertingly fast pace, tugging on the brake lever to slow our velocity. It was then that we realised that the route was, of course, not circular and that we would be obliged to return by the same track: the fast downhill sections were destined to become a slow uphill slog.

The area traversed by the railway line has a rich history that revolves around what is colloquially known as *Le Pain de Bois*, bread of the woods, the humble chestnut. At one time essential to the economy and culture of the region, the *châtaignier* tree covers three-quarters of the entire woodland. The traditional fabrication of fine chestnut slats used in the manufacture of barrels, lobster traps, and *tressées* used in the weaving of baskets, were carried out by artisans known as *feuillardiers*. These solitary men would live and work in little rude *cabanes*, huts made from woven branches, which have been preserved on site. These artisans, living out their lives in the deep forest, with time evolved into basketmakers and producers of fencing and fence posts.

The river Dronne runs through the Périgord Vert for some one hundred and ninety kilometres to the Isle à Coutras in the distant Gironde region, a site of ancient villages and thousands of châteaux. At Bussière-Galant the fast-flowing water was the site of intense activity around the mills, forges and refineries, which utilised the charcoal of chestnut wood. Near the bridge that crosses the Dronne lies *la roche qui pleure*, the rock that cried. Encased in the stone is a cross that bears witness to an ancient legend. This tells of a time when the souls of the dead were trapped in the land of the living. The path crossing the Dronne at Joffreny mill was frequented by the inhabitants of Bussière-Galant en route to Châlus. In passing the rock, the lamentations of the dead souls could be heard, which stuck fear into the hearts of the people. The enterprising parson of the parish organised a procession to the rock, whereby the cross was installed. The lamentations ceased henceforth and the inhabitants could once again traverse the path again without fear.

At the end of the line, the track simply terminated with a buffer in the shade of a leafy copse. Carts were hauled off the tracks and laid on the grass. As the last of the carts trundled to the terminus, some families dove into packed lunches, while others turned their carts around and headed off back up the track. After a respectable rest, our little party decided to head off back.

On this day, the only crying that could be heard came not from a rock but was the pitiful whinging of the Count and I as we hauled our chattering cargo back up the incline on the way back to the start of the line.

A few weeks later, having terminated our lease on the cottage in Kent, it was time for Al to make the final move over to France. I could barely wait for my wife to join me, since my weeks spent alone had been at times stressful and lonely. So, in late September, I drove back to England. Having again commandeered our friend Roy Garrett's old horsebox, which we had used to cart over our initial batch of furniture, we packed everything into the back as best we could and headed for Limousin. While Al and I drove down in our car, tugging the balloon trailer behind it, Roy and his brother Paul brought up the rear at the snail's pace that was dictated by their temperamental vehicle.

It was a strange sensation to realise that we had at last cut most of our physical ties with England. We were now officially resident in France, with a new life ahead of us. Al and I were keen to speed on with our renovations at the *grange*. The massive roof of the barn, for example, still required insulating before the chill of winter hit us, and it was a job that filled me with trepidation. Apart from this monumental task, the rest of our home was basic, yet comfortable. We decided to devote the remainder of the summer and autumn to working the land. Storing the large number of packing cases containing our worldly goods in a room that had been allotted as a spare bedroom, we worked out a plan of action for tackling the great outdoors while the weather was clement.

We had drawn up plans to create a substantial vegetable plot that would provide us with all the fresh vegetables we would need. Neither of us had owned a fully-fledged *potager* before, so I had spent many hours scouring reference books in order to work out how best to prepare the land. I established a detailed notebook, complete with sketches of the intended plot and the produce it would contain. In order to condition the soil, it would be necessary for us to prepare the land now; its heavy consistency, once incorporated with plenty of bulky organic matter, would then become crumbly and workable after the first of the winter frosts had penetrated and broken it down. That way, we would be ready to plant our first seeds the following spring.

The area we had selected for the vegetable garden was little more than a rough area of grass adjacent to the large, open-fronted hangar attached to the *grange*. The terrain, which benefited from full sun virtually all day, sloped slightly along its length, which we felt would ensure good drainage. Marking out the overall plot with a string line and wooden pegs, we debated how large we should make the garden. Greedily enlarging the plot to cram in more produce, we did not stop to consider the heavy workload we were imposing on ourselves. We stood back and inspected the rectangle of nettles and brambles that we had marked out, covering an area of some twenty square metres.

'Now what do we do?' asked Al.

'Get rid of all the weeds, remove the grass and dig it all over,' I replied.

'Not by hand, surely?' Al was aghast. 'That will take us months! Isn't there some machine we can use?'

'We'll have to see if we can hire, or borrow, a rotovator to break up the earth. But meanwhile, we can get rid of the nettles and brambles with our brush cutter.'

'You'll need a *motoculteur* for that,' said a gravelly French voice from behind us. Al and I had been making not entirely successful inroads into our future vegetable plot with a spade and a garden rake. The earth was as solid as rock: in fact, much of it was stone, a dense bedrock of granite. We turned around to see Bruno Bussiere, the ex-*gendarme*, chef and hen-pecked husband of Madame Météo. The years since we had first met had been hard on the elderly gentleman and his previous passing similarity to debonair Scots actor Sean Connery had blurred somewhat around the edges, like a *sfumato* painting. He had gained a considerable surplus of kilograms, had lost much of his white hair, and had become quite stooped and fragile. The crumpled form we saw before us was a far cry from the thick-set man who had single-handedly chopped up several of our fallen oak trees for firewood, taking his share for the trouble.

'*Bonjour* Bruno!' I shouted. 'It is proving to be hard work! I don't suppose you have a *motoculteur* do you?' We had so far been unable to find a rotovator for hire or to scrounge from friends.

'I do!' he called helpfully.

'Any chance we could borrow it then?' I hollered back.

'Certainly!' the old boy responded. 'Any time you like.'

'Have you finished preparing your own *potager*, then?' asked Al.

'No.'

'Why not?' said Al.

'My *motoculteur* is broken,' he replied. Al and I looked at each other bemused. Damn! We had once again fallen into the linguistic trap frequently set by the French in order to snare unwary foreigners. Ask a direct question and you will not necessarily get the full answer, for Frenchmen are apt not to volunteer relevant information.

'Thanks Bruno, but maybe we'll pass on the *motoculteur*...' I said.

'*Comme vous voulez!*' he said, waving, and set off down the lane.

The drought conditions that afflicted Limousin were severe that summer. There had been no rain for many weeks and the huge water butts Al and I had connected to the gutter system of the *grange* and its attendant barns had run dry, leaving behind a black, stinking silt in the bottom into which hapless lizards had fallen and drowned. The communal pond had completely dried up, although our own spring-fed Ugly-Bugly still boasted a respectable level of water. We began ferrying large containers of water from this private source to the house in the back of our estate car, although much of the liquid slopped out during the bumpy drive along the *chemin*. Our flower borders, which did not contain much fertile soil at the best of times, were dry and the plants wilted, their leaves crisp and brown. Only the wisteria and grapevines that clothed the front of the *grange* thrived, since Al and I had also begun the habit of dousing their roots daily with pans of water used in cooking. It was hard to see how the plants had survived at all, since the ground in which they had been planted two years earlier was mainly composed of hard granite. But they thrived: the wisteria produced an admirable display of honey-scented white blooms after the first year of planting, while the grapevines hung heavy with small, juicy black grapes that were delicious to eat, although a little tart on the palate.

One morning I heard a metallic clanking at the front of the *grange* and went to investigate. Véronique, mumbling away to herself, was bent over, busily arranging pans, buckets, bowls and other containers in the lane at the front of her house. She looked up as I approached.

'What's this for, then?' I asked, kissing her the ritual four times on cheeks that were slick with perspiration.

'*Regardez!*' she exclaimed, pointing skywards towards the south. I examined the rich blue of the cloudless sky. 'Rain is coming.'

'Not according to the *météo*,' I responded. The daily ballooning forecast I habitually read on France Météo's Internet website typically offered the fine degree of accuracy essential for aviators. The five-day forecast had predicted that the dry conditions would persist. But Véronique knew nothing of the mysteries of the Internet, nor cared a jot.

'*Ben, dit donc!*' mocked my neighbour. 'What does the *météo* know? Madame Bussiere says otherwise and I would always take her word for it in preference to a load of scientists! She knows how to read the weather by the colour of the sky, the way certain leaves turn on the trees, the smell of the air...' I had my own doubts about this claim, however. Polish-born Jolanda Bussiere had been dubbed 'Madame Météo' by her long-suffering husband, Bruno, on account of her mysterious ability to forecast the weather. But he knew, and I knew for a fact that the old lady actually gleaned her information not from reading the forces of nature but from the hourly weather bulletins broadcast on radio and television.

'So if I were you, Monsieur Richard, I would do as I am doing. Put out anything you can to catch the rain.'

'OK Véronique!' I laughed, and waved her goodbye. I checked the weather forecast again. No change. It was not going to rain, I steadfastly believed.

The following morning I heard the sound of tinkling metal again, but this time accompanied by a distinctly watery dripping. Jumping from the bed, I ran to the window. It had rained heavily during the night and my neighbour's collection of pots and pans were full to the brim with water. Dressing quickly, I skipped gleefully downstairs to examine my water butts, which I confidently expected to be overflowing with water. I flipped off the lid of the first butt. The container was empty. I had foolishly forgotten to close off the tap at the base of the barrel and the night's rainfall had simply flushed through the system and soaked into the dry ground. The second butt revealed the same. Véronique came out of her house and began distributing her freshly gathered water supply to her parched flower pots and containers.

'Madame Météo knows best!' she chuckled. Perhaps there was more to Jolanda Bussiere's mysterious forecasting abilities than I had suspected.

One evening, after a hard day preparing the *potager*, Al and I were relaxing and listening to some soft, tinkly jazz on the stereo. My wife looked up from her trashy celebrity magazine and smiled across the sofa at me. Distracted from the high-brow literary tome I was reading, I caught her eye and returned the smile.

'Rich,' she said huskily. 'Now that we're here in France, in our lovely home, I realise that something is missing...'

'What's that?' I asked. Al raised and lowered her eyebrows simultaneously and her mouth stretched into the broad, Julia Roberts smile that I found so beguiling. Whatever she was suggesting, however, was totally lost on me. 'We've left something behind? What is it?'

'No, it's nothing we've left behind. We've discussed it before... something to complete the picture, make our life here more enjoyable...'

'A swimming pool?' I queried. 'You'll have to wait a few years...'

'No, dork brain!' she cut me short. 'I mean our family isn't quite complete...'

'What?'

'We two are a family, right?'

'Uh-huh.' I nodded, fearful of where this line of enquiry was leading.

'And what would make our family complete, darling?' she was feeding me the lines but some mental blockage was preventing me from articulating a plausible response.

A lump came to my throat. 'What are you trying to tell me?' I queried. 'Are you saying you've changed your mind. And now you want to have a…'

'Two,' she interjected.

'Two!' I croaked. 'From not wanting any, you suddenly tell me that you've changed your mind and now you want two?' I was incredulous. My wife and I had discussed on numerous occasions whether or not we would want to start a family and, whilst nervous about bringing another child into the world when I had already two estranged children from my first marriage, I was not averse to the notion.

Al, conversely, had always maintained a stance of not wanting children at all. She had, in fact, been extremely vociferous about the topic. 'I want to be totally selfish for the first time in my life,' she had told me. 'I want to share my life with you and you alone.' Flattered, I had bowed to her decision, while stressing that the metaphorical door was always open for a change of mind. Now it seemed that the door had been ripped from its hinges and a whole gaggle of offspring were clamouring on the threshold.

'So, darling,' I said, taking a deep breath. I reached out to take her hand in mine. 'You've reconsidered. It's normal. I understand. But two?'

'They'd be friends, growing up together…' Her tone was becoming excited.

'Yes… but…'

'There'd be a lot of mess at first, I admit…'

'I'm certain of it!' The nappy stage had never been a favourite time of my child-rearing days.

'But we could put a lot of newspaper down!'

'Err, yes…'

'And they could sleep in the same bed!' she said, clapping her hands together gleefully.

'Well, yes darling. But we could stretch to a bed each, I guess...'

'So we can have two?' Al had a gleeful expression like a child who had just been promised a brand new bicycle, complete with stabilisers and a bell.

'But Al, what about the age thing...' I had always been concerned about the good sense of starting a family late in life: I was approaching fifty years old, while Al was nine years my junior.

'If we had them at the same time, they'd be the same age!'

'Well, yes, that is true... but you can't guarantee that, Al.' I sometimes worried about my wife's grasp of the way the world worked. Now my fears had been confirmed.

'Of course we can, silly. It's simply a matter of coordination,' she explained blithely. My jaw dropped and my eyes metaphorically stood out on stalks. 'Don't put obstacles in the way.'

'So, let me get this straight. First you didn't want any. Now you want to have two b... b...' I found it difficult to spit out the word.

'They needn't be the same sex!' she interrupted.

'No?'

'Or even the same breed...' Al placed a delicate forefinger to her lips in contemplation.

'Excuse me?'

'Boxers.'

'Boxers?' I repeated, somewhat taken aback. The centime dropped. But I must admit I was a little relieved. A hot flush washed over me.

'Well,' she said. 'We need not necessarily buy two boxers. I know you love the breed, but personally I've always hankered after a beagle. So, what do you say, Rich? We can go and buy a boxer and a beagle pup?'

Research had revealed that *le boxer* was a popular breed of dog in France, although many of the specimens I had seen out and about were stockier than the lithe animal I knew and loved, and frequently sported trimmed ears. I detested this procedure, rife in the States, whereby the animal's naturally floppy ears are snipped to a pointed shape to make them stand up from the dog's head. In my mind there was little difference in terms of mutilation between this and the systematic docking of tails, but this too was commonly carried out on young pups. I had owned a boxer previously. Oscar had been my constant companion after my separation from my ex-wife and it had only been the necessity of taking a full-time London-based job during those unfortunate years that had resulted in me having to find the dog a new home. Since then I had missed the company of a canine companion and wanted to redress the balance by giving a good home to another.

I logged onto to the Internet website of the Boxer Club de France to search through their listings of *éleveurs*, breeders, in or close to our region, from whom we could purchase a pedigree pup. We made several enquiries and prepared to await a favourable response. Meanwhile, we attempted to find a breeder of beagles. So that our two new companions would become fond friends, we intended to coordinate their purchase to within a few days.

Locating a beagle breeder south of Limoges, we set off on a Saturday morning to inspect the goods. Arriving at a rather dilapidated farmhouse, we were greeted by a round-faced, moustachioed man wearing regulation green hunting trousers, jacket and boots, with a matching peaked cap perched on his head, ear muffs folded upwards. As we climbed out of the car, we could hear a cacophony of hoarse barking emanating from a tin-roofed barn at the far side of a muddy yard.

'*Alors*,' the man said, shaking our hands. 'You're looking for a beagle. Good hunting breed…'

'We're actually looking for a pet…' explained Al. The man eyed her quizzically, then shrugged. We followed him across the yard to the barn. Our host unlatched a little door at the side of the building and led us inside. The pervading stench of dog excrement made me retch, but I concealed this unfortunate reaction. As our eyes became accustomed to the dim light, we found ourselves in a long, narrow hallway with iron-barred cells down each side; it reminded me of a nerve-tingling scene from *Silence of the Lambs* and I quite expected to find Hannibal the Cannibal glaring from between the bars. Instead, the cells were filled with a sea of writhing dogs, their coats filthy and wet. There must have been about sixty animals in total and the din was ear piercing. As the dogs scrabbled on the bare concrete slab, which was slick with urine, they could not avoid treading in the heaps of their own turds that covered the surface. It was a pitiful sight. Al grasped my hand and squeezed it tightly as the man led us to a large pen at the end of the corridor, in which there were about a dozen puppies aged, I imagined, about sixteen weeks. He swung the door open and the puppies raced out, ignoring us and heading down the corridor and out into the yard through a hole in the base of the outer door. We followed and watched as these ruffian beagles headed in pack formation for a flock of unsuspecting chickens. As the poultry scatted in all directions, the dog breeder let out a loud whistle and the pack of hounds swerved and came pelting back towards us.

'How old are these pups?' Al asked, confused by the rather stocky, shorter-legged frames of the filthy rabble. Their coats were coarser than beagles we were familiar with, and their colouration much darker.

'What age dog do you want?' replied the breeder, avoiding the question.

'Well, we'd hoped for twelve weeks… once they are weaned…' said Al.

'These have twelve weeks…' said the man immediately.

After a respectable amount of time examining specific pups at closer range, we thanked our host for his time and departed.

'Not like the beagles I remember from England,' remarked Al. I agreed. 'We'll keep looking, eh?' I nodded.

On our way back home, out of curiosity we stopped off at the large pet shop located in a *zone commerciale* on the outskirts of Limoges. Browsing through the line of cages housing jumbles of kittens, white rabbits, guinea pigs and assorted birds, we reached a row of glass-fronted kennels containing various breeds of dog: wrinkly Shar-Pei, silky-eared King Charles Spaniels, fluffy bichon frises, and a large, curly-haired black mongrel which lay sleeping on the sawdust floor. Curled up against its body was another pup, reddish-brown and smooth-coated. As Al and I peered into the kennel the brown pup stretched all four long legs and a head appeared, yawning tiredly and revealing a long pink tongue. Blinking sleepily, the pup regarded us through the glass. One floppy ear hung down, while the other stood erect. The pup's round face was wrinkled and drooped towards a pair of floppy jowls and its snub nose was characteristically turned up. The pup stood up unsteadily and wobbled towards the glass, revealing a smart white bib at his chest.

'Oh, Rich... he's *so* adorable!' breathed Al, waving at the little boxer behind the glass. 'He's perfect...' And that was how the rumbustious boxer pup, who we came to dub Jazz (after my fondness of the music), came into our lives. Although originally intended as 'my' dog, the loveable canine soon won over Al's heart and she discarded any notions of bringing one of the beagles of France into the family. The pair soon became inseparable. So much so that it was often difficult for me to persuade my wife that an invitation to a friend's house for dinner did not invariably stretch to Jazz as well.

Al had an innate ability to communicate with horses in a relationship based on mutual trust and over the coming months she employed a similar method when tutoring young Jazz how to behave in his new family. The pup responded well to her tutelage. She would issue instructions to him in short French phrases: he would, she insisted, learn to recognise the specific sounds and the tone. Should he become separated from us at any time, she professed, the dog would recognise the word '*Arrêt!*' if commanded to stop by any common or garden French person he might encounter; likewise, he would immediately sit at the '*Assis!*' command. She demonstrated the trick by using the English words first. The pup showed no reaction. She used the French words, and he obeyed immediately. Her favourite trick was to crouch down with Jazz and whisper a subtle '*Vas-y!*' in his floppy ears. Fired with enthusiasm, Jazz would suddenly pelt off hell for leather away from his mistress until he heard the shrill '*Viens ici!*', whereby he would execute a tight about face and hare off back towards her, pink tongue lolloping out of the side of his mouth, jowls flapping. As he grew and became more physically solid, this game became a real danger, since he was apt to run at full speed into one's legs, toppling us like ninepins.

The old Zetor tractor

Chapter Six

Working the land

The rampant growth of nettles and brambles surrounding the property had reached epic proportions. While I had maintained a rigorous programme of *débroussaillement*, dousing the weeds with noxious chemicals applied by a pressure sprayer, this brush clearance had been only partially successful. Suitably protected against stings and spikes by thick jeans, wellington boots, a thick jacket, a hat, gauntlets, goggles and facemask, I would wade into a sea of unrestrained growth that in places reached over my head. The intense summer heat – with temperatures in the mid-thirties – made this task, dressed in this way, appallingly uncomfortable and taxing. No sooner had I administered an intensive course of treatment and the plants had shrivelled and died back, than new growth would emerge from the ground to take its place. Even a motor-powered brush cutter failed to keep the twisting, spiky stems of the brambles at bay for long. One of our large fields was accessible only via a narrow pathway, which had become impenetrable. No tractor had been able to gain entry to the field for a decade or more. Although a veritable forest of young oak saplings had been allowed to prosper undisturbed for years, the grass was unkempt and of poor quality. It became clear to us that maintaining our acreage would call for some specialised equipment if we were to make any headway at all.

After much research on Al's part, we purchased a 1970s Zetor tractor, which hailed from Eastern Europe, and a *girobroyer*, or rotary mower. The mower was a large orange slab of metal about the size of a king-sized double bed, which housed three vicious-looking revolving cutting blades beneath. We were assured that this device, which was to be attached to the rear of the tractor and raised and lowered hydraulically, would make short work of slicing through the bramble thickets and nettles, cutting the long grass short into the bargain. We also purchased a box-shaped rear-mounted *bennette*, or carrying bin, and a clanking iron harrow for grubbing out the weed roots. With this equipment, we felt sure, we would be able to care for the land more effectively.

After the delivery of the tractor and its accessories on a low-loader, curious farming neighbours appeared at the hangar attached to the *grange*, where the machinery was housed. To a man, they unanimously declared the Zetor to be '*très fort*', very strong, and *'formidable!'*. I was clapped on the back by calloused, grease-impregnated hands and congratulated in my choice of equipment. I was shy to explain that the bulk of the decision-making in our purchase of a tractor had been due to Al's sterling research and ability to strike up a canny bargain with the salesman. But she was merely *une femme*, and in this neck of the woods, *les hommes* ruled the fields. Rather fraudulently, I felt as though I had been officially admitted into the enclosed and masculine world of the *agriculteur*.

Despite having a practical mind – my specialist subject as a writer is house renovation and do-it-yourself – the mechanical contraptions that lie beneath the bonnet of an automobile have always eluded me. The tractor was no exception. I had soon become practised at greasing the many nipples that protruded from the tractor's body, but the myriad hoses, pipes, nuts, bolts and adjustment knobs, screws and levers that protruded from its oil-smeared engine compartment performed functions that would ever remain a mystery to me. I admired the machine for its kitsch qualities, although its overall design seemed more reminiscent of a child's imaginative misrepresentation of a tractor than of a real vehicle. The tractor was indeed manfully large, with deep-treaded rear tyres that reached almost to my shoulders. The guts of the tractor and its fuel tank were housed within a faded red shell, and the vehicle sported an angular glazed cab and a large orange flashing light on the roof (which I found to be particularly impressive). The light was to be used when the vehicle was driving along the highway but, as I did not have the necessary licence to permit this – the equivalent of a heavy goods vehicle licence is required in France for all tractor drivers – I would be limited to trundling across our own property.

Inside the cab was an enormous steering wheel with a disturbing amount of play in its action, a baffling array of dials that did not appear to function and a bank of levers. But after extensive instruction from Monsieur Dubranle, the agricultural supplier we had bought the tractor from, I was confident that I could control the beast. In practice, my confidence was sorely misplaced.

My first attempts to drive the tractor were sadly deficient, partly due to the fact that the gears were unmarked and – Monsieur Dubranle's instructions forgotten – selection was a matter of pure guesswork. When finally I managed to find a gear and depressed the accelerator pedal, the tractor lurched forwards at an alarming rate like a dragster. The front reared up disconcertingly, the two small wheels leaving the ground completely. The machine then began to pirouette gracefully before its front wheels descended to the ground with a jarring thump. Soon, however, I got the hang of driving in a straight line, which curiously enough called for constantly wiggling the steering wheel from side to side. Attempting to scale the slightest grade, however, would result in the tractor rearing up again.

'You need a *masse*,' advised Jérôme L'Heureux, the farmer from whom we had bought the farm, Véronique's nephew. He still owned and farmed many hectares of land surrounding Le Mas Mauvis, despite the fact that he lived fifteen kilometres away. Even this reasonably short distance, however, took him an hour each way in his own tractor, before he could even commence work. He would frequently be working the land until darkness fell, by the feeble beam of his headlights, before heading off home, exhausted, only to return at the crack of dawn the next day. It was a hard life, for little financial reward.

The burly farmer had for years appeared to regard me from a distance with a critical eye, no doubt amused by my ineptitude as a junior league *agriculteur*. But with the passing of time he had warmed towards me and I to him. In any event I found him hard to take seriously ever since he had developed a predilection for wearing a type of overall *à la mode* with French farmers. The bottle green overalls were dissected by chunky white zips down each leg and around the groin, along each arm and down each side of the torso. Undoubtedly practical, the overalls resembled a man-sized BabyGro. Because of his considerable girth and upper-body musculature, however, the big man's *layette* was always ill-fitting, leaving his hairy forearms and lily-white ankles exposed and his ample crotch severely constrained.

Jérôme had come to realise that, while I might have only a vague notion of what I was doing, I had a stubborn streak that would not permit me to give in or to ask for his help. His help, however, was doled out freely and generously. Jérôme had watched with interest one day as I trundled across the field on only the back wheels of the tractor, and felt honour bound to offer some expert advice. 'The *giro* is too heavy unless you have more weight on the front,' he explained, dismounting from the air-conditioned cab of his own throbbing tractor, which made mine look like a Dinky to his Tonka. He pointed out the stack of huge metal weights clamped on the front. 'This will stop the front from rearing up. It is essential, Richard.' He resolved to locate a second-hand *masse* for me. Meanwhile, he advised me on some technical adjustments to my driving style that would lessen the disconcerting effect. 'Keep the *giro* low when ascending, not raised high like you have it. This will alter the point of balance and transfer the weight to the front of the tractor.'

It seemed that farming was far more of a science that I had thought.

With the mower attached, and mindful of Jérôme's wise words, I began my first cut of the field at the rear of the property. For this historic maiden voyage, I was joined in the cab by Al. She perched precariously on the passenger seat with Jazz in her arms, as we rumbled around the perimeter of the field, first cutting a broad margin. I had been sent a schematic plan on the art of mowing by Al's mother Sheila, a woman who knows tractors. The diagram, annotated with arrows, and resembling a weather chart, indicated the order of play. First, cut a margin around the field two passes wide. Second, proceed to divide the field into two halves with a single pass of the mower. Third, cut the grass in one half by mowing back and forth in straight lines. Finally, repeat the procedure for the second half of the field.

It was a strenuous, long-winded task, which called for raising and lowering the mower at each turn, for it could not be dragged around complex bends. The constant jolting of the tractor resulted in every nerve in my body shaking uncontrollably. After three or four hours I had completed the modest sized field and headed for the shower to cool off before I was able to clamp my quivering hands around a bottle of cold beer.

Tractor driving was not without its mishaps. On one occasion, when rumbling around the perimeter of the field I encountered a slight incline to one side. The tractor responded by leaning at an acute and alarming angle. This motion caused Al and Jazz to leap in panic from the cab while I was left to wrestle the machine back on the straight and narrow. On another occasion, while I was making a technical adjustment to the hydraulics at the rear of the tractor, the hand brake fell off with an audible *ping!* and clattered down the steps to the cab onto the grass. Unmanned, the vehicle started to roll forwards, gaining speed as it headed for the incline and the marshy area below it. Running after the tractor, I managed to scramble aboard just in time to apply the foot brake before the machine plummeted into the dip.

The mower did indeed prove more than able to cope with the forest of brambles that had made huge tracts of our land impassable. With the mower raised, I would reverse slowly into the thicket then, switching on the blades, would lower the contraption. This had the effect of shredding the tangled stems, and even stout broom stalks would be reduced to stubble in an instant. I carefully cut around the numerous self-seeded oak saplings that had been allowed to flourish undisturbed amidst the brambles for several years, with the comforting thought that I would be creating a leafy copse for future generations to admire. Cutting into dense undergrowth like this, unaware of what lay beneath, did have its mishaps: on three separate occasions I punctured the front tyres on glass and twists of metal, which stranded the vehicle on the land. Not possessing a heavyweight jack to lift the tractor and remove the wheel, I was obliged to call out a local agricultural equipment mechanic for help. Embarrassed by my frequent call-outs for the most simple of hitches, I was assured by the kindly mechanic that this was only to be expected.

'*C'est pas grave, monsieur,*' he said, smiling. 'Even real farmers have such problems!'

Although we were equipped with a fine tractor and grass-cutting equipment, we still had no mechanical means of tilling the earth to prepare the vegetable garden for planting the following spring. Hire equipment was a scarcity in those parts and all our neighbours were heavily involved in rotovating their own gardens and could not lend us their equipment. Bruno Bussiere's *motoculteur* was still lying in pieces in his garage. Al and I had continued with our task of turning over the earth by hand. It was backbreaking work and I had already snapped the shaft of my favourite spade. So it was with utmost gratitude that we accepted an offer of help from Jérôme L'Heureux, who arrived one morning with a generous proposition.

'I'll plough your *potager* for you if I can use your tractor,' he explained. 'I've promised to turn over aunt Véronique's plot today – my plough is already here on the *communale* – but my tractor broke down on the way over. *C'est vraiment grave!* The *météo* forecasts a long period of heavy rain, so if I don't get it done today, it won't get done for a while. The ground will be too wet. And I'll get well and truly nagged by my aunt.'

'That is serious!' I concurred. 'Take the tractor with pleasure. The keys are in the ignition. But can I help out at all?' The burly man scrutinised me for a moment, inspecting the long shorts and Wellington boots I was wearing, and the broken spade I held in my hands.

'I asked to borrow the tractor, Richard, because it is strong and reliable…' he said with a deadpan expression.

'I guess that means you can manage on your own, eh?'

'*Tout à fait,*' he replied. Entirely.

While Al and I stood back and watched Jérôme hitch up his big, shiny plough to our dear old tractor, feeling more than a flush of pride, we noticed a familiar figure shambling along the lane towards the house. Bruno Bussiere hove into view, looking extremely down-at-heel.

'*Bonjour* Bruno,' Al said, greeting him with a *bisou* on each flaccid cheek. I shook his hand, which felt limp and puffy.

'*Bonjour*,' Bruno said solemnly, scraping the blue canvas captain's cap from his head. He appeared downtrodden and miserable, which was so unlike his typically jovial self. He was gnawing on a stick of liquorice root as a substitute for the roll-up cigarettes he favoured.

'Taking the morning air, are you?' asked Al. '*Ça fait beau, eh!…*'

'Getting out of the house for a bit of peace, more like…' he grumbled. We knew that he and Jolanda had quite a tempestuous life together – their arguments could often be heard resounding across the village, as could the sound of crockery, pots and pans being thrown – but Bruno normally weathered the brunt of his volatile wife's temper, presenting a smile to the outside world. Today he was clearly in the depths of depression.

'Jolanda at home cooking lunch, is she?' asked Al, trying to buck the old man up.

'*Non*,' he moaned, taking the liquorice root from his mouth and examining the chewed fibres at the end. 'She refuses to cook any more.' He shoved the stick back in his mouth and chewed.

'Why's that?'

'She says that since I was *chef de cuisine*, I can do the cooking from now on. Says I am lazy. Who cuts the wood, eh? Who digs the *potager*? But she hasn't bought any food. Stupid woman.' He began peering into the flowerbeds that ran along the front of the *grange*. Bending down with a groan, he picked up a large brown striped snail, examined it, and popped it into the cap he still held in his hand. '*Donc*, that is why I am here… *les escargots!*' He snatched another snail from the flowerbed and put it in the cap. Peering up at us, his lips curled into a sardonic smile.

'What are you doing?' said Al, as the Bruno bent down again and began to fling more of the big snails into his cap.

'*Déjeuner…*' he said hoarsely. 'And free, too! You have the best *escargots* in the village. Must be attracted by these silly English flowers you insist on planting…' He indicated the fine blue spires of delphiniums that were my pride and joy, thriving as they did in very little soil. One of Bruno's bushy Connery-esque eyebrows flicked upwards and he revealed a mouthful of nicotine-stained teeth.

'Err, I wouldn't eat those, Bruno!' I said. 'I've doused them quite liberally with poison…' I indicated the masses of little blue pellets I had recently scattered on the soil. They had certainly done the trick, luring a laudable clutch of gastropods. Undeterred, Bruno continued gathering snails until he had collected more than a dozen.

'Really, Bruno, you shouldn't eat them. They'll make you ill. You don't want to end up killing yourself and Jolanda, do you?' I elaborated. Our neighbour simply raised another bushy eyebrow and sneered.

'*Pas de soucis,*' no worries, said the old chef. 'I'll flush them through first…'

'But that takes days, doesn't it?' I asked.

'*Normalement,*' he reflected mysteriously. 'Anyway, I'd best get back before she starts squawking. I really ought to strangle the old bird.' With that, he pulled a large discoloured handkerchief from his jacket pocket, placed it over the snails, then jammed the cap back on his head. With that, he proffered a Nazi salute (as was his wont), spun on his heel and shambled off towards his home.

'What do you make of that, Rich?' said Al, sounding concerned.

'Well, the mood he's in, I hope he doesn't feed Jolanda those snails today…'

'Or strangle her!' added Al.

Al, for whom the passage of time had become only a vague notion since she embarked upon her enforced period of unemployment, would frequently ask: 'When exactly did my sabbatical start, Rich?'

'Oh, I don't recall,' I would fib, dismissing the subject and raising another.

'But how long do I have left?' She would sometimes insist. I knew that this deeply sensitive lady felt guilty that she should perhaps be out trawling for another job, now that she was permanently installed in France. On a practical level, equipped with her excellent command of French, I was sure that she could secure a job locally without problem. But I worried about her health deteriorating again, when she had made such sterling improvements. Rather selfishly, I loved the thought of her pottering around the *grange* while I worked at my computer, and was deeply content to see her toiling away in the vegetable plot – loving the physical and mental challenge of taming unruly Mother Nature. Often I would lean out of the upstairs window adjacent to my desk in order to catch a glimpse of Al tending the vegetable seedlings, the little boxer pup never far away from his mistress's side.

While I would generally arise with the first light of day streaming through the un-curtained, un-shuttered windows, I would leave Al to sleep and wake at her leisure. Since our move to France, alarm clocks had been summarily banned from the household. It was fortunate that France exists on a time difference one hour earlier than the UK: I was able to virtually complete a day's work before my colleagues in London had woken, sat on a tube train for an hour, snatched breakfast from a greasy spoon, and made it into the office by ten o'clock. My master plan was to rise early, work until about two o'clock in the afternoon, then finish for the day; the rest of the time could be devoted to gardening or renovation jobs. Sadly, my London-based colleagues did not appreciate this fact and were apt to email or telephone with queries well into the evening.

After I had been working for a few hours at my computer, the sleeping beauty (invariably cuddling the pup, who had surreptitiously sneaked under the covers once I had vacated the bed) would drag herself into the land of the living with some reluctance. I was always amazed at my wife's propensity and capacity to sleep. Sleeping was, she would announce, one of her 'favouritest pastimes'. Preparing an intensely strong milky coffee for us both, she would next don her habitual jeans, boots, T-shirt and straw cowboy hat before hitting the trail, towed along by the exuberant young Jazz for a lengthy walk across the surrounding fields. They would return to regale me with tales of the herds of deer they had seen on their travels, and what stage the various crop fields had reached. Our life was falling into a snug fit rather like a comfortable pair of briefs. So whenever Al asked me about the expiration date of her sabbatical, I would respond by casually adding another few months onto her break from work. My only fear was that we would not be able to continue to survive on one salary: my freelance work was spasmodic, and magazine projects could fail at the first hurdle, or else be canned for financial or other reasons best known to the publishers. I had experienced such setbacks before and, ever the optimist, believed that something would always turn up to save the day.

So until the day arrived when our newfound lifestyle was under threat, I watched with enormous satisfaction as Al's fingers started to turn a verdant green with her growing horticultural experience, and marvelled at how she responded to the challenge of creating our oasis. The farm at Le Mas Mauvis was, after all, the first real home she had ever owned.

With the grass shorn to within an inch of its life, we turned our attention to the next stage: the erection of high wire fencing to prevent our future herd of llamas from leaping out. Whenever we commenced such manual work on our property, the flurry of activity would, sure as eggs are eggs, attract a swarm of intrigued or downright nosy neighbours, who would come to ogle. Perhaps it was because little happened in the hamlet and the fact that French daytime television was predominantly crap. Watching *les anglais* toil was a far more entertaining prospect. Véronique obviously found our antics amusing, as she was frequently driven to waddling over to where we were sinking fence posts, or stretching wire fencing, with a rickety wooden kitchen chair in tow. Without a word, she would set the chair down at the side of the lane a few feet away from us, plonk her self upon it, then fold her arms and stare.

'What will you do with your llamas, Monsieur Richard?' she asked one day. 'Make pillows? My nephew tells me you can make pillows…'

'That's right, you can…' I said, in between hammer blows.

'So their feathers are very soft, eh?'

'Feathers?' I said, regarding her in disbelief. 'Véronique, I…'

'So you need such high fencing to stop them flying out, *j'imagine*?' she interrupted before I could correct her on the llama's physiology.

'Actually, Véronique, a llama is not a bird!' I explained. 'Perhaps you're confusing it with an *autruche*?' It was possible that the old lady, not conversant with the wider world beyond the hamlet, could assume that I was intending to keep ostriches.

'Ah! *Je vois!*' said my neighbour, as if light had just dawned on her. 'You must think me a foolish old woman. Now I realise, I've seen them on *la télé…*'

'*Non non non,*' I placated. 'It's understandable.' My neighbour's horizons were extremely enclosed: in all her seventy-plus years she had rarely ventured beyond the boundaries of her region. The television was her only means of seeing the world that lay beyond.

There was a pause while the old dear considered our conversation.

'So what do the llamas' eggs taste like?' she asked.

Al and I had become a source of amusement and a convenient confessional for some of the locals. Bruno Bussiere would occasionally stop by, tattered dictionary in hand, on the pretext of a chat to improve his command of English. We suspected, however, that this was merely a ruse to cover up a *sortie* for an illicit coffee with Véronique. His domineering, envious wife Jolanda had forbidden the ageing ex-lothario to visit our neighbour *tout seul* for fear her friend Véronique might entice her man with her womanly wiles.

'Madame Bussiere thinks Monsieur Bussiere and I are having *une liaison amoureuse,*' Véronique had coquettishly revealed one day, the chair she had carried close to the fence creaking under strain of her considerable bulk. This astounding revelation was sufficient to distract me from my chore of sinking a fence post. I mistimed the swing of my sledgehammer and all but missed striking poor Al – who was supporting the post – on the head.

Other neighours, I believe, admired what we were attempting to do, however ineptly. Prime candidate was my arch-rival Monsieur Thierry André. The man was a wily individual who had in years gone by seen fit to sneak his herd of cows onto our land whenever we were not in residence and avail himself of free grazing. He tended to put the beasts on our unfenced fields during winter when the earth was damp and the animals had graunched up our fields no end. We had eventually been forced to set the forces of the law upon him, in the form of a legal letter from the formidable Maître Marsolet: the mere mention of the lady *notaire*'s name was enough to strike cold fear into the hearts of mere mortals. After this, the farmer's bombastic attitude had softened and he had come to accept that we were not to be trifled with. Still, he could never be outdone in certain respects. Size, to the burly farmer, did matter.

'Your tool is very small,' he had announced one day, pulling up his tractor at the side of the track.

'I beg your pardon?' I said, looking up from my work.

'I have a larger tool.'

'I'll bet you have, Thierry…' I mumbled.

'A thicker one is better,' he opined, adjusting the hang of his grimy jeans. He was wearing a pale blue – but extremely grubby – T-shirt several sizes too small to encase his magnificently rotund stomach, which ballooned over the waistband of his trousers. On his feet were a pair of green wellingtons. Broad shoulders gave way to a thick neck and balding pate, on top of which was perched a cloth cap that was many sizes too small for his skull. As usual he was bathed in perspiration and this sweaty sheen was accompanied by the rank odour of a man who perhaps bathed only once a fortnight. His complexion was unhealthily ruddy, a sure indication that his

110

blood pressure was bubbling somewhere off the scale. As some inexplicable concession to personal adornment, a grey, spiky goatee protruded from his chin.

In comparing the dimensions of our respective tools, I assumed that the husky-voiced farmer was referring to the long metal bar I was using to create a hole for a round-section fence post: the technique was to ram the bar into the earth, then to revolve it, rather like stirring a large pot of porridge. This was intended to form a snug hole for the post. Unfortunately, the ground was rock hard and I could make no impression on it at all.

'I will fetch my tool!' he growled, unusually helpfully. With that, he sprang onto his tractor, turned it from its intended course and rattled back to his farm. Five minutes later he was back again, proffering a stout iron bar that put my poor rod to shame. Wielding the bar like Yoda with a light sabre , he examined my feeble attempts at forming a hole. Suddenly he raised it above his head on thick, muscle-bound arms then drove it downward with a swift motion that sank the pointed end about a foot and a half into the rock hard earth. He tugged on the rod and revolved it, hauled it out of the hole and rammed it back in again with a grunt. '*Voila!*' he said. 'It's done. You may borrow this tool, Richard.' Deftly, he flipped the bar and presented it to me on the palms of both hands, with a little bow of the head.

'Why thank you, Thierry…' I said, taking hold of the bar. He let go. It weighed about three tons, I estimated. It was all I could do to hold onto it. Stumbling forward, I tripped in the hole the farmer had formed and fell into his open arms. This embrace was, in fact, a most unpleasant sensation. Setting me upright, he clapped me across both arms.

'You will have muscles as big as mine when you've finished with that tool!' He guffawed, clambered back onto his tractor and sped off down the lane to his byre.

Al and I had obviously found favour with the farmer, and this was made abundantly clear late one evening while we were relaxing, listening to some music in the *grange*. Tyres screeched to a halt in the lane outside and we peered through the window to see what the commotion was about. There was Thierry's white van parked outside, headlights blazing. Suddenly there came a loud rap on the door. We descended. On opening the door we were presented with the sight of the farmer, clad in hunter's outfit, thrusting a supermarket carrier bag towards us. The bag seemed to contain something that had recently been alive, for it was dripping with blood.

'What on earth is that?' shrieked Al, backing off warily as the burly farmer proffered her the bulging bag.

'*Regardez*,' said Thierry, opening up the neck of the bag and revealing the gory contents. 'This is yours…' I peered inside the bag. At the bottom, swimming in a soup of thick blood, was an enormous chunk of freshly carved meat about the size of a leg of lamb. But this was no lamb. The flesh was a rich reddish colour with a texture like beef.

'*Pour mangez…*' He mimed feeding something to himself. 'It's yours!' he repeated. '*Tiens!*'

'From the hunt, perhaps?' I asked. The farmer merely winked.

'Oh, but it's not necessary!' said Al.

'*Au contraire!* But it is!' he responded excitedly. '*C'est normale!* And I insist! I will be offended if you don't accept this gift…' Gracefully, I accepted the dripping bag.

'Now be sure to cook it properly! Not in the oven, as this will make it tough. Cook it in a pan on the stove,' he advised. 'And you know how to make a sauce?'

'Yes,' we chirped in unison. 'But what is it?'

'A proper sauce with the blood of the joint?' he prompted.

'Yes, of course. But, Thierry, what is it?'

'Not that disgusting powdered gravy you *anglais* love?'

'Never! But, Thierry…'

He regarded us with suspicion, for he considered that the English had no notion of how to cook. Then he winked again, tapped the side of his nose mysteriously, climbed back in his van and departed.

'Hang on a minute,' I said as the realisation dawned upon me. 'It's not the hunting season is it?'

'No, Rich… but let's not look a gift horse in the mouth, eh!'

Ballooning over Pierre-Buffière

Chapter Seven

Basket cases

Now that I was permanently ensconced in France, I yearned to get back into the air in my balloon. But first there was the question of a fuel supply. A balloon's burner, which produces the hot air that inflates the envelope, is fuelled by liquid propane. In order to fill the flight cylinders that are secured within the basket, I had previously utilised several tall bottles. Attached to the flight cylinders by a long hose, the propane was extracted simply by gravity. This was fine on a warm day, when the pressure within the

114

bottles would be sufficient to allow the liquid to flow freely. But on cold days I would frequently have to resort to pouring boiling water from a kettle onto the bottles in order to extract sufficient gas. This was a laborious and time-consuming job, taking about fifteen minutes for each of the four cylinders I habitually carried. I had promised myself that when I moved to France I would purchase a bulk cylinder, the type that is commonly used to fuel a home's central heating system. With this I would not only have a ready supply of gas for an entire year of flying but also I would be able to fill all the cylinders in just a few minutes.

I contacted a local supplier and made an appointment for their representative to visit Le Mas Mauvis to advise me on the costs and other requirements. On the allotted day, Monsieur Claude Norrin turned up at the house with his son Benoît in tow as a translator, for he spoke no English at all. I explained that my grasp of French was sufficient for me to converse in his language, but Monsieur Norrin had considered that it was only polite to converse in my native tongue. He was a warm, friendly man with a strong handshake. He sported a full, droopy moustache flecked with grey and a thick head of coiffed black hair. His son, shy and apologetic for what he regarded as his poor grasp of English (although his command of the language was admirable), was tall and slender with a closely shaved head. Over cups of strong black coffee we discussed my requirements for the installation of a *citerne*, the large tank that would contain about 2000 litres of propane. Outside, I would be required to prepare a concrete base for the cylinder, which must conform to strict dimensions and be sited sufficiently far from the building.

During our discussions, it turned out that Monsieur Norrin was a keen balloonist too. Although he was not a pilot, he regularly flew in his company's own promotional hot-air balloon and adored the sport. Our common interest in flying soon became the basis of a strong friendship, and Claude would make frequent visits to Le Mauvis whenever he was passing on business. Invariably around lunchtime, we would be alerted to his arrival by the sound of tapping at the front door.

'*Un petit café?*' I'd say, inviting him upstairs.

'*Pourquoi pas?*' Claude would reply. We would then chat for hours while sipping coffee and our friend would smoke several untipped Gitanes, perched on the stool at our kitchen island unit. Claude proved to be an excellent French teacher for both Al and me. The *Professeur*, as we came to dub him, was endlessly patient with my grammatical gaffes and always spoke slowly and distinctly so that I could absorb his words: when delivered at normal break-neck speed, French conversation can at times leave me floundering, unable to decipher the babble or construct a response. But with Claude as my tutor I soon gained the confidence to flourish linguistically.

With the concrete slab cast at the side of the hangar attached to the *grange*, the bulk tank was delivered on the back of a flat-loader lorry and hoisted into place. Due to the different valve connections used in England and France, a special refuelling hose was required. The enterprising Claude arrived one morning with a tool chest and an array of connectors, then proceeded to fashion a unique Anglo-French device that would allow me to fuel my flight cylinders in record time.

I was thrilled when I received in the post an invitation from Monsieur Alain Manhes, president of a ballooning club, *L'Association des Montgolfières du Pays Arédien*, to attend a festival of flying in the town of Saint-Yrieix-la-Perche in the Corrèze *département* south-west of Limoges. It appeared that Claude

Norrin, whose company was supplying complimentary propane during a weekend of flying events, had suggested my name to Monsieur Manhes and he had been only too happy for the 'English Pilot' to participate. For a modest fee, which included accommodation and meals, we would have the chance of flying with some twenty other balloons from the region and further afield. I immediately sent off my inscription.

After loading up the balloon, we met up with Claude, who was to be one of my crew, and headed off on the hour-and-a-half drive to Saint-Yrieix on the Friday afternoon. The area known as the Pays Arédien is situated within the confines of the Limousin and Périgord Vert regions, in a triangle formed by the cities of Limoges in the north, Brive-la-Gaillarde to the south-east and Périgeux to the south-west. It encompasses the *départements* of the Corrèze, the Dordogne and the Haute-Vienne and lies to the east of the beautiful national park of the Périgord-Limousin. Elegant *châteaux* from the fourteenth, fifteenth and sixteenth centuries nestle amongst the lush, rolling green hillsides of this area rich in architectural and historical heritage.

In north-west Corrèze lies the small town of Arnac-Pompadour, dominated by an elegant chateau that was once the home of Louis XV's mistress, the celebrated Jeanne-Antoinette Poisson, who became Marquise de Pompadour. Now the vast estate is the headquarters of a national stud, which specialises in the continuing development of the Anglo-Arab breed of horse. Breeding horses has been a long tradition in Limousin, with successive Lords as far back as the thirteenth century introducing stallions from such far-flung places as Syria. Originally designed as a training ground for horses, a racecourse was created in 1836, with the magnificent chateau as a backdrop. Today it is a popular setting for showjumping, dressage and steeplechases, attracting thousands of eager punters each year.

Saint-Yrieix-la-Perche, the capital of the Pays Arédien, is a town that has played an important role in the history and development of the region. Standing at 370m above sea level, it is dominated by the fortified Collégiale du Moustier. Founded in the Mérovingienne era, the Frankish dynasty that ruled over Gaul and West Germany from 500 to 751 AD, the building is today considered to be one of the finest examples of gothic architecture in all of Limousin.

Noted for its printing works, which supplies the Mairies of France, the town is also proud of its integral association with the production of fine porcelain. In the mines of Clos-de-Barre, near to the town, Jean-Baptiste Darnet first discovered, in 1768, a plentiful source of kaolin. This friable clay is an essential ingredient in the manufacture of the pure white porcelain, for which the nearby city of Limoges has become synonymous throughout the world.

Limousin is a region with a diverse heritage of gastronomy, and Saint-Yrieix is no exception. Not only does its luxuriant farmland support vast herds of the sturdy brown Limousine cattle – source of a robust beef of outstanding quality and flavour – but it is also proud of another local speciality, *Veau de Saint-Yrieix*, a delicately pink veal produced, sadly, at the sacrifice of animals slaughtered at just fifteen months old.

The area is also noted for the *Cul Noir* (black bum) breed of pig, a portly, pink-skinned porker with distinctive black markings. The rich flavour of this tender meat is a marriage made in heaven when combined with the sweet Limousin apples.

This gastronomic *tour de force* does not stop here. Another local delicacy is a dainty *petit four* made in the simple shape of a scalloped shell. We had sampled these delights before and found them to be scrumptious when dipped in tea or coffee. A favourite with Louis XV's court at Versailles, *madeleines* are made from a sponge called genoise – a blend of melted butter, sugar, eggs and flour – and are commonly flavoured with lemon or orange flower water, although they are often infused with chocolate, honey, pistachios or rum. Reputed to have been named in honour of Madeleine Paulmier, cook to Louis's father-in-law, the little dainties were also eloquently described by the writer Marcel Proust in his novel *Remembrance of Things Past*, as a '… little shell of a cake, so generously sensual beneath the piety of its stern pleating.' Al and I made a solemn pact to search out these delights as a matter of priority.

The weather promised to be unkind to the hopeful balloonists: a steady rain was falling and the wind speeds were far beyond the safe and legal limits for flying. But still, aware that conditions could dramatically improve, we continued to the allotted assembly point in school premises near the centre of the town. The appalling weather report was confirmed at the pilot's briefing that afternoon. Pilots and crew had gathered in the canteen of the school, where we would receive a briefing from *la directrice de vol*, the flight controller, Doctor Claude Chauvreau, a petite lady with a mass of curly red hair. Standing on a chair so that she could see and be seen, she confirmed our suspicions that the weather front had closed in, quashing any chance of an evening flight.

'The *météo* has registered winds of forty to fifty kilometres an hour on the surface and some seventy to eighty kilometres an hour at two hundred and fifty metres altitude,' Dr. Claude explained. '*Alors*, as we cannot fly in winds that pass twelve knots – that's twenty-five kilometres an hour – there is no way we can fly today!'

Amidst moans from the assembled throng, she announced that, nevertheless, there would be ample food and drink available by way of consolation. The crowd responded with a tumultuous roar of approval. The ballooning fraternity is generally resigned to the vagaries of the weather and – if unable to fly – pilots and crew are more than satisfied to talk incessantly about the pleasures of their sport, to enjoy the camaraderie of like-minded individuals. Here were people from all walks of life who shared a common enthusiasm: some were dressed in *faux*-pilot's jumpsuits resplendent with ballooning badges, while others wore practical fisherman's style waistcoats and utility pants that boasted ample pockets to contain ballooning paraphernalia. Others were simply casual in jeans and T-shirts, while some were even formally attired in suits. It was similar in England, I reflected. While sports such as cycling, skateboarding, skiing and motor-racing had clearly defined 'uniforms', ballooning had no such encompassing identity.

Briefing over, animated conversations sprang up around the room concerning the very latest innovations in flying apparel – satellite guidance systems, state-of-the-art burners, new grades of nylon for the envelope, and so on – while clusters of serious-looking pilots regaled each other with anecdotes on past flying adventures. Like fisherman's tales, I suspected that claims of aerial bravado were hugely exaggerated.

'Have you ever flown across the channel, monsieur?' asked one of the pilots with whom I had been chatting. He was a tall, portly man with a long goatee beard, extravagant moustache with twizzled ends, and long, shoulder-length hair. He was the spitting image of Porthos from the Three Musketeers, an image that I am certain he had contrived.

'No, I haven't,' I admitted. The feat of flying from England to France – a regular organised annual event – was one I had hoped to perform one day.

'Ah, monsieur! It was a magical experience, there is no doubt!' said Porthos, holding court to the other pilots who had gathered around. 'One hundred balloons set off from Dover on a fine, crisp morning with a favourable wind behind us. We flew low over the water, passing ships along the way. I myself dipped my basket into the channel! How do you English call this?'

'Splash and dash,' I said. The tricky technique of dipping the basket into water and ascending before full submersion was normally carried out in lakes and ponds, but rarely in the English Channel.

'Ah, that is so!' Porthos continued, raising his wine glass to inspect the colour of the liquid. 'But mark my words, flying the channel is a risky business, monsieur. It is easy to take a wrong track. One could find oneself missing La Belle France entirely!'

'I can imagine,' I said. 'I once flew from my home in Sussex and could not find a field free of animals to land in. So I was forced to fly over the South Downs and land on the beach before I was carried out to sea.'

'*Magnifique!*' exclaimed Porthos, clinking wine glasses with me. He was clearly impressed. 'But of course England is such a small, narrow island, this must happen all the time!'

The subject of our extravagant claims moved on to 'scary landings', in which Porthos described landing his balloon on the roof of a multi-storey car park (which no one believed); another pilot described landing on a roundabout at an intersection of motorways (which everyone seemed to have done at some stage); while I regaled them with a classic landing in the midst of a pine forest (which was viewed with a certain amount of scepticism, although it was perfectly true). Al and I began to circulate and, amidst all this camaraderie, encountered a young blonde woman loitering by the door, smoking heavily. She appeared ill at ease. We became involved in a polite conversation with her and it turned out that this was her first foray into ballooning. She had come along with her husband, a pilot, whom she had recently married, and seemed to be suffering from a bout of social insecurity.

'I find all this very strange indeed,' she said, drawing on her cigarette. 'We French are generally formal on social occasions, particularly where we know no one. So this situation is quite bizarre to me…'

'Why is that?' asked Al.

'All I can hear is *'tu tu tu tu tu… tu tu tu tu tu'*. People using the familiar form instead of the formal *'vous'* when addressing complete strangers. *C'est bizarre! C'est pas normale!* It is not how we are brought up!'

'We don't have that distinction in English,' I explained. 'It's just 'you' whether you're talking to a friend, family or a stranger.'

'Yes, but for me this is very odd. My husband, Roger, he says to me, just relax Amélie. Here we are a big family! This is why we use the *'tu'*. We're a big sporting family when we are together! But it is difficult to break the habit of a lifetime and *'tu tu tu'* everyone you meet!'

Just then a tall, dark haired man sporting a jumpsuit and baseball cap joined us. He slipped an arm around Amélie's tense shoulders. She wriggled free and peered at him through slit eyelids.

'*Je te présente Richard et Al,*' said Amélie rather stiffly, introducing us to her husband Roger.

'*Enchanté,*' I said, proffering a hand.

'Hi! How's it going?' drawled Roger, shaking my hand, then Al's. '*Tu es Anglaise, je crois?*'

'*Vous vous vous!*' snapped his wife, shocked at her husband's blatant informality in the presence of strangers.

'*Tu tu tu!*' he responded, glaring at her, nose-to-nose.

'*Vous,*' she snapped back, poker faced.

'*Tu,*' he snarled, teeth bared. This was obviously an argument that had been raging for some time, which had apparently reached stalemate.

'Drink, anyone?' I said, hoping to defuse this squabble over the fineries of French etiquette. As we sauntered over to the bar, I could appreciate Amélie's sentiments, for France has struggled to keep its identity and individuality in the twenty-first century, when globalisation and exposure to the horrors of English and American television had been partly responsible for watering down the language. To purists, this degradation of French culture was regarded as pure anathema.

The following day, after a night spent in the comfortable dormitory of a local college, the balloonists reconvened at the canteen to be told that there was unlikely to be any flying. We would, however, take our balloons to the *Plan d'eau d'Arfeuille*, just outside of the town and monitor the situation. When we arrived at the clearing in the pine woods that surrounded the lake, however, a stiff breeze was blowing and rain began to pour down. Flying duly abandoned, we were advised to spend the day sightseeing, although urged to return to the school for a gourmet lunch. A fascinating visit to the nearby Musée de la Porcelaine with Alain Manhes and his wife

Colette worked up a fine appetite and to my delight we were later introduced to the succulent pleasures of slices of black bum pig with apples.

On the Sunday morning we arose during darkness and returned to the school canteen for a bleary-eyed briefing over cups of strong, black coffee and a plentiful supply of fresh croissants. The day's prognosis was favourable. The weather front had passed, leaving the promise of light winds and clear skies. We joined the convoy of twenty balloon trailers headed for the nearby chateau at Ladignac-le-Long, where we would attempt a mass ascent of balloons. Pilots would participate in a lighthearted flying competition, the *Chasse au Renard*, or 'fox and hounds'. A single balloon – the fox – would launch first, to be followed some minutes later by the rest of the pack of hound balloons. The object of the task was to attempt to follow the fox balloon to its landing site and to drop a marker as close as possible to the basket. The closest three markers would be deemed to have won.

As the sun rose to reveal a rich blue, cloudless sky, pilots and crew laid out their balloons on the dewy grass in a closely packed group and began the process of inflating them. A grey, low-lying mist still hung in the air, blurring the horizon beyond the field. The crack of burners firing broke the morning silence. The cluster of balloons began to fill out and gracefully rise from their prone states to stand erect above their baskets. Here was a colourful array of balloons in various sizes: reds, yellows, blues, multiple-stripes, two-tone patterns like *Zulu India*'s red and black livery; several balloons bore advertising slogans or colourful motifs.

The rules of participation required that balloonists offer places to passengers: I had been assigned, in addition to Claude Norrin as crew member, Pierre the driver of the propane tanker, and a young lady name Chloe who had won the flight in a raffle. When all the balloons were inflated, swaying gently in the breeze, occasionally bobbing harmlessly into neighbouring balloons, we awaited the word of the launch master to release our tethers. Control of a mass ascent is by necessity placed in the capable hands of a fluorescent-jacketed representative of the organisers, whose job it is to ensure that no balloon can inadvertently ascend beneath another, or obstruct the launch of another, for the balloon's envelope – the bag which contains the hot air – obscures the pilot's overhead view.

First of all the fox balloon was given permission to *décoller* (a wonderfully descriptive word, which literally translates as 'unstick' from the ground). Slowly it lifted off and was soon a brightly coloured dot about a mile distant against the blue sky. One by one, the word to launch was relayed to the pilots of the other balloons, which, freed from their tether lines, began to rise through the fine mist into the fresh, clear air. Soon the sky was dotted with multi-coloured globes flying side by side or at varying altitudes in an attempt to locate a wind direction that would take them on a course to intercept the fox. Some hounds got it just right, while others could not locate the correct wind and veered off to the right or left, resigned to the fact that they would not be able to stick with the pack. For about fifteen minutes, I was lucky enough to tag along with a group of four balloons that were on a track destined to carry them very close to the fox. Looking ahead we could see that the fox had descended and was about to touch down in a large field over to our left. One of my flying companions descended and veered towards the same field and I could see that he was on course to win. My own track was such that I would miss the goal by a broad margin, so I decided to fly on.

After about an hour I decided to make a landing on a hillside just before the picturesque village of Pierre-Buffière and set the basket gently down in a grass field with ready access to a lane. It had been necessary to land at the far side of the field, so Claude and Pierre exited the basket and, while I floated the balloon just above the ground, the two men tugged us closer to the gate, where I set it down again. After having deflated and rolled up the envelope we were able to sit down on the grass and admire the splendid view of the village to our west. While we were admiring the panorama Al, driving the retrieve vehicle, appeared in the lane and we had soon packed up the balloon and were heading off for coffee in the village.

Pierre-Buffière is a higgeldy-piggeldy cluster of charming half-timbered houses with tile and stone roofs, built around the eleventh century church of Sainte Croix and the remnants of a feudal chateau. The Renaissance doorway of the church was spectacular, inset with eighteen rich blue enamelled plates, a clear indication of the area's proud connection to the manufacture of fine porcelain. On the lower part of the hill on which the body of the village stands is another, smaller church, that of St. Côme and St. Damien. Through the valley overlooked by the village flow the rivers Briance and Breuilh. The fast-flowing rivers, popular for kayaking, are traversed by the eleventh-century l'Ermitage bridge and at a higher level the graceful arches of a tall viaduct. Beyond lies the modern bridge carrying the north–south autoroute between Limoges and Brive, although it does not encroach on the peaceful setting. After a pleasant sojourn in the sunny main square, we headed off back to St.-Yrieix-la-Perche for a welcome lunch of prime Limousin beef steaks, cooked pink and served with bowls of *frites* and *haricot verts*.

The favourable weather conditions had held during the afternoon and we gathered in the grounds of the *Lycée Agricole de La Faye*, the agricultural college near the centre of St. Yrieix-la-Perche, to avail ourselves of the free propane offered by Claude Norrin's company. Pierre bid us an effusive goodbye and set about this work at the tanker lorry, refuelling the line of balloonists who had gathered in an orderly queue with their gas cylinders. The air soon became rich with the heady stench of propane: not a pleasant aroma by any means but – when blended with the smell of the leather straps that secure my flight cylinders in the basket and the suede basket trim – is one that is evocative of the excitement of an impending flight.

The organisers of the event had thrown down the gauntlet of a second flying task: a competition poetically named *Le Retour au Bercail*, the return to the fold. This involved a rather tricky manoeuvre: the balloons would take off *en masse*, with the object of flying back to land closest to the point of departure. Given the wind direction and speed, however, I doubted that this would be a possibility. A crowd of hundreds of fascinated onlookers from the town and beyond had gathered in the field where the balloons were laid out. Little stalls had been erected at the perimeter of the field and trestles were set up to sell barbecued sausages, *frites*, candyfloss, beer, wine and T-shirts bearing ballooning motifs. The atmosphere was one of a village fête, with much laughter and jollity.

I had been assigned as my passengers a craggy-faced local man named François and his twelve-year-old daughter Sophie, who had won the flight in a raffle held earlier in the day. Also to fly with me was Henri Canou, who appeared with his face all but concealed by a plaster cast. Only his eyes, ears and mouth – and a shock of black hair festooning from the top – were visible. Henri was a pilot also, but on this occasion was helping out as crew wherever needed: he had recently undergone a corrective operation on his nose to alleviate a long standing breathing difficulty, hence the cast. Our flight was calm and tranquil as the light southerly wind carried us towards the town of Nexon. Taking the balloon down for a low approach into a large field, I miscalculated slightly and the basket descended into a deep, nettle-filled hollow just adjacent to the field, dragged slowly up the steep sides, then came to rest gently on the damp soil. The field was generally bare earth, but there were many small cabbages dotted around, the remainder of the crop that had apparently been harvested. As we were packing away the balloon a little old man chugged up on a moped, dismounted and scrambled nimbly up the bank from the lane that skirted the field. He wore blue dungarees, a stained vest, wellington boots and a tatty straw hat. He must have been aged in his mid-eighties, I guessed, and had a wrinkled, nut brown face, his cheeks covered with grey stubble. He scraped the hat off his head to reveal a bald pate considerably lighter in colour than the rest of his head.

'*Bonsoir, messieurs, mam'selle*' he crackled hoarsely. We responded and shook the bony hand he proffered. He then bent down and began pulling up little cabbages and stuffing them into his upturned hat.

'Ah, so are you the *propriétaire* of this field, monsieur?' I asked the old man, for it is only polite for balloonists to ascertain ownership of a landing field before a balloon is removed. The old man looked up at me with a puzzled expression.

'*Mais, non… pourquoi?*'

'Oh, I just wondered… the cabbages, you see…' I said, pointing to the vegetables he had taken. The old man grinned, revealing only one yellow tooth poking from his bottom jaw. He put a finger to his lips, said 'ssh…' and promptly jammed the hat back on his head. Leaves poked out from under the brim. He waved us goodbye, scrambled down the bank, remounted his moped and sped off.

Our presence had become the subject of much curiosity from other locals, who had emerged from their houses and farms to cluster around and watch the spectacle. The owner of the field – a rotund man in his forties wearing identical blue dungarees to the cabbage thief – made himself known to us and spent many minutes examining the fabric of the balloon, before uprooting several cabbages and handing them to me.

'*Je vous remercie,*' he said.

'Thank you?' I queried. 'For what, monsieur?'

'For landing here in my humble field. *Merci.* It is an honour, monsieur.' He bowed extravagantly. Never before had I encountered such generosity of spirit from a farmer whose field I had cheekily chosen to land my balloon in. In England one is frequently met with a demand for money as a landing fee. But I was extremely grateful, stuffed the cabbages into my flight bag and shook the man's hand.

Soon we had packed away the balloon and were heading off back to St.-Yrieix, just in time to attend a prize-giving ceremony held at the plush l'Hotel de Ville. Champagne and *hors d'oeuvres* were served in celebration of a successful day's flying. Winners of the *Chasse au Renard* were presented with their trophies – magnificent silver cups – then all pilots were given a commemorative china dish depicting an image of the black bum pig, plus baskets of *madeleines* donated by the lady mayoress. Deeply honoured, I was even given a rapturous ovation as the guest pilot from across the channel.

'We must thank our English guest, Richard Wheels, for attending our little event,' announced Jean-Claude Dupuy, one of the event's organisers. Just then Henri Canou, who had been otherwise engaged, slipped into the room. 'Ah, and here is one of Monsieur Wheel's passengers, just back from hospital!' All eyes turned to the bandaged Henri. 'A bumpy landing, eh, Henri?' Henri grinned beneath his plaster mask and waved. All the assembled audience guffawed.

Grouping together for a photograph, the happy family of balloonists all resolved to meet again the following year for a repeat performance of this charming event.

Cul Noir, *Black Bum pigs*

Chapter Eight

Winter's chill

Bent double, weeding the neat parallel furrows of the vegetable garden that had been created by Jérôme's plough in less than twenty minutes, I became aware of a heady, drain-like stench wafting in the warm, late summer air. The unpleasant odour was not entirely unfamiliar to me: it had become increasingly detectable indoors, emanating from the bathroom. We had not worried unduly about the problem, since *fosses septiques,* septic tanks, are notorious for escaping smells. It was, nevertheless, a mite embarrassing when visitors called. However, we had assumed that the bad odour was simply par for the course. With this kind of essentially rudimentary system it is necessary to add a biological activator each week, flushing sachets of powder down the toilet. On first detecting the stink, I had simply added a double dose of sachets and thought no more of the matter. Until that day.

Following my nose, I headed off towards the point at the back of the *grange* where the septic tank was buried. I lifted the three concrete lids one at a time: the chambers beneath the first two were clear, but that beneath the third was full of a disgusting grey sludge. Whatever it was, the sludge had backed up all along the leech pipes that were supposed to filter the water – a bi-product of the sanitation system – into the field and discharge it harmlessly to the deep earth. I replaced the cover and wandered into the field, following the route of the perforated underground pipes to the inspection chamber at the end of the system. The slab covering the chamber had been dislodged by the malodorous crud, which was bubbling slowly and forming a substantial lake. Swarms of horseflies buzzed madly around the chamber, then dived into the mire and carried away great dollops of it. The stench was utterly foul and I found myself gagging.

'What is it?' said Al, approaching from behind me carrying two cups of tea, little Jazz at her heel. She took one look at the gloop bubbling up from underground and stopped dead in her tracks. 'Shit!'

'No,' I said, taking her literally. 'Not shit…'

'Grease,' confirmed the Count, who had dropped in for a social visit, only to find Al and me scooping bucketfuls of the stinking sludge from the inspection chamber. 'The *bac dégraisseur* must be full.'

'*Bac dégraisseur?*' I repeated through the lint facemask I had been forced to wear. Al, made of far more sterner stuff than I, simply waded deep into the sludge in her wellingtons, without need of a mask. As she delved into the inspection chamber with nothing but a pair of pink rubber gloves and a cut-down water bottle as a scoop, I bristled with admiration for her strength of character – or lack of sense.

'Grease trap,' my brother translated from the shore of the lake. 'It collects the grease from the 'grey', soapy water draining from the washing machine, dishwasher and kitchen sink before it reaches the *fosse*. It's probably why your house always stinks.' Al and I both stared up at him, hurt and embarrassed.

'I don't think we have one of those,' I revealed, ignoring his impudent jibe about our odour problem. I tossed another bucketful of gloop as far away from the epicentre as I could.

'Oh dear,' replied my brother. 'Then you'd better get onto the cowboy that installed the system and get him over here...'

Several unanswered phone calls later suggested that Monsieur Marcel Fugère, a local tradesman specialising in sanitation, roofing and masonry work who had installed the system, was unavailable for comment. Meanwhile, with continued use of our plumbing and lavatorial facilities the grey sludge poured from the inspection chamber. The bad smell in the bathroom had become considerably worse, and now drifted upstairs into the kitchen, seemingly wafting out of the sink and dishwasher.

'Frankly, I'm not sure I trust the old boy any more,' I remarked, when Al had put down the phone a final time. 'After the débacle with the window, I'm not sure he'd be up to putting right this mess with the drainage.' I was referring to the episode the previous winter when Monsieur Fugère, had installed three windows in the rear façade of the *grange*. The sweet, soft spoken and gentle old boy liked a surreptitious tipple, even when tottering around on a high rooftop. A mistake with his measuring up had resulted in him positioning the central window too far to the left. I had been obliged to tear him off a strip and make him right the wrong at his own cost. The resulting repair had been far from perfect, but Al and I were reluctant to drive home the point: the old man had seemed genuinely stressed to be taken to task.

Later that week, when we had still not managed to contact Monsieur Fugère, and the problem with the sludge was becoming a serious hazard to anyone within sniffing range, Al looked up from the pages of *Le Populaire*, the local newspaper she had been reading, ashen-faced.

'No wonder we couldn't get a response from Monsieur Fugère,' she said, her voice tinged with sadness.

'Why? Has he won the Loto and given everything up?'

'No. There's an obituary here… he died last week.'

Al made some discreet enquiries and discovered that Monsieur Fugère, who, it turned out, had suffered for many years from a deep form of clinical depression, had reached the end of his tether and in desperation had recourse to take his own life. His poor wife had discovered him hanging by the neck from a beam in his garage. Heavy drinking had been the old man's way of coping with a tragic family accident that he somehow blamed himself for: his youngest child had, many years previously, drowned in the garden pond. I felt deeply shocked about the old boy's death, and a little guilty that I might have contributed to his anguish by ticking him off about the mistake with our window. His life had obviously been a precarious balance, a challenge that he felt unable to cope with.

I telephoned our English neighbour, Jeff Dedman, a hard-working general builder who lived in Le Mas Mauvis, directly across the communal swathe of green at the centre of the hamlet. Leaving a message on his answering machine, I briefly described our problem with the *assainissement* and requested his urgent presence. The next morning, Jeff arrived to survey the situation. Confirming that the lack of a grease trap had clogged up the underground system of perforated filtration pipes, he explained that it would be necessary to modify the system and install a new *bac*.

'That should cure the awful stink in your bathroom as well,' he brutally confirmed. We agreed a price for the job and Jeff left, promising to order the grease trap and mini digger that would be required to sink it into the earth alongside the septic tank and return as soon as possible.

In the same week that we had learned of the death of Monsieur Fugère I had encountered Véronique waiting on the doorstep of her house, dressed in a sombre coat and hat. She explained that she was awaiting a lift to attend a funeral in the nearby village, that of her cousin, Cyrille Laborde. This announcement was the second poignant blow Al and I had received that week. Monsieur Laborde, a perennially jovial, wildly enthusiastic local tradesman, had been responsible for installing the electrical and plumbing systems in the *grange*. Although his installations were somewhat basic, rather messily rendered and prone to failure, he had been a frequent source of advice and assistance to us, when we were mere strangers in this land. Sadly, we had witnessed him, over the subsequent years, wither and fade as he succumbed to cancer. He died after a protracted and torturous battle against the disease.

Two deaths in one week. I wondered what, or who, would be next. The answer was not long in coming. Bad news had a habit of arriving in threes, it seemed to me. A few weeks later we learned that Jolanda Bussiere, the ubiquitous Madame Météo, had passed away in the middle of the night. Alarm bells started ringing in my head.

'My God!' I said to Al. 'You don't suppose…' I remembered our last few encounters with Bruno and the disparaging way he had spoken about his wife, his collection of poisoned snails and his rather blatant comment about strangulation. Al looked at me and shook her head, despairing of the fantasies my mind was apt to conjure up. 'No, it couldn't be…'

It seemed that, thankfully, my over-fertile imagination had got the better of me once again.

'Blood clot on't brain,' clarified the Yorkshireman, who lived next door to the Bussieres. 'Died quietly, sudden like. Bruno's reet distressed, of course. For all their mithering and bickering, they were inseparable, that pair were.'

Bruno was disconsolate after the death of his wife. He became reclusive, rarely venturing out of doors, and no longer seemed to have recourse to visit his friend Véronique for coffee and conversation. For a while he even neglected the garden he adored and his pride and joy, a well-stocked vegetable plot, became choked with weeds. In time, however, his grief subsided and gave way to happy memories of his fifty or more years of marriage. I like to think that he began to recall the good, bad old times, the good-natured squabbles and phoney bad moods that had punctuated his life with the volatile Pole, and was happy that he had spent his days with her. Soon we would see him pottering in the garden once again, feeding the small flock of ducks, a couple of geese, and the several hens that provided him with eggs and meat. Gone, however, was the noisy cockerel that used to make a ruckus that could be heard across the village, morning, noon and night. Bruno had strangled the old bird, a *chapon*, or castrated cock, which he had been fattening up for the table. The scrawny bird, it turned out, had been one of the last meals the ex-chef had enjoyed together with his wife.

With the *potager* ploughed, weeded and thoroughly dug over, Al and I took advantage of a timely offer by Thierry André to help him disperse the steaming dung mountain that had accumulated in his pony paddock at the rear of our property.

'Take what you need!' he said. 'You'd be doing me a favour! I have more shit than I can handle!'

We trundled down the lane to the field in our tractor and helped ourselves to several *bennette* loads of the fresh manure, transported it back to the vegetable garden and dumped it on the soil for later incorporation. This source of fresh manure would, we anticipated, enrich the neglected soil, give it the much-needed bulk it required, and enable us to produce a fine crop of vegetables the following spring and summer. While we were grateful for the free manure, we had always wondered why Monsieur André kept ponies at all. The gruff farmer was hardly the sort to be found instructing young children in the art of riding at local gymkhanas. The ponies themselves were, although well fed, unshod and their coats never groomed. Their hooves were in appalling condition, curling at the ends and splitting. One poor animal limped constantly because of its cracked, malformed feet. We could only assume that the farmer regarded the ponies as agricultural animals rather than as pets or companions. This was quite a disquieting thought, particularly for Al, who was after all a fervent horse lover. There were times when it could be distressing living in the heart of a farming community where animal welfare was never high on the agenda. But what agricultural value was there in a pony, after all?

After starting with just a pair, André now boasted a modest herd of eight plump ponies. The grass in the paddock was sparse and even during summer André was obliged to dump a large bale of hay on the ground for the animals to consume. Each year the mares were put to the haughty little palomino stallion and his harem soon increased. The resulting spindly-legged foals grew, were weaned from their mothers, and then were summarily hauled away in a trailer. Their separation from the mare and subsequent removal generally occurred late at night or very early in the morning. An unholy fracas would erupt, rousing Al and I from our slumber. Peering out of the *grange* window we could see the distressed stallion galloping madly around the byre into which he had been penned while his offspring were carted off. His distressed whinnying was accompanied by a frantic shaking of the head and angry snorting through flared nostrils. He would stamp the ground and buck at the aluminium door separating him from his family.

'Why does Thierry keep ponies anyway?' I had asked font-of-all-knowledge, Véronique one day while we were partaking in a *petit quatre*, afternoon coffee and biscuits, in her airless kitchen. 'Does he breed them to sell to riding establishments?'

Véronique, hunched over a large bowl of black coffee as if it was a witch's cauldron, choked on a morsel of the biscuits her strict diet forbade. 'Monsieur Richard, Al...'

she wheezed. 'You know what Monsieur André's *métier* was before he became a farmer…' I'll swear she even cackled like an old crone delivering a fearful prophecy. Dipping another stick of *gateau* into her bowl of coffee, she cursed '*merde!*' as the end of the confection dissolved and fell with a plop into the liquid. She began to fish it out with a tablespoon and slurp it from the end.

As I contemplated the old lady's words, Al's eyes met mine. The corners of my wife's mouth curled downward as the sad thought occurred to her. Véronique's spectacles had steamed up from her close proximity to her coffee bowl. She pushed them back up her nose and peered at me through the fog. '*Boucher. Charcutier…*' she intoned ominously.

'So they're slaughtered for meat?' I sought her confirmation. The French had a predilection for eating horsemeat but I did not think that this included ponies. Suddenly I recalled the delicious joint of meat that Monsieur André had kindly given us a few weeks previously. We had cooked it and gorged ourselves upon it, believing it to be a succulent cut of venison from a *cerf*, or deer, illicitly shot out of season by the wily hunter. Having consumed the evidence, chewed the bones and licked our greasy fingers, we had felt guilty in our minds, but replete and satisfied in our stomachs. Now that I harked back to the occasion, our generous donor had acted very mysteriously that evening, skilfully avoiding an explanation of where the joint had come from: or indeed to which species of animal it had once been attached to.

'What does horsemeat look like?' I asked Al nonchalantly, when we had made our way back to the *grange*.

'Oh God! Why ask me? Don't mention it! I don't even want to think about it!' Al said, covering her ears. 'The thought of eating horsemeat gives me the willies!'

I could discern that, since moving to France, Al was beginning to crave the occasional horse riding excursions she had enjoyed while back in England. She had long since retired from the world of professional equestrianism and had taken a lengthy break from riding. She would regularly be on hand to help exercise Dickens, her late sister Claire's horse, in the company of their mother and her own steed, Thunder. Together, mother and daughter would canter across the somewhat bleak Ashdown Forest in Sussex. On moving to France, Al had even talked of owning her own horse again. We certainly had the stable space.

'I wouldn't want anything super-duper,' she stressed. 'Just a steady neddy. One I can take on a gentle plod around the lanes, riding western style, long in the saddle, unhurried…' I suggested that, until we were ready to invest in our own horse, she should locate a livery stable where she could maintain her enthusiasm. Not wanting to incur too much expense when she was not working, she nevertheless promised she would make some enquiries. It was a curious fact, however, that although we knew there to be a horse-riding fraternity in the *département*, riders kept an extremely low profile. Not once had we seen a rider out on the quiet lanes in five years of owning the property. We had never seen family ponies being put through their paces in makeshift jumping arenas found in nearly every rural village in England. Certainly there were horses and ponies: I frequently passed them in the paddocks as I ran. Claude Norrin's daughter Auriel owned her own horse, kept in livery near her home. The nearby town of Le Dorat hosted regular *concourse hippique*, show jumping events at their arena in the centre of the town. So where were all the horses and riders? It seemed that rather than hacking out on the lanes – a common sight in England – riders in our part of France confined their sport to the fields, or an indoor school or *manège*.

On the advice of the physiotherapist, and hoping to be able to run again, at night I would tie a long length of fabric around the balls of my feet, stretch it to just above the knee and tie it around my leg. This maintained my feet at right angles to my lower legs while I slept. It was not particularly comfortable and frankly I felt ridiculous, but I was determined to persevere. Sometimes I would forget about the restraint and attempt to exit the bed on waking in the mornings, resulting in me tumbling onto the floor in a heap. However, this bizarre treatment had apparently not been a cruel joke at my expense, since it seemed to do the trick admirably. Allied to an enforced break from running, I soon experienced a vast improvement in the condition of my legs. The shin pain had all but disappeared and my troublesome knee had also benefited from the rest. I chanced a little gentle trotting out on the lanes, keeping to the grass verges wherever possible to cushion the jarring blows to my knees. Within a few weeks, with no discernible side effects from the exercise, I began to increase my mileage until I was able to run for an hour or more without a recurrence of pain. The lure of the Paris Marathon in just six months' time was almost too powerful to ignore, but I knew that Al would be worried about my ability to complete the course, and the damage I could do to my body in the attempt.

'What's this?' she demanded one day, finding a magazine stowed behind a cushion on the sofa and slamming it down on my desk.

'Umm, a magazine,' I admitted bashfully, as if I had been caught reading explicit porn.

'A running magazine. Open at a marathon training schedule…' my wife elaborated.

'Oh gosh, so it is!' I said with mock surprise.

'You'll never learn, will you Rich?' she said sternly.

'Well, there's no harm in reading, is there?'

After the claustrophobic heat of the summer, the month of October brought about an intense chill, which continued until Christmas loomed close. Winter had fallen upon us with a vengeance, leaving us somewhat unprepared. I awoke from a restless night, freezing cold and with stiff joints. Lying shivering in my bed, it was a toss-up between which part of my anatomy was the coldest: I felt vaguely for my nose with numb fingers but could discern no tactile sensation from either. I suspected, however, that my feet would win the toss hands down: a chilly wetness at the bottom of the bed told me that the rubber seal on the stopper of my Doulton's Improved Foot Warmer had not, in fact, been one of its major improvements. The contents of this ancient hot water bottle – boiling when added the previous evening – had apparently seeped out during the night, no doubt after being kicked over in my cold-induced delirium, soaking the sheets, my feet and the thermal socks I was wearing. Plummeting temperatures had subsequently turned the liquid to ice, or so I suspected. I peered at my feet in the gloom beneath the duvet and pondered on what would be the first visible signs of frostbite. I attempted to wiggle my toes, but down at the foot of the bed nothing stirred.

The foot warmers were part of a job lot of rustic artefacts my mother-in-law had imagined would form an attractive decorative collection for our new home; they were one of her better junk-shop finds, and far more useful than the marble egg collection she had tried to foist upon us. Al and I both religiously clung to a pair of these old ceramic foot warmers each night, in addition to those stationed at our feet, during the first bitterly cold winter since we moved to our woefully incomplete barn conversion.

Peering tentatively out from the cocoon of pillows, two layers of duvets, two blankets and an eiderdown, I exhaled and watched my breath rise in a hazy mist. High above my head I could see what looked like a bloom of frost on the bare undersides of the clay roof tiles. I cursed to myself that we had not managed to insulate the roof before then. Where had the time gone? Knowing how bitter the winters could be here in Limousin, how could we have left ourselves so vulnerable? I turned over on the mattress and outstretched a shaky hand to see whether Al was still alive. Apparently so. She seemed relatively warm, in fact, I thought jealously. It was only my stubborn streak that prevented me for dressing appropriately for bed, as she did: somehow I could not bring myself to put on more clothes when retiring for the night than I wore during the day and persevered with a tee-shirt, a pair of thermal long johns and a woolly hat to protect my balding pate. However, my resourceful wife's nightly policy of donning a pair of tights, two pairs of fisherman's socks, thick denim jeans, two tee-shirts, two jumpers, a scarf, a pair of gloves and a fetching woollen balaclava, seemed to conserve some of the heat she had managed to eke from our wood-burning stove.

I slipped from beneath the mound of bedclothes and shoved my wet feet into a pair of trainers. Pulling my dressing gown on, I adjusted the rake of my woolly hat and tiptoed across the room to the kitchen island, rubbing my cold hands together in an attempt to restore blood circulation. Filling two huge bowl-like cups with milk, I put them in the microwave, set the timer and watched as they revolved on their carousel in the glow of the interior light, covetous of the fact that the milk was being lovingly warmed from the inside out. When the milk was frothing I added coffee and sugar and stirred the brew. Shuffling back to the bed, I happened to squint absently out of the front window that overlooked Véronique's vegetable garden, noting how every surface glistened with a thick layer of white frost. I saw a curl of smoke from her chimney and reflected that the old lady must be inside her draughty kitchen, huddled around the stove. What kind of life was it that she led, I lamented? She received very few visitors and she had confided in Al that she was so desperately sad and lonely she 'hoped that God would take her soon'.

I had noticed of late some strange behaviour in the elderly lady, and had meant to take up the matter with her nephew and guardian Jérôme when next he paid a visit. For the last few mornings I had witnessed Véronique standing outside her house dressed in her night attire, an overcoat and a fur hat, shouting and waving her big stick at someone or something across the grassy area in the centre of the hamlet. When I identified what she was calling out, I was shocked and more than a little confused.

'Jeff!' she yelled. 'Jeff, you *canaille*!' Now why, I wondered, was Véronique shouting after our English neighbour? 'Just you wait until I get hold of you! You're *méchant*!' she growled. This was intolerable. What on earth had poor Jeff done to deserve being called a wicked scoundrel? As far as I was aware, the hardworking builder barely knew Véronique. In any case, I considered, Jeff was unlikely to hear her insulting jibes, for he was extremely hard of hearing and obliged to wear a hearing aid.

No, quite clearly, the old dear had completely lost her marbles. Suddenly, I caught sight of something that made me stumble over my own feet, spilling the coffee. My shoes clattering on the floorboards and my subsequent shriek made Al sit bolt upright in bed. Lying there in the vegetable garden, sprawled across the ice-hard furrows of the soil, I saw Véronique. I could clearly make out the shape of her body, clad in her usual blue-and-white-checked house coat.

'What is it?' hissed Al in panic, scrambling out from the bedclothes to join me at the window. This was possibly the fastest she'd ever exited a bed in her life.

'It's Véronique!' I cried. 'She's lying spark out in the garden! She must have collapsed and now she's frozen to death!'

Al peered into the morning haze, at first doubting my outrageous claim but then, seeing the unmoving mound of checked fabric, frozen on the furrows, her jaw dropped. 'Quick! You go out to her! I'll phone for an ambulance!' She grabbed the telephone.

I raced for the stairs, stumbled down to the front door and out into the bitterly cold air. Scrambling up the bank on the other side of the track that separated our two properties, I attempted to negotiate the rickety fence at the perimeter of our neighbour's vegetable plot. I slithered down the slippery slope, then undeterred immediately struck out again for the summit. Véronique's corpse was clearly visible now. In the dim light of dawn I could even make out her poor head lying on the soil.

Just then, from the corner of my eye, I noticed a pall of smoke trailing out of her chimney. A light clicked on in her kitchen. The sound of a key turning in a lock broke the silence in the still air and I watched in disbelief as our neighbour's grey head poked from around the opening door. Pushing her spectacles up her nose she peered at me quizzically. Straddling her fence in my gaping dressing gown wearing nothing but a pair of long johns and a T-shirt, at six o'clock in the morning, I felt rather foolish as the old lady regarded me.

'*Oh là là!* What are you doing outside in this cold, Monsieur Richard?' she croaked. 'You'll freeze to death!' Then she cast her gaze towards the mound in the vegetable garden and shook her head woefully. 'I don't think that even my *salade* will survive this cold, although I've covered it up!'

I swung my leg back over the fence, tightened the cord of my gown and looked back at Al's now grinning face at the upstairs window. Before dialling for the emergency services she had obviously realised that the corpse in the garden was not, in fact, Véronique, but merely one of her old house coats draped over her precious crop of lettuces in a vain attempt to protect them from the intense cold. I looked back at the mound: the old lady's 'head' had transmogrified into nothing more than a frost-blighted *frissée*.

'Bonjour, Véronique,' I mumbled, rubbing my hands together then blowing on my icy fingers. 'It is a little crisp this morning, isn't it?'

Still, as the chilly day wore on, I was unconvinced that our neighbour had not gone completely bonkers. When I had warmed up sufficiently to risk leaving the relative comfort of the bed in order to stoke up the stove, I could hear Véronique in the lane outside, intent on her latest pastime, baiting poor Jeff for whatever perceived offence he had committed.

'Jeff! Jeff!' she hollered across the green, brandishing her gnarled stick. 'Don't you turn a deaf ear, you evil *chiure*!' I could not believe the language I was hearing, uttered from the mouth of a dear, grey-haired old lady! As if making reference to Jeff's hearing problem was not bad enough form, calling him an 'evil shit' was just going too far! I made a mental note to have a quiet word in Jeff's ear, if this shameful behaviour should carry on.

Laid-back Jazz

Chapter Nine

They eat horses, don't they?

The only means Al and I had of heating the huge sixteen by eleven metre area of the barn's upper *grenier* was a chunky woodburning stove purchased for a song from a London commuter friend and hauled over to France in the back of our car. But its promise of keeping us snug in the winter months had proven to be wishful thinking. During our first Christmas at Le Mas Mauvis we realised that the stove was going to be slightly less than effective at warming up the huge volume of the largest bedsitter in the world. This was partly due to the absence of insulation on the underside of the massive tiled roof. The heat we generated by burning our own supply of oak logs simply rose – as heat has an irritating habit of doing – and literally disappeared through the roof.

Undeterred by the cold, we had simply wrapped up well and clustered around the stove to consume an unconventional but delicious Christmas lunch. At this time of year the French consume a vast amount of seafood. The ice-chilled fish counters in supermarkets and shops are filled with an abundance of lobsters, crayfish, mussels, whelks, prawns, clams and other shellfish. Wooden crates of oysters are stacked up in the aisles attracting clusters of knowledgeable French folk, who seem to use the occasion as a means of meeting up with friends and neighbours. Animated discussions abound on the relative merits of particular types of oyster. Alongside the crates of oysters are packs of lemons and rows of champagne bottles, the sparkling liquid considered the perfect accompaniment to the somewhat acquired taste of the seafood.

Although most of this produce of the sea was available *vivant*, Al had obtained an already cooked lobster from the local market stall in Magnac-Laval. We selected a recipe that would complement the subtle taste of the magnificent creature – and which would be possible for us to concoct with only a single-burner camping stove. The lack of a real cooker and oven had never prevented us before from experimenting with *la haute cuisine* and we had proudly developed an efficient system of cooking multiple dishes with only the little gas burner. Precarious towers of pans and steamers tottered atop the stove, cooking the various ingredients in order of priority. The complexity of our meals frequently surprised us, although we had judged on this occasion that roasting a turkey was beyond even our creative capabilities. The top of the wood-burning stove, nevertheless, not only acted as an efficient hot plate ideal for cooking vegetables but also, beneath its lid, concealed a smoking chamber that could be used to imbue the flesh of fish, chicken or other meats and cheeses with the delicious oakiness of burning wood.

Our first experiment with the smoker had not gone well: sliding the heavy and very hot cast iron lid to one side with gloved hands, we had both been choked and momentarily blinded by the acrid, billowing smoke that poured forth. Lowering the two plump fillets of *lieu noir*, coley, into the furnace on cunningly-designed slings made from aluminium foil, we had replaced the lid and wiped the smut from each other's faces while we waited until the fish was cooked. The enticing aroma that seeped from the stove told us that the fillets were ready and we again slid back the lid and entered the smoke cloud to retrieve our meal. Although the fillets were cooked to perfection, the foil slings were charred to a crisp. They promptly disintegrated and deposited our deliciously smoked fish into the bowels of the stove. The *grange* smelled distinctly fishy for several days after that failure. A valuable lesson learned, we improved and strengthened the design of our foil slings until the stove became yet another versatile part of our culinary armoury.

Full of festive spirit during that first *Noël*, we had bought a sizeable Christmas tree – amazed at how cheap it was compared to equivalent trees in the UK – set it up in front of our central upstairs window overlooking the lane that passed in front of the barn and adorned it gaily with ribbons and lights. Huddled around the stove for warmth we enjoyed a romantic first Christmas in France. We were only too aware that the barn would probably become uninhabitable during the harshest of the winter weather, which was still looming on the horizon. There was only one solution: to invest in enough insulation to seal the vast room.

I had decided that the best form of insulation was a relatively new product, which promised a high degree of heat retention in the winter, while preventing the oppressive heat of the sun from entering the house in summer. The material consisted of a plastic bubble-wrap sandwiched between two thin films of aluminium foil. Only seven millimetres thick, it was equivalent to the insulating properties of mineral wool blanket over a foot thick. Sold in long rolls, the sheet material could be simply stapled to the undersides of the rafters, then clad with plasterboard. The only problem was going to be safe working access to the underside of the pitched roof, some six metres above our heads. Erecting scaffolding was going to be prohibitively expensive and would be a quite inflexible system as well: it would be necessary to work from one end of the room to the other, a distance of sixteen metres.

'We'll borrow Jeff's three-section ladder,' I explained to Al at an informal planning meeting. 'Our ladder just won't reach up to the apex. We can feed lengths of insulation over the main structural timbers of the roof – which we're leaving exposed anyway – so they'll be supported while I staple them to the rafters.' So our plan was formulated.

Jeff Dedman was only too pleased to lend me his long ladder, and even helped me to carry it back to the *grange*. 'You're going to fix the insulation from one ladder?' he said, and I confirmed this. 'You must be off your rocker!' Jeff was so busy that he barely had time to be with his wife and two young children. The roof of his own house had been in the process of retiling for over a year, and we were still waiting for him to come and install our grease trap.

'How's the old lady?' he asked, changing the subject, as we walked along the lane carrying the ladder between us.

'Who? Al?' I said.

'No. Not *your* old lady. The old lady Véronique,' he clarified. I craned my neck around to look him in the eyes. He winked at me.

'Why?' I asked.

'Just being neighbourly, like. Haven't bumped into her for a while.'

'She's fine, I think.' I was nervous, half expecting Véronique to spring from her doorway, wrestle the builder to the ground and club him to death with her stick. But he was spared this indignity, as I was spared the embarrassment of having to separate the pair of them.

Before we could fix the insulation it would be necessary to spray all the exposed roof timbers with insecticide. For this we had decided to use a pair of garden pressure sprayers, which would apply the fluid evenly to the surface of the rafters, tiling battens and other structural members high up in the huge roof. After having grouped together the furniture and covered it with a protective polythene film, the pair of us dressed for battle in old clothes, rubber gloves sealed at the wrists with elastic bands, goggles and facemasks. Al wore a baseball cap into which she had scooped her long, dark tresses, while I opted for a bandana.

Al worked from a pair of stepladders on the lower level of the rafters, applying a fine mist of liquid to the timbers. Meanwhile, I leaned the top of Jeff's fully-extended three-section ladder onto the highest horizontal beam and scaled up the rungs nervously, the pressure sprayer slung over my shoulder. Although a pilot, I am not good at heights. Happy in a wicker basket floating thousands of feet up in the air, I am vertiginous when still connected with the ground, such as looking out of a top floor window. And from my shaky perch high up in the roof, the world below me looked a distant place, the rungs of the ladder seeming to disappear into infinity. My knee caps started to quiver uncontrollably and my teeth began chattering.

'Shit bugger shit bugger shit bugger ...' I intoned as a kind of mantra intended to focus my mind. The words came muffled by my mask.

'What did you say, darling?' called Al's similarly muffled voice from a speck many miles below me.

'Nothing,' I squeaked. Get a grip. Focus. Grasping the sprayer's trigger, I aimed the nozzle towards the rafters and squeezed. The nozzle dropped off and plummeted into the abyss. A spurt of noxious insecticide hit me full in the face, spattering my goggles. 'Urgh! I'm blind!' I wailed, my feet clattering on the rungs as I lost my balance. I regained my grip. Just then the whole ladder began to shake violently. I lifted the smeary goggles and peered down into the gloom, where the minute figure of Jazz had the bottom rung in his vice-like grip and was attempting to drag it across the floor.

'Jazz!' called Al. 'Naughty boy! Leave daddy's ladder! *Au lit!*' At the command of his mistress, the mutt relinquished his grip on the rung and scuttled back to his bed. I descended rapidly to the safety of the floor, quivering like a jelly. Al looked across from her perch. 'My, you're a quick worker! Run out all ready.'

'Can't talk. Need drink,' was all I could utter.

The second time I scaled the heady heights – spray gun repaired – I was more determined to succeed. Possibly the bottle of beer I had just knocked back was an unwise idea, but there was no way I was going back up there again without some kind of nerve-numbing drug coursing through my veins. Able to get into a rhythm, I had soon completed a substantial area of the rafters and tile battens. It was, nevertheless, a soul-destroying job. Since the insecticide was colourless it was as if I was merely spraying a fine mist of water. To make matters worse, the liquid soaked into the dry wood rapidly and after a few minutes it was difficult to see any progress at all. The noxious smell of this 'odourless' product revealed that the air was indeed thick with fumes. By moving our ladders along periodically, we had, after several hours, completed a single coat of fluid. Then it was time to start again and apply a second coat. The next day we had to endure a repetition of the process by applying a third, and thankfully final coat.

At last we were able to fix the insulation. Cutting sixteen-metre lengths, we fed the first over the two beams that divided the roof into three sections. I mounted my ladder, hauled the insulation over my head and attempted to align it on the rafters. This was more difficult than it seemed, since the insulation was very heavy. Al, having suffered a neck injury in a traffic accident years previously, found it difficult to look upwards. Standing below, she propped up the sagging insulation with a broom while I stapled it to the rafters. We had, after about an hour, fixed up one strip.

Fixing the overlapping strip above it was even more difficult, since the increased height and the acute angle of the ladder meant that I would have to balance the insulation on my head, while trying to staple it. Even then, to staple the top edge, I would have to reposition the ladder so that it leaned precariously against the topmost beam. Al developed the cunning knack of viewing my progress from below through the reflection of a hand mirror, enabling her to protect her delicate neck. At the end of the day we had fixed the insulation to the lower third of the roof slope on both sides of the room.

Exhausted, we sat on the hearth next to the wood-burning stove and sipped wine, both wondering how on earth we were going to cope with insulating the upper two sections. The telephone rang.

'*Oui, allô?*' I said.

'*Riche! Comment ça va? C'est Claude...*' Our friend the *professeur* had called for an update on our progress with the insulation.

'It's going slowly, Claude,' I explained.

'*D'accord, mon ami.* Benoît and I will arrive tomorrow morning to help you.'

The next morning, true to his word, Claude and his son duly arrived at the *grange* with a long, extremely heavy pair of iron stepladders and a staple gun. After an obligatory coffee and the iced buns the pair had brought along, we set up our combined access equipment and commenced fixing the insulation to the central section of the roof. The job was much easier with the four of us and we evolved a method of fixing shorter lengths of the silver material, which proved to be less problematic, but still very tricky. With the aid of my brother's tall, narrow scaffold tower we made rapid progress. Claude, always the joker, delighted in standing at the base of the scaffold and shaking it violently whenever poor Benoît ascended, laughing heartily.

The following day only the top segment of the roof, where the two pitches met at the apex, was left. Claude and Benoît were not available, so it was down to Al and me to struggle again. The weather outside had deteriorated and it was necessary to light the stove to keep warm while we worked. Up in the apex

154

of the roof was extremely hot, where the hot air had risen and become trapped by the insulation. I had become more used to working on high and took to abandoning the ladder and clambering about in the arrangement of oak beams that supported the roof.

Meanwhile, matters came to a head with the battle that raged between Véronique and Jeff. Each morning the old lady would be out there in the lane yelling abuse across the hamlet. To his credit, if he was aware of the feud, he said nothing and gave no outward reaction. However, I was spurred to take preventative measures one morning when Véronique's fury had given way to action.

'Jeff! You little shit!' she shouted. 'Right! You're going to have to be castrated!' With that, she set off at a fast waddle down the lane towards Jeff's house. She had already reached the *poubelle* before I managed to catch up with her.

'Véronique,' I said, clasping her arm. 'Don't you think this is far enough?' She was making threatening gestures with her stick. Not far away I could see Jeff clambering into his van. He seemed oblivious to his terrible fate. The old lady strained at my grasp.

'He's *méchant*!' she wailed, slamming her stick into the tarmac.

'Jeff's not wicked, Véronique,' I said. 'Why do you think he's wicked?'

'He never comes when I call,' she sobbed.

'Why are you calling him anyway?'

'He's a randy dog, Monsieur Richard,' she said, fixing me squarely in the eyes, unblinkingly.

'Whaaat?'

'He's after every bitch in the village…'

'I beg your pardon?' I was stunned.

'… And probably the males, too!' she pronounced solemnly.

'Excuse me?' I said, truly mystified.

'Laurent wouldn't be too pleased at that, now would he?'

'Laurent? Who's Laurent?'

'Monsieur Richard. What's the matter with you? You know my nephew Laurent? He is Jeff's master.'

Just then, Jeff's van rolled onto the lane and headed towards us. Véronique drew me aside as the van came alongside. 'Step back while Monsieur Dedman passes.' She waved politely at Jeff, who grinned back at us from the cab, and in a moment was gone. 'Right, you can help me catch that wicked *chiot*. Look, there he is now!' She pointed towards Jeff's house and the kennel outside, where a young, lithe brown pointer with dark, spotty markings was attempting to have sex with Jeff's dog, Charlie the floppy-eared hound. Not unreasonably, the hound was at pains to reject the amorous advances of the hunting dog.

'Hah! The dog's called Jeff,' I said, as reality dawned. 'The dog's called Jeff as well… hah!' Véronique glared at me as if I was crazy. So she hadn't been calling Jeff an evil *chiure*, or shit, but an evil *chiot*, or puppy!

'Yes, Monsieur Richard, I know. But if he keeps running off like this he'll have to be castrated. It's a good job that Laurent gets back from holiday tomorrow. I'm fed up with looking after the stupid *chiure*.' As I set off to apprehend the canine rascal, I reflected that perhaps I had not misheard the old lady after all.

With the roof of the *grange* insulated, we could detect a vast improvement in the building's ability to retain the warmth we generated, but there existed a cold barrier at floor level where the thin floorboards were the only components that shielded us from the unheated ground floor of the building. Purchasing rolls of mineral wool insulation, we began filling the spaces between the ceiling joists in the hallway, bedrooms, bathroom and ancillary rooms on the ground floor. The job was horrendously uncomfortable. The intense itchiness created by the tiny fibres of the insulant managed to penetrate our clothing, no matter what precautions we took. Tight-fitting cuffs, over-wrapped with rubber gloves, minimised the problem, but our hands became sweaty and wrinkled with the moisture. A hat, goggles and facemask protected our faces to some degree, although the simple function of breathing tended to steam up the goggles and made it difficult to see what we were doing.

Cutting the rolls of insulation in half, we fed the material into place, retaining it between the joists with large nails. This was marginally successful, although the insulation sagged. Eventually intending to fix plasterboard between the joists to conceal the insulation while leaving the bulk of the oak beams exposed, we temporarily stapled vast sheets of *bâche* to the undersides of the joists, covering the ceilings. The thin reinforced plastic tarpaulin is widely used in France for anything from protecting an un-garaged car from the weather, to covering stacks of logs left outdoors to overwinter. In true make-do family style, this method was eminently suitable in the short term, if grossly unattractive. Soon we could feel the benefit of our newly insulated home.

Friends and relations who came to visit, however, failed to appreciate the efficiency of the system. Many remained well wrapped in coats and scarves – despite a roaring fire in the stove on the hearth – while Al and I, whose bodies had adapted to the cold conditions, flounced around in T-shirts.

My suspicions that Al and I had consumed one – or at least part of one – of Monsieur André's ponies was plaguing me. It was not that I had a particular aversion to eating such an animal: I had in my lifetime consumed bits of kangaroo, alligator, ostrich and frog. But I knew my wife would baulk at the thought of munching a creature she had regarded as a friend since she was a wee nipper. To satisfy my own curiosity, I decided to find out just what the truth of the matter was. But, if indeed the farmer had palmed us off with a portion of pony, should I break the news to my horse-loving wife, or keep mum?

Was Monsieur André running a sideline in equine meat, I wondered? If he was, with less than a dozen animals it was hardly a business he was ever likely to float on the stock market. Could it be that he had simply discovered a cheap, trouble-free way of filling his own freezer cabinet? But what about the ponies that I had seen driven away? As a former butcher he would have no qualms about dispensing with the ponies and converting them into a range of delicious cuts of meat. In any event, I was curious about the truth behind the common perception that the French regard the horse (and perhaps its smaller relation) as a gastronomic speciality rather than a noble beast and one of man's most enduringly faithful companions. While Al was out walking with Jazz, I began by consulting an Internet search engine. I input key words such as 'pony', 'horsemeat', 'france' and 'butcher'. A wealth of information sprang up arguing for and against the consumption of horsemeat by, amongst others, the French, Belgians, Canadians, Germans and Japanese. There was nothing that mentioned ponies per se, but I was intrigued.

I was most surprised by the apparent popularity of horsemeat, not just in France but throughout the world. In

Quebec, Canada, horsemeat was said to be readily available in supermarkets, vacuum-packed for longevity. In Iceland the meat was used as an ingredient in strong-flavoured stews or dipped into fondues. In Japanese cuisine raw horsemeat was known as *sakura*, meaning 'cherry blossom'; this referred to its vivid pink colour and the delicacy was employed in many dishes, even somewhat bizarrely an ice-cream called *basashi*. Netherlanders apparently had a penchant for breakfasting on *paardenrookvlees*, a sliced meat made from smoked horsemeat. It turned out that the poor Brits, with whom eating horse was generally taboo, had unintentionally scoffed minced steed (along with diced donkey) in the form of salami and chorizo sausages. The Food Standards Agency, in 2003, had investigated the inclusion of these ingredients in produce widely sold in the UK, without them being listed on the label and despite a legal requirement to do so. Most disgusting of all, to my sensitive mind, were the culinary practices carried out in Kazakhstan, including the manufacture of *karta* from a section of horse rectum, which was smoked and boiled.

From an historical point of view, consumption of horsemeat had been common in pre-Christian Europe, although it was regarded as unclean under Moslem, Islamic and Jewish laws. Although it was proscribed from the French *table d'hôte* during the Middle Ages, during Napoleon Bonaparte's Russian campaign cold and starving French soldiers had butchered and eaten their own steeds. In France, a nationwide famine in 1866 saw the ban on eating horsemeat lifted. In 1870, during the siege of Paris, hungry, desperate citizens had found horsemeat much more palatable than the rats, mice, dogs and cats they had been forced to eat when the butchers' shops were forced to close their doors. It seems that the French had developed a taste for horsemeat, *viande chevaline*, and 'hippophagic butchers' sprang up in every major town across the country. These specialist shops – *boucheries chevalines* – were readily distinguished from conventional butcher's premises by the gilded horse's head suspended over the entrance, and their window frames painted a rather blatant blood red. The meat was sold in distinctive pink paper embellished with the picture of a stallion's head. The obvious suggestion was that by consuming the meat one would be invested with the noble steed's vigour.

France and Belgium held the record as the most rapacious *hippophagistes* in the world. Horsemeat, cheaper than beef or pork, was also regarded as being a leaner, sweeter and tastier meat. It was also higher in protein, vitamin B12 and zinc. It was once recommended by the French health authorities that children should eat at least one horse steak a week. The meat was low in cholesterol and easily digestible. Its vivid red colour denoted its richness in iron. Horsemeat was immensely popular in France up to the 1980s, when pressure from publicity campaigns waged by gutsy former film actress Brigitte Bardot and the International League for the Protection of the Horse resulted in a decline in its consumption. In the late nineties, the equine equivalent of mad cow disease struck more than four hundred people and caused the French authorities to ask the European headquarters in Brussels to outlaw imports of horsemeat from Eastern Europe. The outbreak of food poisoning had been caused by the threadworm *trichinella spiralis*, resulting in diarrhoea, vomiting, fever and a swelling of the face, neck and limbs, with potentially fatal consequences. The parasite was thought to have entered infected horses when the plant-eating mammals were fed animal protein, most likely pig carcass.

The decline in horsemeat's popularity was to be short lived. Mad cow and foot-and-mouth disease resulted in an increase in the consumption of horseflesh in 2001, as carnivores sought alternatives. 'Over the last few months, our profits have soared thirty to forty percent,' claimed a happy Michel Beaubois, president of the Féderation de la Boucherie Hippophagique de France. 'And we expect to sell more than fifty thousand tonnes of horse next year.' Because of the escalation in consumption, meat sellers were unable to meet demands. Cases of horse rustling were reported: in some cases domestic horses and ponies were pilfered from their cosy stables only to reappear in black market outlets.

Nowadays, the French consume over three hundred thousand horses each year, knocking their *hippophagique* rivals into a cocked hat. Not all the animals are slaughtered in the country: the USA is one of the major importers, although equine carcasses also come from Argentina, Canada and other European countries. But where did the raw materials for the horsemeat actually come from? It seemed that few horsemeat producing countries actually raised horses for meat in the way that cattle, pigs and sheep are. Instead, meat came from ex-racehorses, retired stable and work horses. It was something of a relief to discover that meat from injured horses that have been put down by a veterinarian with a lethal injection is not used for consumption.

So the question still remained: was Monsieur André raising ponies for consumption, conversion into sausagemeat, or was he merely making a few extra euros by selling foals as steeds for the children of Limousin? I decided that the answer to that question needed to come straight from the horse's mouth.

In the grip of lierre

Chapter Ten

Mad cows and Englishmen

Al and I were determined to involve ourselves in the local community as much as we could, so when we saw a notice posted in Magnac Laval announcing *Donnez du Sang!*, we agreed that this would be an ideal way to contribute. Blood donors were being sought and we resolved to give as much as we could spare. I had never given blood before, which I regarded as a huge failing on my part. It was time to set the record straight. The blood-letting event was being held at l'Hotel de Ville in the village the following week.

Presenting ourselves at the enrolment desk, we were handed official forms to fill in. We spent fifteen minutes translating the many questions about our previous and present health status and other personal details, and duly handed them in to the smiling lady behind the desk. Reading through our responses, her eyes suddenly widened and her smile disappeared. She coughed in barely concealed embarrassment.

'I think there is a discrepancy, *madame et monsieur*,' she announced, shaking her head sorrowfully.

'*C'est quoi ça?*' said Al, peering at our forms. 'Have we made an error?'

'*Non, pas d'erreur.* But you are English, *non*?'

'Yes. Why?'

'Then I believe we cannot take your blood, *madame et monsieur…*'

'Can't take our blood? Why ever not?' asked Al.

'I will call a doctor to explain, *madame*. Please sit.' We obediently took seats in the waiting room while the lady entered the main hall. Through the open door we could see that many beds had been set up in neat rows, and on them other donors were lying while their blood was extracted. I began to feel a mite queasy, but hid this from Al, a seasoned blood donor. In an adjoining room a small cafeteria had been provided, where individuals post-donation were relaxing and partaking in the free tea, coffee, biscuits, bread and cheese that were provided. The atmosphere was that of a pleasant coffee morning, where friends and family had gathered to chat.

Eventually we were summoned to an office located off the main hall, where a serious-looking, white-coated lady doctor sat, gloomily surveying our enrolment forms. We were asked to take the seats in front of the desk. The doctor peered over her half-spectacles at us.

'Do you live in France permanently?' she asked solemnly.

'Yes,' we said.

'And for how long have you lived here?'

'Not long. Just three or four months,' explained Al.

'Oh, not years…'

'No, just months.'

'Ah! Then we do not want your blood,' the doctor stated definitively, slapping her palms on the desk and pushing our forms away from her as if we had been wasting her valuable time.

'Don't want our blood?' I questioned. 'Why not?'

'It is poison.'

'Poison?' I turned to look at Al, whose face registered utter incomprehension.

'Poison,' repeated the doctor ominously.

'Oh, so do you think we have some terrible disease then?' I asked, rather insulted by her offhand remark as to the condition of our blood, but also beginning to feel a little worried. What on earth could they have discovered about our blood without even making the merest of pinpricks?

'Yes,' came the stark response.

'And what disease would that be, then?' asked Al.

'Mad cow disease,' came the blunt response.

'We have mad cow disease?' I confirmed.

'*Naturellement.* You are English.'

'So all the English are infected with mad cow disease then?' I sought her clarification.

'Perhaps not all. But there is this risk. We do not want to bring this disease back into France. You English gave it to us in the first place. So, you may keep your blood, thank you. I am sorry.' She stood. We stood. The lack of a proffered hand to shake was apparent to Al and me, 'unclean' as we were. Showing us to the door, the doctor added, almost as an afterthought: 'Feel free to stay and take tea and biscuits.' Rather deflated by our rejection, however, Al and I chose to depart and take our diseased bodies back home, to drown our sorrows with red wine and ruminate on the number of beefburgers we had consumed in our lives.

Our assimilation in French society had taken a turn for the worse, but I was intrigued as to the circumstances of our rejection from the blood bank. Research revealed that the French had become paranoid about the safety of donated blood since a scandal in 1985, when more than four thousand people had contracted the Aids virus from blood transfusions. In the aftermath of the affair, many victims had died and numerous government officials were brought to trial. While that particular furore had nothing to do with the outbreak of Creutzfeldt-Jakob Disease, the human form of mad cow disease, the French were on high alert. The brain-wasting ailment originated in Britain during the late 1970s, as a mutation of a disease found in sheep. The spread of the disease was believed to be caused by animal feed made from meat and bonemeal from infected cattle. Although this dubious practice was banned in the UK in 1998, figures from Customs and Excise showed that in 1989 France imported more than 15,000 tonnes of meat and bonemeal from the UK.

The main source of the French population's exposure to BSE was believed to originate from imports of infected bovine carcasses from the UK. By the mid-1990s France had recorded tens of thousands of cases of BSE each year. In 1996, the European Union banned imports of beef from Britain and millions of British cows were slaughtered and their carcasses incinerated. When potentially infected beef from British cows was discovered in three Parisian supermarket chains in the year 2000, the French fears about the disease and its health risks to humans had reached a peak. Consumers panicked and beef sales fell. Meanwhile, the government had taken steps to prevent the spread of the disease by banning blood donations from people who had spent more than a year in Britain between 1980 and 1996. Al and I, of course, fell within this category. The measure was precautionary, said the government, since there was no proof that CJD could actually be transmitted through the blood.

The newspaper *Le Monde*, however, stated that health officials believed the ban would have the effect of eliminating a large number of people who regularly gave blood, and that these people would have to be replaced by a significant rise in the number of new donors. It was pointed out that since France was the major market for British beef during the period when cattle were first infected by Bovine Spongiform Encephalapothy, innocent donors who had never left the shores of France would have been just as exposed as those who had visited Britain.

While only three French people had contracted variant CJD, compared with eighty-two in the UK, two had died. French doctors predicted that these figures could rise dramatically. The number of cases of BSE in French herds had tripled, the epidemic concentrated around Normandy and Brittany, where most imports of animal feed from Britain wound up. France began a testing programme of all cattle aged over thirty months, which could have eaten more contaminated meat and bonemeal-based feed than younger animals. Twenty thousand animals were tested each week, at a cost of five hundred francs an animal, and those infected were destroyed. One of the reforms necessary to prevent the spread of the disease was to ban the use of meat in cattle feed, but French farmers said that they would not accept the substitute that was suggested – American rapeseed – since it might have been genetically modified.

The BSE crisis was not the only food-related health scare to afflict this nation of gourmets. The French were also being assaulted by revelations closer to home. Poor hygiene standards proliferated in slaughterhouses and on farms. Shoddy veterinary controls were cited, along with lapses in animal welfare. Studies of French meat products such as paté, minced beef and sausages brought to light horror stories of poultry tainted with harmful dioxins, and calves that were fed on sewage. The French defences were up. They had a reputation to uphold.

To cap it all, three-star Michelin award-winning chef, Alain Passard, owner of the expensive eatery l'Arpège in Paris, publicly denounced the use of meat in his establishment. In future his menu would comprise only vegetable creations (although he was keeping his options open with a selection of poultry dishes). Passard stressed that his decision was not an overreaction to the BSE crisis but one of personal choice. 'I can no longer stand the idea that we humans have turned herbivore ruminants into carnivores,' said the long-time vegetarian chef. 'But also, I can't get excited about a lump of barbecue meat. Vegetables are so much more colourful, more perfumed. You can play with the harmony of colours, everything is luminous.' Poetic words indeed, but in a country where *les végétariens* are regarded with utmost suspicion and a large plateful of derision, this was a bold move by Monsieur Passard.

As the winter wore on the tasks that we could complete outdoors were limited. Heavy rainfall had made the fields boggy and inaccessible to the tractor. There was, however, one job that had become an important consideration. Whilst strolling across our land with the Count one day we had come across a recently fallen tree. The once majestic oak had been felled simply by the weight of the ivy that clung to its trunk and branches. It had been a process that had taken, perhaps, some twenty years, when the smallest strands of the *lierre* had first entwined around the trunk of the tree. Left to grow unrestrained for decades, the parasitic ivy had swollen and taken hold of the tree in a death grip. The main, woody stem of the plant had attained the thickness of a man's thigh, curled around the trunk, while its clinging tendrils gripped the branches.

We had realised that freeing our trees of the ivy was an important task but the premature toppling of the tree – which still had much life inside – revealed that it was now a priority. Of the hundred or more trees that marked the boundaries of our fields, some ninety percent were in the process of being strangled by ivy.

'You're going to have to get rid of this ivy as soon as possible,' said the Count, who was in the process of communing with one of my stricken oaks by giving it a warm, comforting hug. 'If you don't, you're going to lose all your trees. Mark my words! Why the farmers leave the stuff there from year to year I'll never know!' It was common throughout the region to see aged trees that had been left in the murderous grip of prolific ivies for many decades without intervention. Eventually the ivy would win, after perhaps thirty or more years.

'Perhaps it's a process of natural selection,' I suggested. 'The farmers allow the ivy to topple the weaker trees after a number of years, saving them from having to cut them down. Then they chop them up and use them as firewood.'

'Yes, could be,' agreed the Count. 'But they never replace trees that fall, or which they cut down. So eventually there won't be any trees left at all. It's criminal. The bastards ought to be guillotined.' Although my brother tended to to espouse rather excessive views on punishment, I had to concur in part. I had been saddened to see hundreds of oaks felled in previous years by farmers out to make a fast buck from a rich resource: trees were either cut up for firewood or sold abroad as the raw material for the manufacture of fine oak furniture. This was acceptable in itself, but there seemed to exist no policy of reforestation. Huge areas of the countryside had been denuded of this valuable resource to the environment. Why could they not simply plant a sapling to replace a tree that was felled?

One thing was certain: we would have to act promptly before any more of our trees were brought down by the ivy. Fired with enthusiasm, the Count agreed to return the following weekend with his trusty chainsaw and, along with Stephanie and Al, we would venture forth into the woods on a mission of mercy. And so it came to pass that, armed with two chainsaws, axes and wheelbarrows our little troupe set off from the *grange* just as a light snow was beginning to fall. Little Jazz tagged along at our side, wearing a cosy dog jacket to keep him warm. By the time we had reached our first patient – a stout-hearted oak about two hundred years old, under attack by two thick ivies – the snow was falling in large, wispy flakes.

'It won't settle,' assured the Count, who swore by the forecasts of his electronic weather station, despite the fact that its accuracy was frequently thrown into some doubt by actual climatic conditions.

Stephanie and Al began to cut away the brambles from the base of the tree and its neighbours, while Phill and I started up our chainsaws and began to perform delicate surgery. Slicing great wedges from the main stems of the ivy, close to where they emerged from the ground, we would allow the ivies to die back naturally. Although the ivy stems were entwined tightly around the branches of the tree, we felt sure that, starved of nourishment, they would become dry, wither and eventually fall off, leaving the tree to continue its previously restrained growth with renewed vigour.

By the time we moved on to rescue our second and third trees, the ground was thick with snow several inches deep, and even more was falling as a howling blizzard whipped across the countryside. Jazz, whose jacket had collected a thick coating of snow, considered that there was a limit to being man's best friend and snuck back to the shelter of the hangar to await our return. The Count said nothing more to defend his dubious weather forecast. Although we were well wrapped in scarves, thick jackets and jeans, the horizontal wind was bitingly cold on our exposed faces. Despite thermal gloves, my fingers, prone to the detrimental effects of low temperatures, were unfeeling and bloodless. My brother also suffered from this debilitating condition – Raynaud's Phenomenon – and we would frequently have to pause our work to restore the feeling and colour by stuffing our hands into our relatively warm armpits. Inside my wellington boots, my triple-socked feet had also become numb. I stamped my feet in a vain attempt to restore circulation. Undeterred by the deteriorating weather conditions, however, we worked systematically along the boundary line between our property and our neighbour's, freeing the oaks from their cruel bondage. Some poor specimens, sadly, were beyond salvation and had already begun to lean at an alarming angle as their thick roots were lifted from the ground, taking with them a skirt of earth.

'Ok, so we'll inevitably lose some trees,' I hollered through the whistling wind. 'But we can use the timber as firewood, once it's been stored in the dry for a year.'

After a brief lunch break, during which we returned to the warmth of the *grange* to thaw out and consume bowls of home-made leek and potato soup and fresh bread, we returned once more to the fray. By the end of the afternoon, when darkness was beginning to descend upon us with rapidity, we had managed to rescue more than thirty trees. I casually wondered whether the trees, which had been partly supported by the ivies for many years, were feeling a little insecure right now, standing as it were on their own two feet. They could be forgiven for feeling a little wobbly, I told myself, but they would thank us one day. Strange what the cold does to a feeble mind.

We tree surgeons were satisfied that we had made an impression on what was a mammoth task. We appeared to have also made some kind of an impression on our neighbour. From the stifling warmth of her kitchen, Véronique regarded us as we wended our way through the thick snow, chainsaws slung nonchalantly over our shoulders.

171

Balloon inflation

Chapter Eleven

Up, up and away!

On St. Valentine's Day, February 14, I had invited friends to partake in a gentle balloon flight in *Zulu India* over the countryside of the Haute-Vienne. Claude Norrin, his delightful wife Martine and our new English friend Jill Farrell were to be my passengers. The promise of a post-flight bottle of champagne was undoubtedly a lure for my passengers. I was only sorry that Al could not fly with us, but her duties lay in the role of Golden Retriever responsible for chasing the balloon to its landing place and returning us home afterwards.

Martine was a strikingly attractive, petite lady with delicate features and short, wavy brunette hair. For all her delicate profile this mother of two teenagers seemed to command inner physical strength: in her job she drove one of the huge articulated 'bendy buses' that wend their way through the narrow streets of Limoges. This was indeed a picture to imagine, as it was hard to see how she could see over the steering wheel.

We had met Jill after she had telephoned out of the blue one day. She had spoken to Al during one of my absences in the UK. Her husband had recently passed away and her grief had been lightened by a gift from a friend in England: a copy of my book *Bon Courage!* had been delivered to her because of the sentiments in its title and the fact that we appeared to live a mere stone's throw away from her. Jill had not heard this phrase exhorting courage in adversity until, on the death of her husband, all her French friends and neighbours had used it to comfort her. We had soon befriended this funny, effervescent lady. Jill always beamed with an infectious, broad and open smile, wore her straight chestnut hair in a shoulder-length bob with a fringe at the forehead and was rarely without the pair of large gold hoop rings that dangled from her ears. Although Scottish by birth she spoke with the Cheshire accent she had adopted when living south of the border.

In the months after her husband Steve's tragic death, Jill had struck up a relationship with the mayor of her commune. Jean-Michel, a divorcee, lived just across the road from her, and had been a close friend to her and Steve since their arrival in France three years previously. On Steve's death, Jean-Michel had done all he could to look after and support Jill in her grief and their friendship had developed into a loving partnership. Monsieur le Maire was a tall, upstanding man in his mid-fifties, with closely cropped, receding grey hair. Always immaculately dressed, this quietly spoken, intelligent and caring man wore wire spectacles, to the arms of which were attached a pair of minuscule hearing aids. During his time in military service, Jean-Michel had been in the artillery corps. In the days before ear defenders became compulsory, the constant pounding of weaponry had irreparably damaged his hearing.

'Jean-Michel can't hear a bloody thing when he takes his specs off!' Jill would joke, whenever her partner removed his glasses to polish them during a conversation, rendering him oblivious to what was being discussed. Often he would not wear his glasses at all, in order to 'give ze ears an 'oliday', as he would say. Early in their relationship, Jill had telephoned him early one morning for some lovey-dovey pillow talk. The mayor, prematurely aroused from his sleep, and of course without his spectacles, answered the phone call bleary-eyed and thus virtually deaf.

'*Bonjour mon coeur,*' Jill had breathed sexily into the mouthpiece. '*Je t'adore!*'

'What's that you say? The dog's dead? I'll be right over, *cherie!*' came Jean-Michel's panicky voice as he launched himself from his bed and into his dressing gown and slippers.

These minor hiccups aside, the pair conversed mainly in French – Jill's accent rich with her dulcet Cheshire tones – although Jean-Michel loved to practice his English. Jill had naughtily taught him some choice English phrases, and he often came out with such gems as: 'Ee, I'm bloody knackered', delivered in a rich French accent. He generally spoke to me in his native tongue, while I would respond in mine. The mix made for a curious conversation to the onlooker, but it worked well for us. Because of his mayoral duties, Jean-

Michel was not able to fly with us, but he had agreed to come along to assist with the launch and wish us a happy flight.

We had decided to fly from Jill and Jean-Michel's home village of Cromac, close to Lac du Mondon. Jean-Michel had arranged with a local farmer that we could take off from his large, flat field. Al and I arrived at the mayor's abode to collect him and Jill, with Claude and Martine following behind in their car.

'All set?' I said, greeting the pair.

'*Oui, Riche,*' said the mayor. '*Mais, d'abord, j'ai un gros saucisse!*'

'I beg your pardon?' I said, somewhat taken aback. Perhaps I misheard.

'I need to visit *la toilette…*' whispered Jean-Michel, heading for the house. 'I will be just two minutes…' When he had disappeared indoors, I looked confusedly at Jill, then at Al. Both ladies appeared confused, too. Jill was blushing.

'Did he say what I thought he said?' I queried.

'What did you think he said?' asked Al.

'That he was going to the loo because he had a "*gros saucisse*"… a fat sausage…'

'That's what I thought he said,' agreed Jill.

'No use asking me,' said Al, shrugging. 'I'm a deaf old bird at the best of times. And I haven't had my eardrums blasted by gunfire!'

'Well,' said Jill. 'It's not the kind of thing you'd expect the mayor to say. I've never heard him say that before. I'm quite shocked. He's such a polite, well-spoken man. Normally!' Just then, Jean-Michel reappeared, rubbing his hands together and looking very pleased with himself.

'*D'accord!*' he chirped, looking at our blank faces. 'All ready?' We nodded, smiled and clambered into the car. We soon put it to the back of our minds and concentrated on the flight.

The maize in the launch field had been recently cut, leaving short stalks protruding from the ground. It was an ideal site to lay out the balloon and inflate it. Only Claude had flown before, so I would need to thoroughly brief the others in what was to be expected of them – and what they should expect. We tugged the basket from the trailer and set it on the ground, then I instructed my friends in helping to rig it for flight. Once the burner had been attached, we tipped the basket onto its side and attached it to the front of the car via a long tether line. We dragged the bulbous bag from the trailer and hauled out the voluminous red and black fabric. Spreading it out on the ground in the direction of anticipated travel, I connected its flying wires to the burner frame.

Jill and Martine were detailed to hold the mouth of the envelope open while I inflated it with cold air from a motorised fan. Claude manned the crown line attached to the metal ring at the top of the envelope, used to steady the balloon during inflation.

'Jean-Michel,' I said. 'You can come to help me fit the parachute at the top end…'

'Parachute?' wailed Jill. 'Hang on a minute, darlin'. What do we need a parachute for? You didn't say anything about parachutes. I'm not jumping out the flippin' thing!'

'No, don't worry! It's a parachute valve that seals the big hole at the top of the balloon.'

'Big hole? What big hole? I've changed my mind, m'darling. I'm not coming!'

'Jill, trust me; it's OK,' I stressed, putting a consoling arm around her shoulder. 'The valve seals the hole and it's how I vent hot air from the envelope when I want to descend. It's perfectly safe. It's held in place with strings and Velcro tabs.'

'You've got to be kidding, mate! Bits of string and Velcro? Are you mad?' It took some convincing my friend that balloon flight was, in fact, very safe and the parachute valve a tried and trusted device.

I started the fan. The fabric started to billow. Trotting up to the top end, I entered through the hole at the apex and retrieved the nylon parachute valve, then with Jean-Michel's help fixed it in place. The envelope began to fill with air rapidly and assume its smooth balloon shape. Claude had pulled out the long black line attached to the crown and was leaning back against it.

Back at the basket, I fired up the burner and blasted a huge yellow flame into the open mouth. Repeated bursts of flame began to heat up the air inside and the fabric became more taut, then the balloon rose slowly. I stepped backwards nimbly into the basket as it flipped onto its base.

'Put your weight on the basket,' I shouted to the others above the noise of the burner. The balloon was now erect – some ninety feet tall.

'OK, passengers on board!' I said, and my three friends clambered over the side of the basket. After briefing them, I applied more heat to the envelope, then tugged the quick release to free the tether. The balloon lifted off gracefully and silently. I squeezed the trigger that fired the burner just enough to carry us safely over the treetops at the far end of the field, then applied a more prolonged burst of heat to make us ascend more rapidly. I glanced back at the field, where Al, Jean-Michel and some curious onlookers were waving farewell.

In a few minutes we had reached one thousand feet and I could see clearly the track along which the light northerly wind would carry us. Although I had not flown in this area before, the countryside was familiar to me and I found no need to study the map. It was a simple matter to navigate by picking out distinctive points of reference: a pond, the church spire of a distant village, the intersecting line of one of the rod-straight tar roads that connects the neighbouring communities.

To my joy – truly a case of *bonne chance* – we were being carried roughly on a course for my own hamlet and our home at Le Mas Mauvis. Soon we were passing over St. Léger Magnazeix. The main square was, as usual, totally devoid of human life. We continued onward towards Le Mas Mauvis. As we passed over an area of crop fields surrounding the hamlet, I gazed below and noticed several waving arms, and could hear muffled cheers, as farmers paused their grass-cutting and clambered from their tractors to witness the spectacle of the balloon's passage. I later learned that this was the first time a balloon had ever been seen in this vicinity.

We flew over a group of about a dozen hunters and their dogs, who waved their shotguns in the air. At first I thought they might be angry that we had disturbed their hunt, but they seemed only too pleased to see the balloon. The dogs, reacting to the presence of this large red and black object in the sky and the occasional crack as its burner broke the silence, barked and raced about madly, no doubt scaring off their masters' quarry into the bargain. But the hunters did not appear to mind. Claude indicated four young deer just out of sight of the gunmen, bounding through the long grass and into the cover of a copse.

Flying parallel with the road that led between St. Léger Magnazeix and Magnac Laval, some ten kilometres distant, we could see that Al in the retrieve vehicle had managed to keep pace with us. Soon she sped ahead and I could see the car and trailer turn onto the lane that led into Le Mas Mauvis. By the time that the balloon drifted over the hamlet, Al had summoned Véronique from her kitchen. The two of them stood in the lane outside the *grange*, gazing upwards as I guided the balloon directly over the top of our house at a height of about two hundred feet: I had allowed myself this slight breach of aeronautical protocol, whereby an aircraft must not descend below five hundred feet unless taking off or landing. I reasoned that, in any case, there was a slim chance that I might be able to set the basket down in our own field at the rear of the property in an intermediate landing.

As we drifted over the buildings, my passengers calling out to the figures below, I could see that Al was waving frantically, while our neighbour simply stood stock still, transfixed by the balloon's presence: it would be, she later told me, a memory she would treasure forever. My chance of landing in the field was gone as the gentle breeze carried us out of range and I fired the burner again so that we ascended to an altitude that allowed me to survey the lay of the land. At two thousand feet the countryside was laid out beneath us as a tapestry of light and dark green pastures and woodland, the yellows and browns of cut and ploughed fields. The sunlight reflected in the numerous ponds that dotted the terrain and we could see clusters of houses and farmsteads like models far below. Herds of cattle and flocks of sheep appeared motionless from this height, as the animals grazed contentedly in their fields.

Some minutes later I realised that we were heading directly for the centre of busy Magnac Laval, where a livestock market was in full swing. I knew that I would have to make the decision to gain height and fly on to avoid causing havoc amongst the penned animals, or to select a landing field immediately before the village. Weighing up our options, I chose to land.

'OK, I'm going to select a field and set us down,' I announced to the passengers. 'Remember what I told you: hold onto the rope handles inside the basket, facing away from the direction of travel and when I give the signal, crouch down slightly to absorb any slight bump! Stay down until the balloon has come to a complete rest and I've told you to move. You understand?'

'*Oui!*' shouted Claude over the roar of the burner. He positioned Martine so that she stood in front of the rope handles and selected the pair next to them.

'OK darlin'!' yelled Jill, assuming the landing position.

'And whatever you do,' I added. 'Don't get out of the basket until I tell you it's OK; the sudden loss of ballast could make us take off again!'

'Ballast?' said Jill. 'Who are you calling ballast, cheeky sod?'

In one hand I grasped the red line that I would use to rip the parachute valve from the top of the envelope, then looked ahead at the rapidly approaching collection of buildings at the centre of busy Magnac Laval. I could just make out the animal pens on the village square. To my irritation, the wind speed had picked up substantially and without warning, carrying the balloon along with it at a fair lick.

'This might be a firm landing!'

'What d'you mean, 'firm'?' croaked Jill nervously. 'You didn't say anything about 'firm'!'

'I mean we might hit the ground quite hard…'

Looking ahead, I could see a large field conveniently free of animals and other obstructions, which at the outset seemed an ideal place to land. Beyond it was the agricultural college, set within the grounds of a turreted eighteenth century chateau; I knew there to be many animals within the surrounding fields, so it was imperative that we land now. A hot-air balloon passing too close to penned-in animals can cause panic and result in a stampede. I leaned on the rip line for about three seconds, opening the parachute valve to evacuate just enough hot air to cause the balloon to lose height. It refused to budge. I leaned on the line again. This time we began to descend, rather too rapidly for my liking. I fired the burner again to arrest the descent. Keeping my eyes fixed on the centre of the field I then began to fire the burner in a series of short 'blips': this would keep the balloon on a steady descent at a shallow angle that should allow me to pop the basket into my chosen field. I say 'should', for few things in ballooning can be determined with any degree of accuracy when you are up against the vagaries of the weather. As we skimmed over the treetops towards the field, the leaves rustling against the basket's hide bottom rim, I scanned ahead of me in search of any previously concealed electrical cables or telephone wires that might be strung across our path. Thankfully, there were none. Despite the increased wind speed, we were still heading directly for the centre of the field. About twenty feet from the ground, I gave a final short burn then switched off the burner's pilot lights.

'Right! We're touching down...' I told my passengers. Tugging the ripline, I released more air from the envelope. Braced against one side of the basket, with only the line to hold onto, I saw the ground racing up towards us at a somewhat alarming rate. Suddenly the basket made jarring contact with the ground. There was the sound of creaking from the wicker as the weave absorbed the impact. I instinctively bent my knees to absorb the shock, then stood up again to make sure we were not in any danger. I saw that Claude, Martine and Jill were slumped in the bottom of the basket, winded due to the violent jolt.

'Oh, bloody hell! We're going to die!' I heard Jill scream as the envelope sagged over, tipping the basket onto its side. In a moment, the envelope, which still contained a vast volume of hot air, had re-inflated and rose into the air suddenly, whipping the basket off the ground.

'It's OK guys! Just stay there! We're coming down again…' The wind had veered to the left and we now lurched off towards the side of the field. The basket was swaying violently from side to side and I could hear groans from the tangle of passengers at my feet in the bottom of the basket. I toyed briefly with the idea of re-igniting the burner and taking us aloft again but decided that it would be safer to deflate the envelope as rapidly as I could and bring us back down to earth once and for all. One eye was on the barbed wire fence that loomed ever closer at the perimeter of the field, which could potentially rip the wicker of my basket to shreds. But my overwhelming horror was the sight of an enormous steaming heap of fresh cow manure that lay directly in our path. One of the most bizarre phenomena of ballooning is that if there is one object in a field that you wish to avoid – be it fence post, dung heap, tree, pond – then you're bound to head straight for it like filings to a magnet.

As if to prove me correct, the basket collided firmly against the stinking heap with a muffled 'Whumph!', sending up a spattering of black, wet and sticky manure which showered down into the basket. Without further ado we were airborne again, the basket having twirled around the manure heap. Although contact with the dung heap had acted as a kind of air brake, slowing us down considerably, we were now on a direct course for the barbed wire fence. There was no time to re-ignite the burner and ascend. There was nothing at all I could do.

'C'mon *Zulu*!' I said to the balloon. 'Up you come!' Fortuitously, the basket gained just enough height to clear the fence by a margin of mere inches, whereby I breathed a silent sigh of relief. I had had quite enough of these shenanigans. I hauled on the red line and kept reeling it in as the parachute vent was ripped free from its Velcro tabs. The basket smacked knee-jarringly back down to earth, promptly lifted off again, then made firm contact once more, tipping over onto its side as the partially-deflated envelope dragged us for several yards through the lush, grassy field and the numerous mounds of fresh sheep excrement that lay in its path. With a jolt, the basket righted itself. Finally, as I continued to haul in the ripline, sufficient hot air was released and the basket came to a standstill. I gazed upwards. Slowly the envelope began to crumple and descend upon the basket. I realised that if we did not take prompt action, we would be gift-wrapped by a voluminous nylon shroud. Claude emerged from the bottom of the basket, his glasses skew-whiff on his face and his normally coiffured hair in complete disarray. His shirt had been rent open to the navel. Nevertheless, he was grinning from ear to ear.

'*Allez Claude, très vite!*' I shouted, unclipping the crown line from the burner frame and handing it to him. '*Tiens!* Jump out and pull this rope as far as you can over there!' My friend, still somewhat befuddled, adjusted his glasses, grabbed the end of the thick rope, vaulted nimbly out of the basket and began to run in the direction I had indicated. As he tugged on the crown line, the top of the envelope was diverted from its downward descent and was soon flopping over, just clearing the burner frame. In a few minutes the fluttering fabric was lying stretched out along the ground to one side of the basket. Claude, hauling on the crown line, stuck a thumb in the air. I tied off the ripline around one of the burner supports so that an unexpected gust of wind could not re-inflate the envelope and drag us skywards again.

I looked down into the bottom of the basket. There was Jill, flat on her back, arms and legs akimbo. But where was poor Martine? Surely she couldn't have fallen out of the basket during one of our false landings? Hearing a muffled squeak, I looked closer and could make out a pair of arms and a leg beneath the prostrate body of Jill. Hauling her to her feet, we discovered Martine lying in the bottom of the basket, where she had been crushed beneath the joint weights of her travelling companions. We helped the little lady to her feet and smoothed down her rumpled hair. She adjusted her clothing, which had become twisted and disorderly. Despite her ordeal, she smiled broadly, then burst into fit of uncontrollable giggling. She then whacked me hard on the arm. Soon all three of us were madly chortling about the rather eventful culmination of our flight. Claude appeared at the side of the basket looking as if he had been dragged through a hedge backwards.

'I thought you said ballooning was a gentle experience, you little bugger!' said Jill, grabbing me in a headlock and tweaking my nose.

'Did I say that?' I squawked. 'How remiss of me…' Had I not explained that every landing is indeed a 'controlled crash'?

Al arrived with the trailer in the lane adjacent to the field to find four juvenile adults giggling hysterically and nursing our respective bruises. We packed up the balloon, returning it to its trailer and headed back to Le Mas Mauvis, where Jean-Michel had just arrived. Our little ballooning party then celebrated the flight of *Zulu India* with glasses of champagne, which seemed to ease the minor aches and pains.

Sowing seeds

Chapter Twelve

Salad days

Walking with Jazz one fine morning on the muddy lane that curled around the back of our property, I noticed Monsieur André attempting to load a reluctant pony into a horsebox, assisted by a man I did not recognise. The pony was neighing frantically, tossing its head from side to side. We stopped to watch as the little animal bucked and strained against the halter, wedging its hooves into the slope of the horsebox ramp. Eventually the men succeeded in tugging, pushing and cajoling the pony into the box and slammed the ramp closed behind it.

Monsieur André, wiping his sweaty forehead with his enormous, hairy forearm, caught sight of me and waved. I wandered over to the horsebox and shook the farmer's wrist that was offered to me, while the stranger disappeared inside the box through its small front door, carrying a bulging hay net.

'Another one off my hands!' said André gleefully, rubbing his palms together. He was wearing a pair of oil-stained denim jeans, the waistband of which hung below his ample pot belly, and a pale blue granddad vest that was worn to holes. On his head was a grubby beanie hat, which appeared to have been stolen from a child. It sat perched on the very top of his head. He bent down to fondle Jazz, who – undiscriminating in his friends – was straining at the leash for some attention. 'Down to the last few now…' the farmer growled, indicating the dwindling herd of ponies, silently grazing in the adjacent field. 'You don't fancy a little pony, do you?'

'No thanks,' I said, quick as a flash. For all I knew, I'd already had a little pony.

'*Tant pis,*' he shrugged. He wiped his forehead again.

'So you'll be breeding some more will you?' I asked tentatively, almost afraid of his likely response.

'*Non, ça suffit.* I think I've had my fill of ponies for now…' He belched as if to demonstrate the fact.

'What do you mean?'

'A lot of trouble for little reward. And I'll be selling this barn soon,' he explained. 'The stinking government impose too many restrictions for my liking.'

'How so?'

'New laws! Modernisation! *Putain!* It's no longer going to be possible to run a farm this close to habitation…' He indicated the tall, stone house across the muddy farmyard, no more than ten metres from the filthy, decrepit barn that was home to his veal calves during their short lives. André owned not only the ancient barn and its attendant hectares, but also a vast, iron-framed, corrugated roofed *bouverie*, or cattle stable attached to it. The stable was packed to the gunnels with huge round bales of hay, the winter feed for his animals. Twice a day he and his cowman – a swarthy, shifty-eyed individual of gypsy stock who never seemed to speak – would drive his herd of cows along the lane from the fields surrounding his main farm on the edge of the village to the barn. The veal calves within the barn could be given their quota of mother's milk, before the cows were driven back to the fields again. It was a monotonous existence for the men and the animals, and highly impractical given that the farmer owned a substantial spread with ample space for cattle stabling closer to hand. I could not imagine why on earth he continued the practice. There seemed no logic in it.

The house adjacent to the tumbledown barn had been the home of our English neighbours, the Timpsons. The couple had, about a year previously, disappeared form the face of the earth. Rumour had it that they had moved to the southern coast of France for the sake of Maureen's health. As a sufferer from multiple sclerosis, the rather damp, cold winters of Limousin had been a daily trial for her. Their sudden departure had been a mystery, but also a source of sadness to those of us who had considered the couple our friends. Since then, the house had remained empty. Monsieur André had been a close confidante of the couple and seemed to know more about their disappearance than he cared to let on.

'*Alors*,' continued the farmer. 'I'm obliged to sell up and move my *entreprise* close to my own farm.' He scowled. 'That, and the fact that my two boys don't want to carry on with the farm, means I might just as well retire!'

'That's a pity,' I said. Farms were commonly passed on from father to son, but André's two boys – one in his thirties, the other just twenty – had their eyes fixed on a less demanding and arduous style of life. Lured by the bright lights of nearby Limoges, they would be unlikely to remain in the isolation of the countryside for long. In any event, once their father passed on they would inherit all his property, lock, stock and barrel.

'*Non*, for me it would be a welcome break. I'm sick of farming anyway,' he leaned rather too close to me so that I could smell his rank odour. 'I'm not short of *l'argent*, you know...' he whispered. 'I still own some other businesses...' He winked. Monsieur André was always keen to brag about the fact that he was not without funds and other means.

'Such as?'

'*Boucherie*...' he drawled. 'I was one of the biggest butchers in the Haute-Vienne, *parbleu!*' You'd better believe it! I believed him. 'I don't suppose you want to buy this barn, and the fields?'

'How much?' I said, simply out of curiosity. I was in no position to buy another property, even if I had wanted to.

'Seventy five thousand euros,' he rattled off. He had got to be joking: the tumbledown barn, byre and surrounding hectares of land could not be worth more than twenty thousand euros.

'That's a lot of money,' I said.

'*Oui, mais ecoutez...* I have to sell this barn. I don't have a choice. It's useless to me if I can't farm here. So I have to build another barn on my existing land. That will cost me seventy five thousand euros. So that's why I'm asking this price.' The man displayed a twisted kind of logic that would have been admirable, had it not been completely insane.

'I'll think about it!' I said, if only to shut him up.

'*Bon!* Anyway,' he said, changing the subject. 'Have you seen Monsieur Gordon?'

'Gordon Timpson?' I asked.

'*Oui*, he's been back in the hamlet driving a flashy sport's car… The house has been sold.' He rubbed his forefinger and thumb together.

'Who to?'

The grimy farmer leaned in far too close again and took hold of my arm in a vice-like grip. 'Now who do you think? *Les Anglais, naturellement…*' This went without saying, for most properties in the region seemed to be snapped up by English buyers. I found myself wondering who our new neighbours would be. Monsieur André released my arm and grinned. '*Deux hommes…*'

Bidding farewell to the farmer, I wandered back towards the lane. 'Oh, by the way, Richard! I've meant to ask you,' he called after me. 'Did you enjoy *la viande*?'

'The meat? Err, yes we did… err, it was, err, *délicieux…*' I took a few steps back towards him. 'But, Thierry… what exactly was it?'

'What was it?' he retorted, raising his eyebrows in surprise. 'Only the finest piece of *cerf* I've shot this year!' I must have visibly relaxed. The meat had been venison after all. My wife's aversion to eating friends of the family had not been compromised.

'I thought for a moment it might have been pony!' I laughed, rather too ridiculously. The farmer stared at me for a moment without any discernible expression on his grimy face. Then he began to laugh raucously. The other man stuck his head out of the trailer, grinning.

'Pony! Ha ha ha! Pony!' howled the farmer. 'Pony! *Ecoutez*, Gerard!' he called to the man. 'Oh, you *Anglais*! Ho ho! Not all Frenchmen eat horses, you know!'

'Well, I just thought...' I mumbled, somewhat embarrassed.

'Gerard here finds good homes for my ponies...' he said, suddenly poker-faced. 'That's right, isn't it Gerard?'

'Good homes,' repeated the man, nodding.

'You didn't think we were dealing in illicit horsemeat, did you?'

'No,' I said. 'Not at all.' What a thought!

Back at the *grange*, Al greeted me excitedly with news that Gordon Timpson had been sighted in the hamlet, driving a bottle green, open-topped sports car. What was more, Véronique's informants had discovered that the Timpons' house had been sold to two English men called Keith and Peter.

'Do you think they're gay?' asked Al.

'How on earth would I know?' I replied. 'They might just be friends, brothers or cousins...'

'Well, it could be nice, couldn't it! They have such good taste,' she opined.

'Who do?'

'Gay men. Professional couple, two disposable incomes, no children. In touch with their feminine side...'

I raised my eyes to the rafters in hopeless despair. What an over-fertile imagination my wife had, jumping to such conclusions! Thank God I was on hand to inject a sane, practical influence to our lives.

Prolific budding on the wisteria and grapevines trained up the façade of the *grange* and the first shoots of green to poke through the soil of our flowerbeds announced the gradual and welcome return of spring to France's rural heartland. It was early April. The winter had been harsh, but we were consoled by the fact that it was of relatively short duration when compared to the winters generally endured by England. Our homeland, we reflected, could expect another few months of cold and darkness. The overall level of light increased with each passing day, and the hours of the day themselves seemed to stretch out their cramped limbs.

Al and I began to prepare the soil of the vegetable plot for planting the first seeds and seedlings. The backbreaking task of turning over the heavy earth was in fact a welcome and satisfying reawakening of muscles that had become slothful during the winter. There were, of course, machines that could prepare the tilth quicker and more effectively, but perversely we both enjoyed the physical challenge of tackling the work by hand. Dividing the plot into easily manageable segments, Al and I dug down a 'spit', or spade's depth, turning over and aerating the soil. Next we broke down the clods into a more friable structure. Finally, we used a rake to produce a fine seedbed a few centimetres deep.

We purchased seeds from a nearby *pépinière*, or nursery shop. Like children set free in a sweet shop we could not resist the abundant choice, and came away with far more packets of seeds than we could possibly use in one season alone. Staunch lovers of *salade* of all descriptions, we chose the bitter-tasting, curly endive *frisée*, a red-edged *feuille de chêne* or oak leaf lettuce, and the upright *batavia*, or romaine lettuce. I formed shallow furrows in the soil with my draw rake, while Al followed along behind me, scattering the tiny seeds along the lines. In our misguided eagerness we sowed far too many seeds in one go, a fact brought to our attention by Véronique, who had come to monitor our progress.

'You should sow much less seed at once, but repeat the sowing every *quinzaine*,' she advised, using the peculiar term for a fortnight, which actually translates as fifteen days rather than fourteen.

'We plan to thin out the seedlings,' explained Al. 'And we will be able to eat the baby leaves.'

'Eat the baby leaves?' she clearly baulked at the concept. '*De mauvais goût!*' Tasteless. 'Thinning out is an unnecessary *boulot*. Why make more work for yourselves? Simply sow less. With a plot of this size you will never have the time to sleep!' the old lady opined, quite wisely, it turned out. Once the hundreds of lettuce seedlings had begun to sprout from the soil we found ourselves inundated with more baby leaves than there were meals in the week. As the days passed and the seedlings became stronger, fighting for ground space with their neighbours, we began the tedious task of thinning out, transplanting the more spindly specimens to any spare space we could find in the garden, or merely condemning them to the compost heap. With all the other produce we had sown or planted, space was at a premium. At one stage we even expanded the garden itself by reclaiming part of the adjoining field, and also planted pots and window boxes with our burgeoning crop of *salade*. As the lettuces matured, however, we were rapidly overwhelmed with full, flavoursome heads, which bolted and set seed faster than we could eat them.

Our compost heap was bursting at the seams, not only from our garden and kitchen waste but also from our excess of vegetables. Enclosed in an assembly of wooden palettes and chicken mesh, the heap was observed with suspicion by our neighbours. None seemed to practice the art of kitchen garden management, considering a compost heap to be nothing less than an attraction for rats and other vermin.

We selected three varieties of potato that would provide us with early and late crops. Arranging them, rose up in rows, we placed the potatoes in the full light that streamed through the *grange* windows and left them to 'chit', or sprout prior to planting in ridges. We planted six long rows of potatoes, banking up the earth over them. The shoots appeared rapidly and became firmly established as the plants grew and spread. Soon a flush of white flowers appeared, signifying that the tubers were developing beneath the soil.

Checking on the garden each morning – *comme d'habitude* – coffees in hand, Al and I were horrified to note how some of the potato plants had withered and collapsed. Some leaves had been roughly torn or stripped away, while others were stained with an oily black deposit. Closer inspection revealed the black and yellow striped wing casings of the dreaded *doryphore*, the Colorado beetle. The insect, *Leptinotarsa decemlineata*, is a perennial menace in France, although it is not a notifiable quarantine pest as it is in the UK. The insect had first been accidentally introduced from the USA to the Bordeaux region of France in 1922, after hitching a ride on cargo ships. The beetle had then spread rapidly throughout the region. It was a difficult foe to defeat, for a breeding colony of the insects could be established by a single fertilized female beetle escaping detection.

The insects, measuring about nine centimetres in length, were clustered around the leaves and stems of our plants in their hundreds, along with shiny, juicy orange-brown larvae. These grubs have legs and can move around the potato crop with ease, munching away at the leaves. The black deposit we could see was the insects' excrement. Dousing with a special spray formulation seemed to be successful but for only a day or so, since the insects would reappear to decimate our potato plants.

'If the insects attack after the flowers have appeared, your *pommes de terre* should be fine, since they will already be formed,' Bruno Bussiere explained one morning, passing along the *chemin* to inspect the communal pond for rare signs of fish. He had been amused to see Al and me frantically picking off the beetles one by one and collecting them in a plastic bag, later to squish under our feet with enormous satisfaction. We took him at his word, while secretly worried that once it was time to harvest the spuds we would find nothing more than mouldy tubers beneath the soil.

We also invested in carrots, leeks, parsley, peas, haricot vert and flageolet. Only when we had returned home did we discover that the peas and beans were not quite what we had expected. The packets each bore the French term *nain*, which was unfamiliar to both of us. A dictionary revealed it meant dwarf. This seemed to be a boon, for it meant that we would not have to construct cane supports for the plants.

Red onions, white onions and shallots were planted in neat rows along the edge of the potato bed, and I also experimented by planting individual cloves of garlic. Courgettes were widely available as small seedlings, which Véronique recommended we buy instead of seeds. 'Mark my words, the seeds will never germinate in our soil,' she claimed with her lifetime of experience in the region. 'Don't waste your time.' Accompanying us on a trip to her favourite *pépiniériste* in Magnac Laval, she advised on the selection of suitable seedlings. 'These are the long, dark green courgettes, Monsieur Richard,' she said with a mischievous gleam in her eye. 'Not the big, pale green ones shaped like a pear...' To the French, the many members of the squash family are frequently all referred to as *courgettes*. I recalled the time a few years previously when our kindly neighbour had presented us with an array of vegetables of weird shapes and sizes, all which she claimed to be courgettes. We bought eight plants and installed them in the bed specially set aside for them.

We had also come away with the seedlings of bell peppers and chilli peppers, which we planted adjacent to the courgettes. Ten tomato plants was undoubtedly an extravagance, but we simply could not resist the mouthwatering thought of being able to pick our own shiny red fruit direct from the plant. The kind climate of Limousin meant that these delicate plants could be grown directly in the open soil rather than under glass.

Although I do not watch much television, I am an unashamed addict of cookery programmes. It was one of the things I missed most about living in England. I could watch them all day, and frequently did when in the UK, working from home. With the temptation of a television set next to my desk and an entire channel devoted to food and its preparation, I was continually distracted from my work. I had been entranced by a television series featuring the Italian chef Antonio Carluccio, and subsequently bought his sumptuous cookery books. I was intrigued by his recipes for the flamboyant Swiss chard: it was the first time I had seen the plant with its huge, glossy green leaves and thick, celery-like white stems and distinctive veining. My mouth watered as the maestro described how to prepare a thick, cannellini bean soup using the chard. Although I had never tasted the vegetable, I trusted Antonio's judgment and knew that I would simply love it. Consequently, I had been overjoyed to discover huge bunches of the vegetable languishing in a French supermarket. The plant, it appeared, had originated in France in the 17th century, where it is known as *carde*. Rushing home with my purchase, I had prepared an approximation of the soup and from then I was hooked. And now I could grow my very own chard.

After a few days of hard work, preparing small furrows in the soil for the seeds, planting the different varieties and covering them over, Al and I had filled our very large vegetable plot. In a second wave swoop on the garden centre we returned home with even more seeds, lured by the bait of pumpkin, beetroot, celery, butternut squash and a range of herbs, including basil, coriander, flat- and curly-leaved parsley, plus our favourite salad ingredient, the peppery *roquette*.

With a touch of beginner's luck, all of our produce flourished with the sad exception of the poor *roquette*, which was decimated at the first instance by a tiny black bug known locally as the *puce*, or flea beetle. Véronique's advice to scatter woodash around the base of the seedlings had only minimal success and the plants that survived were pitted with tiny holes.

A vegetable garden of such immense proportions gobbled up most of our free time, as we attempted to keep pace with the rapid growth of the produce. On some days we were too exhausted even to take young Jazz for his twice-daily constitutional. The pup did not seem to mind, however, since he loved to hang around while we toiled. Often he would be found curled up in the shade of the enormous spread of the courgette plants, hugging the coolness of the soil that was still damp from our watering of the previous night. He had also appropriated as a kind of canine independent state the mountain of building sand that had been dumped adjacent to the *potager*. When not burying tennis balls in its midst, or excavating into its depths, he would lord it at the peak of the mountain, surveying all below him with a rather snooty look on what my brother the Count described rudely as his 'squashed-in face'. Concerned that her juvenile charge would suffer the detrimental effects of heatstroke, Al planted a parasol on the top of Jazz Island. The pup would lounge beneath this shade during the hottest part of the day, content with his regal lot in life.

Our burgeoning mountain of fresh vegetables was partially alleviated by the huge chest freezer we bought. We blanched and froze as much as we could, and concocted scrumptious soups, and rich, spicy *pomodoro* sauces from the flavoursome tomatoes that hung pendulous from our plants. We froze these prepared dishes, too, for use throughout the following year.

Visiting friends was a very satisfying way of offloading our glut of produce, and we were able to keep the Count and Stephanie supplied with fresh vegetables during their first months as permanent residents in France. That summer, my brother and sister-in-law had bitten the bullet and departed from England's shores once and for all, determined to make a new life in France. Their daughter Hollie, however, had remained behind. For a girl of seventeen there appeared to be little amusement and few employment opportunities in rural France.

The Count Forgeron

Chapter Thirteen

Cheese, tradition and travesty

My brother Phill, otherwise known as the Count, had been involved in selling arts, crafts and antiques all his working life, but craved the opportunity to put to use his considerable practical talents in metalwork and woodwork. Before leaving for France he had attended a full-time college course, from which he had graduated with distinction as a fully-fledged artist-blacksmith. Shipping over the weighty forge he had constructed, he installed it in the detached stone barn on his property and began to experiment with different forms of his new trade.

A lover of the natural world, the majority of the Count's creations in metal incorporated recurring motifs: delicate leaves, the heads of animals, snakes and insects. Some items were intended as practical fireside accoutrements, mirror frames or candlesticks, while others were sculptures in their own right. Finding an outlet for his work in France became a priority, while the couple were able to keep financially afloat thanks to Stephanie's work, maintaining the accounts for clients back in England.

There is a culture in France for the use of metalwork as a means of protecting and adorning houses, more so than in the UK. Metal embellishments are part of the local vernacular, in the form of iron fencing, window security grilles and decorative panelling for doors. Working with metal was much more popular in France than it was in England and many *bricoleurs,* do-it-yourselfers, were keen welders. Specialist equipment was widely available in do-it-yourself outlets.

Allied to this enthusiam for metalworking is a centuries-old tradition of knife-making. There exists a thriving knife culture in the country, particularly among the hunting fraternity. Every Frenchman enjoys the inalienable right to carry a knife – his personal *couteau*. The knife might simply be a utensil for cutting and eating food: I have witnessed many a Frenchman dip into his pocket and produce a shining blade to simply cut a slice from a proffered *saucisson* or sausage. It might otherwise be a means of idly whittling wood, skinning a dead animal, undoing a screw where no *tournevis* is available, or picking the teeth after a hearty meal.

One of the centres of the *coutelier's* craft is the town of Thiers, in the Auvergne region, twenty kilometres from the city of Clermont Ferrand. The art has been practised there for more than four hundred years. But perhaps the most famous French knife is the Laguiole, which hails from the small mountain town of the same name, located in the southern Aubrac region, made up of the *départements* of Aveyron, Cantal and Lozère. These blades will be a common sight to anyone who has visited a French *buraliste*, or tobacconist's shop, or one of the many specialist hunting shops, craft and gift stores countrywide. Glass cases of the knives generally take pride of place.

Laguiole, a name that originated as *La Gleisola*, meaning 'little church', referring to the tiny chapel around which the town was built, is not merely that of a specific company, as many people assume. The term refers to a style of knife developed in the town, invented in 1829 by blacksmith Pierre-Jean Calmels. The inspiration for the original Laguiole knife was said to be a marriage between a locally used *couteau* called the Capuchadou, with a fixed blade, and the Spanish Navajas, with a folding blade and a distinctive pistol grip. The handle, into which the blade folded, was originally made from the horn of the Aubrac cow.

Authentic Laguiole knives carry an identifying decoration that is open to interpretation, resembling either a bee or a fly. Legend has it that the bee is a tribute to Napoleon and the Battle of Waterloo in 1815, while the fly could refer to the spring head, known to knife-makers as the 'fly', into which the base of the blade folds. Also a traditional embellishment for authentic Laguiole knives is the 'shepherd's cross', a design made with rivets set into the handle, which marks the junction of the three *départements* of the Aubrac region.

At the end of the Second World War the tradition of knife-making in the town declined, as did its population. Eventually, however, cutlers in Thiers, further to the north, began to manufacture Laguiole blades again.

The resurrection of the craft in Laguiole itself occurred in 1981, when the Forge de Laguiole was set up. When the famous designer Philippe Starck designed not only a range of knives for the forge but also its modern factory, the company gained international recognition, attracting more world-renowned designers. There are, however, numerous companies producing knives that bear the name 'Laguiole', including foreign makers who mass-produce the cutters. An authentic Laguiole, however, should be hand-made from the finest materials.

Laguiole is also home to the fawn-coloured Aubrac cows, with their beguiling dark eyes, which provide the area's main source of prosperity. The cows' meat is tender and its milk is churned to produce the delicious Laguiole cheese. It was the peasants who tended these cows who first carried the famous knife blade that became their daily companion on the austere hillsides. In May the cows leave the mountain and trek for three hours to their summer pasture. The tradition, known as the *transhumance* from the Latin meaning 'across ground', attracts flocks of visitors to watch the spectacle, as the cows' necks are strung with bells and their horns adorned with flags. A strange sight on the flat fields of Limousin, our neighbouring farm, Sejotte, is home to a herd of these mountain-dwelling cows, with their magnificent twisting horns. Their neck bells could be heard tinkling night and day, a tuneful, beguiling sound that I came to associate with our home and its sense of wellbeing.

Whilst my brother the Count could not hope to compete with the mammoth sales potential of the Laguoile name, he hoped he could slice out a niche for himself producing quality hand-forged blades. He began to experiment with different shapes, sizes and styles of blade – shutting himself away in his cold forge for days on end – until he had fashioned a knife that would conform to his exacting standards. The knives he produced were beautiful objects of art, while being eminently practical, whether a delicate skinning knife, an efficient hunting knife, or a deadly looking bowie knife. He equipped his blades with sumptuous handles hewn from exotic woods such as ebony, zebrano, piquia amarello and Mexican rosewood, or various types of horn, and embellished them with brass, copper or nickel-silver guards and pommels. Some blades were fashioned from the complex, multiple folds of Damascus steel, which could in itself take weeks to create.

Like many Frenchmen, Claude Norrin was of the opinion that the heathens who lived across the channel knew nothing of gourmet food and how it should be cooked. While I suspected that there might be a grain of truth in this – for I was hard pushed to bring to mind a national dish of particularly outstanding pedigree – I felt honour-bound to defend my homeland's battered reputation. Claude's particular bugbear was the subject of *le fromage*.

'The cheeses of France are *excellents*! The finest in all the world!' he claimed outrageously one afternoon over coffee. 'There is no such thing as a bad French cheese!'

Now I am all in favour of a challenge and Claude's statement had fired me with the wish to prove him wrong. While I adored strong, characterful cheeses, Al was unable to share my enthusiasm; her rather delicate digestive system did not cope well with animal fats. I needed an ally in my search for the foulest of foul French cheeses.

So it was that my brother the Count and me embarked upon a quest to find a French cheese that would challenge Claude Norrin's ludicrous claim. We were both loath to admit, however, that our mission could prove nigh on impossible. Each week we would invest in a different cheese, but each week we failed to find anything that was stomach-churningly dreadful. Some cheeses came close, however.

I purchased a Livarot, widely recognised as a cheese with an arresting flavour and an odour that would assault the nostrils. The 'Colonel' – a nickname that referred to the *laîches*, five stripes of green sedge grass surrounding its girth, reminiscent of a French officer's badge of rank – was one of the oldest washed-rind, cow's milk cheeses to hail from Normandy. The sedge cummerbund was originally used to support the midriff bulge of the cheese as it sagged during its three months maturing, although nowadays this was deemed superfluous and strips of green paper are commonly used instead.

The Count and I would approach our cheese tastings as if we were performing an autopsy. When unwrapping the Livarot, we were immediately assailed by its pungent odour. The vivid orange colour of the rind was due to frequent washings in brine coloured with annatto, a dye produced from the South American rocou plant. The rind itself was ridged, pockmarked and cloyingly sticky to the touch. Not to be put off by the gaudy exterior, we took a knife and bravely delved inside. The slightly pitted paste was golden yellow with a piquant flavour reminiscent of well-hung meat.

The taste of the cheese, we agreed, was comparable to other Normandie stalwarts we had sampled previously, the subtle, fruity Pont l'Evêque and the earthy Pavé d'Auge. Although the Livarot, *viande du pauvre* or poor man's meat as it was once called, was a force to be reckoned with on the cheeseboard, we found it to be a delightful counterpoint to a glass of Calvados or full-bodied red wine.

The Count came up with the Valençay Cindre, a truncated pyramid of goat's milk cheese from the Berry region of the Loire Valley. The shape of the cheese was by legend attributed to Napoleon. Stopping off in the region on return from a disastrous campaign in Egypt, he considered the perfect pyramids of cheese too reminiscent of his failure, whipped out his sword he lopped the tops off. The drained curd of the cheese, after being placed in a mould, was coated in salted charcoal ashes. As it ripened it assumed a bluish colouration. The creamy paste, we found, while decidedly goaty in flavour was not overpoweringly so, and displayed fresh undertones of citrus.

Next we sampled Saint-Nectaire from the mountainous Auvergne region that abuts Limousin. A pressed, uncooked cheese made from the milk of the hardy Salers cows, and traditionally matured on rye straw in vaulted, mountain cellars, it had a greyish-brown rind with a bloom of white, red and yellow mould. The semi-hard, silky-textured paste within was rich with the flavour of mushrooms, nuts and the volcanic soil of the region.

Phill introduced me to a cheese from the Quercy region, south of Limousin, which is also renowned for its *foie gras*, duck and goose liver, and truffles. Part of the *cabécou* family of cheeses, the tiny Rocamadour – named after the astonishing cliff-hugging medieval village of the region – measured only four to five centimetres in diameter and one and a half centimetres high. What it lacked in stature, however, the cheese made up for in its powerful lactic flavour and nutty aroma. Beneath the thin, yellowish rind the paste was lusciously creamy and delicious when eaten with nothing more than a slice of crusty bread. More adventurously, I discovered how sublime it was served melted over a salad of goose liver, walnuts and crispy bacon lardons.

My brother and I were getting nowhere with our search for a bad French cheese, but we had discovered some wonderful cheeses. My favourite was Cantal, sometimes called the 'French Cheddar': mild and buttery when young, but developing a tangy bite when aged. As a soft cheese, I preferred the rich, creamy texture of Coulommiers, made with raw or pasteurised cows' milk, to the rather bland Brie, its more popular family member. Most powerfully flavoured of all was the famous blue cheese made from ewe's milk; Roquefort, matured for over four months in the limestone caves of Roquefort-sur-Soulzon, had a creamy, soft texture and the metallic tang of the *penicillium roqueforti* that is added during production.

Every cheese we sampled was either truly scrumptious or, if displaying some doubtful characteristics, had its redeeming features. Every cheese, that is, with the exception of one particularly foul curd I had obtained from Daniel, whose mobile shop visited the hamlet each week. As part of my education *à la française*, I had attempted to purchase a new variety of local cheese from the van each visit. This time it had been the turn of the evil Gouzon, a round, soft cheese made from unpasteurised cow's milk, which originated in the Creusois town from which it takes its name. Basically creamy white, its soft rind was tinged with brown stains so that it resembled an extremely ancient and mouldy Camembert: in fact, it is described in some circles as *'le parent pauvre de Camembert'*, the poor parent of Camembert. Not a good indication of its pedigree, to my cynical mind.

The cheese was wrapped in plain, waxed paper and came with an ominous warning. 'Be sure to keep Le Gouzon in the *frigo*, Richard!' Daniel had urged. 'Or you will be plagued by flies.' A Frenchman advising that a cheese should be refrigerated? What sacrilege was this? Although I was aware that proper etiquette demands that cheeses such as this should never be refrigerated, I had been driven in desperation to this sacrilegious act, having not at first heeded the warning of Daniel. The *grange* was visited upon by a veritable pestilence of flies. Thousands of the insects swarmed around the mesh dome beneath which the foul cheese festered. Now I was not averse to sampling pongy cheeses and had eaten many rancid varieties that others would curl up their noses at. But this particular cheese stank to high heaven from day one and each day its stench became increasingly unpleasant. Even my brother, who had popped in for a visit, was fearful of getting downwind of the horrific curd: and this was a man generally regarded as having an adventurous palette (or, in my opinion, his selectivity was highly suspect).

Not to be considered cowards in each other's eyes, however, we brothers had shaken hands for perhaps the last time in our short lives and had bravely nibbled a corner of the cheese. Resisting the urge to throw up there and then, Phill had eloquently described it thus: 'It has a taste reminiscent of the inside of a byre at milking time.' I had to agree. The cheese was imbued with the very essence of cow. In effect, it tasted like I imagine cow slurry would taste. I hereby apologise to the brave producers of the cheese – but this delicacy is one whose pleasures escape my sensitivities.

'So would you care to take some home with you to your delightful wife?' I tempted, having swilled my mouth out with Coca-Cola in an attempt to rid myself of the foul and pervading flavour of cow shit and stale milk.

'Thank you, brother, but I would not,' the Count had responded flatly, looking quite green around the gills. 'Not if you paid me. Never in a million years. Pass the Coke, please…'

Why I did not cast the deadly curd from the house then and there I will never know, for I had no intention of ever eating it again as long as I lived. But I had stubbornly kept it for another two weeks, buried deep within the fridge, on the off chance that Claude Norrin would pay me a visit. This cheese, I felt sure, would have him on his knees begging for mercy. How wrong I was.

'So there's no such thing as a bad French cheese, huh?' I said to Claude, who had arrived on cue for a morning coffee, just when I was considering burying the stinking Gouzon in the field at the back of the house. I smiled inscrutably. Ha! I thought. I have you now, Frenchie!

'*Non,*' he responded firmly, tugging proudly at his droopy moustache.

In an attempt to counter this ludicrous claim, I retrieved that particularly pungent example of the French cheesemakers' repertoire, currently in a state of icy stasis, double-wrapped and incarcerated within a Tupperware container buried deep in the furthest recesses of my fridge.

I set Le Gouzon on the table in front of my friend and delicately unwrapped it, trying not to infect my fingers with its noxious oozing. During its incarceration, I noticed, it had assumed a pallid, sepia hue. Claude's porcine eyes widened and I could detect beneath his bushy moustache the pearly glint of his two front teeth. The madman was grinning at the cheese. '*Oooh, un petit Gouzon…*' he purred. I thought he was about to stroke the damned cheese, so handed him a knife. He cut off a large triangular portion and popped it straight into his mouth. Without chewing, he seemed to suck the creamy slime from within the rind, then swallowed.

'*Délicieux…*' he breathed ecstatically, promptly cut off another chunk and downed that, too.

'You must be joking!'

'Now *that* is a cheese!' he said, smacking his lips. 'A little cold, perhaps, but – you are *anglais*; so what do you know about how to keep a cheese? – it does have subtle flavour. It just goes to prove what I said, Riche. How can your puny English cheeses hope to compare with that?' Why would they want to, I mused? Now I had a healthy respect for the cheeses of Britain and this cavalier Frenchman could not be allowed to cast this ill-considered aspersion so freely. Although I adored French cheeses – and had sampled a good selection in the last few weeks – I found that there was little to compare, for example, with the firm texture and intense flavour of a good, strong Cheddar.

'Right!' I said. 'You've asked for it, Claude! I challenge you to a duel!'

And so the cheese challenge was conceived. On a brief working trip back to England, I scoured the supermarkets and cheese shops for a selection that would typify the finest the country had to offer, including some staunch old stalwarts. I managed to gather one dozen examples of cheeses representing a healthy cross section of the counties of England, Scotland and Wales. Exporting this melange of odoriferous produce had been mildly embarrassing, however. When taking the train to the airport, while waiting in the departure lounge, and when sitting in the cramped aircraft seating on the hour-long flight back to France, the heady air of putrid socks had surrounded me like an aura. Curiously, I had managed to commandeer three seats to myself.

We had arranged for Claude and Martine, Jill and Jean-Michel to join us for an English style Sunday lunch at Le Mas Mauvis. The meal kicked off with slices of roast beef, crunchy-skinned roast potatoes, steamed cabbage with black pepper, and florets of broccoli tossed in walnut oil. I had also prepared my *pièce de résistance*, two large, square, crusty Yorkshire puddings, after the recipe of my Auntie Mary (who had been universally adjudged, at least in our family, as the person who made the best Yorkshire Pud in all the world). The course was served with lashings of unctuous gravy made from beef stock. The French contingent eyed the bulging platefuls with curiosity and a large measure of suspicion.

'So this is a pudding?' queried Claude, slicing a portion of Yorkshire pud and transferring it to his plate. I nodded. 'But you serve it with the main dish?'

'Yes,' I said. He raised a doubtful eyebrow. 'But it's not a pudding as in a dessert. It's made from flour, eggs and a little water.'

'So it's batter,' said Jean-Michel, matter-of-factly.

'Well, yes.'

'You English love your batter,' said the Mayor with a wink.

Despite their reservations as to the inclusion of a wodge of batter in the meal, they all tucked in with relish, although Claude had shyly asked for a chunk of baguette to accompany it. Although I attempted to explain that bread was not a traditional English accompaniment to a good old roast, this archetypal Frenchman could not imagine a meal *sans pain*.

'I am just a simple *paysan*,' he murmured by way of explanation.

After a dessert of treacle sponge and custard, we sagged back in our seats to take a breather before bringing out the bulging cheese board. First, we placed on the table a selection of cheese accompaniments: brown-tinged pickled onions, bright yellow piccalilli and Branston Pickle, along with water biscuits, Bath Olivers and Scottish oat cakes.

I had arranged the slabs of cheese on a round, revolving wooden board and set it in the centre of the table, giving it a gentle twirl for dramatic effect. Concealed beneath each wodge was a label to prompt my memory, should I forget which was which. Claude and Jean-Michel, as one, adjusted their spectacles and regarded the yellow, white, orange and blue-veined chunks of cheese. In unison, both men rubbed their jaws thoughtfully, intoning 'Hmm, hmm, hmm!' as I rattled off the names of each cheese and its place of origin: 'Organic Lancashire; Oxford Blue; Shropshire Blue; Organic Cheshire; Clifton Leaf, a goat's cheese from Avon; Stilton, Extra Strong Mature Cheddar, Wild Garlic Yarg from Cornwall; Old Worcester White; Sussex Yeoman; Caerphilly; Wensleydale...'

Claude picked up a knife with a flourish and, holding his other hand above the board seemed to be in receipt of ethereal vibes emanating from the cheeses. Making his choice, he carved off a portion of the deathly white Lancashire, which promptly crumbled into many pieces. I winced. This trait, common to Lancashires, clearly confused the Frenchman, for in his book no self-respecting cheese should do this. Nevertheless, he scooped the pieces onto his plate and popped a morsel into his mouth. The look of distaste that befell his face, however, revealed what he thought of the cheese. Bad start, I thought.

Jean-Michel had carved himself a portion of the Oxford Blue, a vegetarian blue cheese first made from cow's milk by Baron Robert Pouget in 1993 as an alternative to Stilton.

The mayor smeared the creamy, blue-veined cheese onto a fragment of Bath Oliver, sniffed it, and popped it into his mouth. His round, open face assumed a look of extreme pleasure and his lips curled into a broad smile. '*C'est bon, ça! C'est très bon!* I can taste dark chocolate and white wine!' he announced floridly. Prompted by this, Claude followed suit and also had to agree that this was indeed a fine cheese. '*Toutefois*, it does have all the hallmarks of a classic French cheese,' he added, not to be too generous. 'Yes, it is aromatic, spicy and I can detect a hint of tarragon.'

Next up was the Clifton Leaf goat's cheese, a mild, creamy cheese made from unpasteurised goat's milk. The decorative leaf was peeled back and the cheese within sampled by all. '*Champignons!*' said Claude, wide-eyed. 'It has a subtle mushroomy flavour…'

Our guests treated the cheese tasting with the utmost seriousness and Claude even produced a little notebook and wrote down comments on each, apparently to be used in the final judgement. The other cheeses were tasted and commented upon with a variety of grimaces, wan smiles, pitying expressions, but also with a number of positive nods between the two hypercritical Frenchmen. Some cheeses were even given a second tasting.

One of the cheeses that intrigued our guests most was the Cornish Wild Garlic Yarg. Long, narrow garlic leaves wrap the semi-firm, rindless cheese and impart an herbaceous aroma to the butter-coloured interior; not blatantly garlicky but perhaps tinged with flavours suggestive of onion and spinach. The cheese obviously found favour, since it was soon dispatched, leaving only the decorative wrap behind. 'And this word 'yarg',' mused Jean-Michel. 'It is a word from an ancient Cornish dialect, I expect?'

'Oh, I'm sure!' I bluffed, ignorant of the truth. Later research proved otherwise: it is simply the name of the cheese's creators, spelt backwards. Allan and Jenny Gray, however, based the cheese on a thirteenth century recipe in which the leaves of chestnuts, grapes or nettles were used as a protective wrapping.

At the end of the event votes were awarded by all our party and the out and out winner was adjudged to be the Cornish Wild Garlic Yarg. At the bottom of the ratings languished the poor crumbly Lancashire cheese, whose similarity to polystyrene was unavoidable in the eyes of all our guests.

As our guests departed in the early evening, I felt satisfied that I had in some way helped to salvage the reputation of British cheesemakers in the eyes of at least two critical Frenchmen.

The sound of a car's approach drew me to peer out of the upper window of the *grange* in time to see Gordon Timpson's green, open-topped sports car screech to a halt in the lane. Atlhough I knew that he had been sighted in the hamlet, I was nevertheless surprised to see him on my doorstep. Dressed in khaki shorts and a polo shirt, he clambered, out, gazed up at the window and waved. I gesticulated to him to enter. It was good to see him again, and I was pleased to note that he looked in exceptionally good health, and still sported his characteristic cheeky grin. His similarity to the diminutive Scottish comedian Ronnie Corbett was still apparent, albeit without the large, horn-rimmed glasses.

We exchanged greetings and Gordon took up my offer of a cool beer. Apologising for his sudden departure from the hamlet without so much as a goodbye, he explained how Maureen's health had taken a dramtic turn for the worse and the only thought on his mind was to transport her to a kinder climate. She had spent a long time in a wheelchair, unable to get about on her own. Thankfully, although her illness had worsened, she had regained strength and reached a period of stability, to the extent that she had now discarded the wheelchair again. During their initial months in the south Gordon had been unable to think of anything but his wife's wellbeing. Even once Maureen had improved in health, he had found it increasingly difficult to then re-establish old contacts in Limousin. A kind of inertia had gripped him.

'My house renovation days are over!' Gordon claimed with a certain degree of relief in his tone. 'We have a modern flat near Montpellier, it's warm, it's dry, and we're very happy. It's on the second floor, believe it or not, but Maureen would rather tackle the staircase than use the lift. She adores the climate and we're just a stone's throw from the beach.' He explained that an advertisement in *The Times* in London had finally found a buyer for the house at Le Mas Mauvis. He had driven up north that very weekend in order to sign the sale contract and hand over the keys to the new owner.

'So who are our new neighbours to be?' I asked. 'Al's frantic to know. And village gossip is that you've sold the place to two guys called Keith and Peter... tell me more.'

Gordon grinned. 'Not Keith and Peter,' he said. '...but Keith and Peta.'

'Sorry?'

'P-e-t-a,' he spelt out. 'Peta's a woman.' Damn. All these years in a staid, traditional hamlet waiting for a minor scandal to erupt and our hopes are crushed in one fell swoop.

Keith and Peta were, however, a welcome breath of fresh air. A hilarious, witty couple in their fifties, they operated as a polished double act, playing off each other's quips with quick-fire responses that told of a strong bond.

Keith, the most unabashed comic of the duo, had a bone dry sense of humour that could catch the unwary off guard. Of medium build, with a balding, tanned head, hair trimmed close to his skull at the back and sides, and a pair of sleepy, heavy-lidded eyes, he had a penchant for wearing gaudy, floral Hawaiian shirts (which, it turned out, Peta had made for him). His arms were the type that would not be out of place on a sailor, sporting tattoos of naked ladies and words inscribed in blue ink, which had long since lost clarity or meaning.

Peta was a radiant, cuddly woman with a round, smiling face, a pair of wire-rimmed spectacles, and straight blonde hair cut in a neat bob. Her voice had the light, melodic tone of a typical west-country girl. The couple exuded a relaxed, comfortable air, always ready to make visitors welcome in their home. Peta was a keen and adventurous cook, constantly baking biscuits and cakes. Soon after their installation in the hamlet, she was bringing around plates of these confections for her neighbors to sample.

On our first visit for *apéritifs* – accompanied by the Yorkshireman and his other half Dennie – we had sat in their kitchen chatting idly about this and that, our conversation punctuated by the sound of flies being zapped on the wall-mounted, electrical gadget they had installed. In such close proximity to Thierry André's rancid barn, they fought a losing battle: flies were ever present in the house. Peta and Keith were both armed with swats and would slap these down on the table every few minutes to dispatch the most aggravating pests. Something of a chain smoker, Keith lit another cigarette. His wife, also rarely without a cigarette, also lit one. Al followed suit. Dennie, who abhorred the filthy habit, coughed loudly.

'So what do you do, Keith?' asked Dennie, taking a sip of red wine.

'I spend a lot of time in the pub, drinking beer,' he replied.

'No, for a living…'

'I look in people's ears,' he said, completely deadpan.

'Keith's an audiologist,' Peta elaborated. 'He has his own practice.'

'And you Peta? What do you do?' asked the Yorkshireman, taking all this smoking as a good excuse to light up himself. Dennie frowned.

'Anti-social behaviour,' she said.

'Peta runs a local government department in Oxford dealing with juvenile delinquents, sex offenders and drug addicts,' Keith elaborated. 'I'm very proud of her. She locks up naughty boys.'

The couple both had jobs that were physically and mentally demanding, so it was not surprising that they played hard, when released from their responsibilities. Keith had bought the house without his wife ever having seen it, while on a trip to France with a friend to check out availability of properties. The friend had dithered in their intended plan to share a holiday home, but Keith had been entranced by the house and its surroundings. Peta was at first unsure whether she would be able to adapt well to life in the depths of the French countryside. After a few visits to the house, however, she had announced that she intended to take three months' sabbatical from her stressful job and spend the time at Le Mas Mauvis to recuperate. Keith's work pressures – a new audiology practice he was in the process of setting up – meant that he would be unable to stay on at the house with his wife. Peta had found herself alone. After a period of difficult adjustment, during which she occupied her time painting pictures and watching the English television soap operas she adored, she soon began to absorb the *calme* of her new environment. When it was time to leave, she wept buckets, reluctant to be parted from her oasis. She and Keith had decided that this was the life for them, and were putting plans into action to spend more time there, with a view to moving over from England entirely.

This sociable couple loved to entertain, and often the house was filled with a dozen or more friends – many who were professional musicians – on weekend breaks from the UK. Everyone would muck in, whether cooking, washing up or clearing away the debris from the musical soirées that brought new life to the old house. Dinner guests were lucky to escape without having to sample alcoholic concoctions from their well-stocked booze cabinet, and their parties would frequently last until the early hours.

'What are you going to do with the cottage and outbuildings?' I asked one evening over drinks. The property included a small, semi-derelict house and three unconverted barns.

'We're going to open a pub,' said Keith.

'Oh my God!' I gasped. Horror of horrors. 'You're going to open an English pub in the middle of rural France?' I asked, incredulous.

'What's the matter with that? It'll be great! You'll see!'

'An English pub? Here?' I repeated. I was appalled by the concept.

'How about an Irish pub then?' offered Keith, obviously not to be dissuaded.

'That sounds better,' I remarked, a little relieved. The French had a love for all things Celtic, the myths, the music, the dancing, the beer – and of course the hard spirits. There was, in fact, a lively bar in the nearby town of La Souterraine, with a distinct Gaelic flavour. Called *Le Pub Loch Ness*, the French-owned bar sold 'pints' of a Guinness-wannabee stout and stocked a vast selection of Scotch and Irish whiskies. Live music frequently featured Irish fiddle bands and Scottish jigs were sometimes performed by Frenchmen wearing kilts. At other times, blues bands from the deep American south would entertain with music that paid lip service to the Celtic tradition. To the French *clientèle* who frequented the establishment, there was no difference between the different countries represented in the music and the drink. It all came out of the same cultural cauldron.

'Ok, we'll open an Irish pub,' said Keith. 'But it won't be for the general public. Just for us and our friends. Just think, we'll be able go to the pub in the evening, get rat-arsed and stagger to bed blind drunk, without ever leaving the property!'

I had considered Keith's plan to be a wild dream until the day he showed me the original 1970s Space Invader tabletop game – just as I remembered it from my ill-gotten youth – and a fully-functional pinball machine, which were stored in a back room. 'My brother supplies this kind of gear to pubs in England,' he explained. 'And he was able to get me some redundant stock.' He also had a full set of spirit optics, pub posters and other British boozer ephemera, awaiting the day when Le Mas Mauvis would have its very own Celtic pub with beer from the wood drawn up by authentic hand pumps.

The enterprising Yorkshireman had come across a stuffed boar's head at the local *déchetterie* or dump and thought it might be useful as a pub sign. The head had obviously been burned in a fire and was rather singed. Keith was not worried: 'It's OK. We can call the pub Ye Olde Roast Pig.' Whether our new neighbours' dreams would ever bear fruit was debatable, but if they ever did the peace and tranquility of this village backwater could be under threat.

Personal best at the Paris Marathon

Chapter Fourteen

On the run

Feeling hot to trot once again, I decided to try my legs out on a local *course à pied*. It would be my first participation in a French running race and Les Foulées de Bussière-Poitevine, held at the nearby village in the Haute-Vienne, offered just the challenge I was seeking. The race, covering twenty kilometres – just under a half-marathon – promised a picturesque route across rolling countryside, passing along small country roads and forest trails. Donning my running gear on the morning of the race I kissed Al goodbye and set off in plenty of time to register my entry before the nine-thirty start. Queuing up at the registration tent near the start, I began jogging on the spot, just like my fellow entrants. I could feel the excitement and adrenalin of the challenge before me. I loved the pre-race atmosphere almost as much as the event itself, so it was with a heavy heart that I was faced with a sudden stark reality.

'*Licence!*' demanded the official sitting behind the registration table, without looking up. She held out her hand.

'*Licence, madame?*' I queried, puzzled.

'*Licence ou certificat medical, monsieur…*' the lady elaborated, quite impatiently, and waved her hand at me. My glum look brought out a deep sigh and rolling of the eyes. '*Anglais?*' she said wearisomely. People in the line of runners behind me were starting to grumble about the hold up. The man behind me tapped me on the shoulder. I turned around.

'*Je m'excuse, monsieur,*' he said politely in French. 'but to run in France you will require a licence from the *Fédération Française d'Athléticisme*, or a certificate from your doctor testifying that you are fit to run…'

My face fell. A licence? This was news to me. I looked back at the official, who was sitting with her chin resting in her hands, strumming her fingers on her cheeks and looking bored. 'I'm sorry,' I apologised. 'I did not realise… this is my first race in France…'

'Not your first, monsieur, because I cannot permit you to run without this licence…' snapped the official, waving me aside rudely. 'Next please!' she called to the man behind me. I left the file of runners feeling dejected and wandered off towards my car. A few moments later the runner who had helped me at the registration tent came jogging up behind me, patting me on the back in consolation.

'I apologise for this woman...' he said. 'France is full of petty officials such as this... I should know, I am one myself, but perhaps not so rude as her!'

'Quite the opposite,' I smiled gratefully. The man handed me a slip of paper on which he had written an Internet website address.

'If you plan to run regularly in French races, you must obtain this licence, the *Pass' running*... you see, even we are using English words! *C'est marrant, non?*'

'Yes, funny!' I confirmed, accepting the slip of paper. 'Thanks for your help.'

'*De rien!*' he replied, breaking into a jog. 'But now I must warm up a little before the race...'

'*Bonne chance!*' I called as the man trotted off with a backward wave. I remained and watched the field of runners depart, then wended my way home, connected to the Internet and determined how I could obtain my licence to run.

On 23 March 1999 Law no. 99-223 was passed by the French Assembly to protect the health of sportsmen and women and to prevent the consumption of illicit drugs. The law required that all sportsmen produce proof of their fitness to participate in competitions organised by sports federations. The proof was to be in the form of a medical certificate issued by a doctor following a medical examination. A certificate was valid for twelve months. Regular runners could obtain a *Pass' running* – an abbreviation of the franglais term *passeport running* – by applying to the *Fédération Française d'Athléticisme* each season. Introduced in January 2004, the credit-card sized licence also ensured automatic insurance for reimbursement of inscription fees should the holder be injured forty-eight hours prior to the event.

I discovered that it was not merely runners who were obliged to produce a licence or medical certificate: the ruling applied to anyone wishing to participate in any sporting events whatsoever, including weekend football and rugby matches organised by local clubs, athletics competitions, horse shows, swimming and other team sports. No such requirement existed in England for entry to sporting competitions: anyone could enter, for example, the London Marathon, whatever their state of health. I could see that, under the French scheme, potential health problems could be identified prior to competing in a sporting event, although it was no guarantee that, for example, a runner would not suffer a massive heart attack during a race and die. Cynics believed that the French system offered no protection for the person participating in the sport, but indemnified the event organisers against legal action should an injury or death occur.

Whatever the case, if I was to participate in any official races in France, I would require a licence. Paying a visit to Doctor Boely, I received a thorough medical examination and was referred to a clinic in Limoges where I would also be obliged to undertake an active electrocardiogram: wired up to a sophisticated monitor I was asked to pedal a stationary cycle for ten minutes, as the consultant periodically increased the pressure, forcing my poor old heart, lungs and muscles to go into overdrive. As I pedalled, perspiration pouring from my forehead, the consultant scrupulously consulted the graph that spewed forth from the machine. At the end of the day I was pronounced fit and healthy and was discharged from the clinic clutching my valuable certificate.

A few weeks later, after submitting the requisite documentation to the FFA in Paris, I received in the post my *Pass' running*. A slogan printed on the plastic card promised me *des kilomètres de liberté*, kilometres of freedom. I raised a quizzical eyebrow: at almost one hundred euros for the examination, ECG and application fee – which would need to be renewed annually – the freedom to run in France came at a high price.

In early April, Al and I took the three-hour train journey to Paris. We were to spend the weekend in the capital, during which I would run in the annual marathon, alongside some 30,000 other misguided individuals who reckoned that running forty-two kilometres was a good way to spend a Sunday morning. I had trained long and hard on the roads of the Haute-Vienne in order to gain a level of fitness that would enable me to beat my own record. In order to collect my running bib and the microchip that I would carry on my shoe during the race in order to register my times, I had to attend a registration event held at the Parc des Expositions de Paris at the Porte de Versailles on the Friday.

Later we paid a visit to the Eiffel Tower. Riding up one of the huge girder legs in the glass-sided elevator, we were crushed by a gaggle of other tourists, unable to move. My nose was pressed up against the glass, all that separated me from plummeting to the ground below. I felt a little nauseous.

'Stop it!' said Al suddenly, irritation in her tone. She slapped my hand.

'What?' I asked, puzzled. She glowered at me. I continued to look out of the glass wall, seeing the ground drop away most disconcertingly.

'Stop it, Rich!' she said again, through gritted teeth.

'Whaat?'

'Look, I'm getting really cross. Stop it!' she grabbed my hand and pinched the skin on the back, digging her fingernails in.

'Ouch!' I yelped, snatching my hand away.

'Well see how you like it!' she snarled as the door opened and we were carried out to the viewing platform by the sea of tourists.

'What have I done?' I pleaded.

'You know, you bugger! Nipping my bum all the way up in the lift…'

'I never touched you,' I said in all innocence. We both looked back at the lift, which was starting its descent again. As it disappeared from view, we caught sight of the young male lift operator's grinning face and the huge wink he gave my wife.

'I'll report the cheeky whippersnapper when we get back to ground level!' I promised gallantly.

My wife pouted, blushing. 'No, don't worry. It's not serious. Just a bit of fun…' she said coyly. I shrugged. Huh! When she thought it had been me, her boring old husband nipping her arse it was an irritation. But when she saw it was some fit French youth, she came over all gooey. I sulked for a while, until the dramatic view from the top of the edifice melted my resolve. Al smiled and cuddled up to me as we drank in the sight of the Paris spread out below us, one of the most romantic locations on earth.

In the evening we met up with the Yorkshireman, David, and his lady friend Dennie, who had also come to the capital as spectators of the race and to meet up with David's daughter, Anna, who was also in the city for a short break. We dined in a typically Parisian restaurant presided over by a loud, brusque *madame* serving the tables while her husband, who played an abnormally loud and discordant accordion, entertained the customers. After each number, the proprietors would commence a round of applause themselves. The diners felt obliged to follow their lead. At one stage, one of the male waiters put down his tray in the middle of serving a table, and began to sing loudly to the accompaniment of the accordionist.

On the Saturday morning I arose very early and headed off on the metro for the UNESCO Headquarters on Place Fontenoy to participate in the lighthearted *Course du petit-déjeuner*, the Breakfast Run. This fun run would follow a winding course of 5.2 kilometres through the streets of Paris, ending on the Avenue Foch, where the following day's marathon would also finish. About ten thousand people of all nationalities had gathered for the event. Many wore fancy dress. A flurry of flags waved aloft on poles, although the many nationalities represented were suitably watered down in the *melée* of this cultural broth. Music blared from a temporary stage that had been set up alongside the starting line on that crisp, cold morning. An old flatbed truck was positioned at the front of the field, and the members of a ten-piece brass band – entirely clad in pink – sat in the back.

At 7 a.m. the starting pistol fired and the gaggle of runners set off at a shuffling jog, trailing behind the truck. Immediately the band struck up its first number, a barely-recognisable pop classic rendered in true Oompah style. As we ran, crowds of spectators lined the route and cheered us along. The course carried us along cobbled streets by way of the Avenue Bourdonnais, flanking the Champs de Mars and passing close to the Eiffel Tower at its far end, along the Quai Branly and over the River Seine by the Pont d'Léna. At the half-way stage we circuited the Place du Trocadéro et du 11 Novembre, soon bearing right along the edge of the Bois de Boulogne and finishing in the Avenue Foch, a broad road that opened onto the vast Etoile, dominated by the Arc de Triomphe. The avenue – which was to host the finish of the marathon itself – was lined each side with a long row of canvas awnings, beneath which trestle tables groaned under the weight of boxes of cakes, fresh fruit, sandwiches, bowls of raisins and bottles of water and juices and fresh coffee. The runners swarmed around the trestles, gathering handfuls of the free fare and taking it into the centre of the avenue. There they sat and consumed this relaxed breakfast, serenaded by pop music that blared from huge speakers. While the atmosphere was pleasant and friendly I could not help noticing that many people had appropriated cardboard boxes discarded by the helpers, and were working their way along the line of trestles filling the containers with far more than they needed.

On the morning of the marathon, Al and I travelled via the crowded metro to the Champs Elysées, the start of the race. Al seemed to be a magnet for eligible young men. Not only had she scored with the lift attendant at the Eiffel Tower but now one of the young runners, dressed in nothing more than shorts and vest, cheekily helped himself to a seat on her lap for the duration of the journey, smiling constantly at her.

Emerging from the metro station we found ourselves part of a mass of thousands of runners, their supporters and spectators. Amusingly, and in true Parisian style, the constantly busy Etoile had been left open to traffic, despite the presence of thousands of pedestrians making their way along the road to the starting bays. Horns blared as irritated drivers tried to negotiate the roundabout, which was blocked. Many runners – already dressed in their skimpy running gear, despite the fact that the start of the race was more than an hour away – wore black plastic bin bags with holes cut for head and arms, as a means of keeping warm. The Champs Elysées was already crammed with tens of thousands of runners, jostling for position within the bays, which were denoted by coloured balloons. A runner's position in the field was dictated by his or her previous running form and predicted finishing time. Having run a magnificent London Marathon the previous year, I was on this occasion lucky enough to be part of the sub-three-hour section. I did, however, privately doubt that I would be able to run fast enough to complete the course in less than three hours. My strategy was to try to keep close to the pacers of my group, who would be identified by red balloons suspended from their waists.

Standing in the midst of the pen, I removed my plastic bag, warmed as I was by the bodies surrounding me. Al watched me from behind the metal barrier at the side of the bay. As the countdown to the start commenced, broadcast over loudspeakers, runners discarded their plastic bags, old sweatshirts and other gear they had worn to keep warm and tossed them over head towards the side of the pens. A shower of sweaty garments rained down upon Al and the other spectators. These discarded items would later be swooped on by hordes of homeless Parisians and the families of Eastern European refugees who plague the metro lines, picking over the detritus of the departed field like vultures.

Suddenly the starting pistol sounded and the mass of runners started to shuffle off along the broad Champs Elysées, taking care not to trip on the bags, clothing and plastic water bottles that littered the cobblestone surface. Several runners did fall, but were soon hauled to their feet by other competitors before they could be trampled to death. As I passed under the inflatable arch that marked the starting point of the race, I pressed the button on my heart-rate monitor to start recording my time. The screen of the watch remained blank. Interference from the thousands of other transmitters around me had jammed the device from receiving the signal sent from the chest strap I wore. No matter, I thought: all runners had a microchip attached to their shoe laces, which would record starting and finishing times. My only worry was that, without the watch, I was unable to monitor my pace accuractely as I ran. The field thinned out surprisingly quickly and I found that I was able to break into a steady run. My eyes latched onto the nearest red balloon and I made off after this pacer, nevertheless feeling that I was running far too fast this early in the race.

At the end of the *boulevard*, the route took the runners across the vast Place de la Concorde. The largest public square in the city, it was designed by Jacques-Ange Gabriel, architect to Louis XV, with the intention of displaying an equestrian statue of the king. Completed in 1763, the square – actually an octagon – had been surrounded by moats, although nowadays is bordered by the Galerie Nationale de Jeu de Paume (once Napoleon III's indoor tennis court), the Musée de l'Orangerie, the US embassy, the Hôtel Crillon and the Hôtel du Ministère de la Marine. The square lies at the intersection of two axes: the Axe Historique or *Voie Triomphale*, the triumphal way, it is a perfectly straight line running east-west from the Musée du Louvre, through the Jardin des Tuilieries, up the Champs Elysée to the Arc de Triomphe, nowadays culminating in the Grande Arche of La Défense. The second axis runs north – south from the Palais Bourbon, headquarters of the French National Assembly, and down the Pont de la Concorde across the Seine.

When hordes of revolutionaries seized power during the French Revolution, Louis' statue had been removed and replaced with a guillotine. The square became the site of public executions, where Louis XVI, Marie Antoinette and almost three thousand others were beheaded. Legend holds that the smell of blood was so strong in the square that a herd of cattle once refused to cross. We runners had no such compunctions as we swept across the square, scattering plastic water bottles in our wake, past the Obélisque de Luxor. The sharp, pointed tip of the pink granite edifice today replaces the sharp edge of the guillotine. A gift to the French in 1829 by the viceroy of Egypt, the monolith – over three thousand years old and adorned with hieroglyphics – once stood the entrance to the Amon temple at Luxor.

Exiting the square, we ran into the arrow-straight *rue de Rivoli* with its mile-long arcade of souvenir and fashionable shops concealed behind graceful arches. The road runs parallel with the beautiful Jardin des Tuilieries, which hugs the north bank of the Seine between the Place de la Concorde and the Musée du Louvre. The garden stands on the site of kilns that once supplied many of the city's roof tiles, and from which it takes its name. Originally created for Catherine de Médicis around 1564, redesigned in 1664 by landscape architect André Le Nôtre, and renovated in 1996, the formal layout is perfectly aligned with the Axe Historique. The gardens, lovingly rendered on canvas by impressionist painters such as Monet and Renoir, had been familiar to me long before I had ever visited the city, when I was an art student in my youth. Al and I had visited this most central of the city's parks several times. We had delighted in strolling along its neat gravel paths past elegantly trimmed lawns, fountains and statues, or in taking coffee in one of the cafes nestled within the trees that flank its central avenue, dissected by three pools.

Now, however, all I could do was sneak a fleeting glimpse of this oasis of green within the grey city, as the route of the marathon carried me along with the tide of my fellow runners.

Like a mob of rampaging revolutionaries, we stormed past the Musée des Arts Décoratifs with little appreciation of the sumptuous artefacts it housed: we were more intent on avoiding collision with the traffic bollards in the centre of the road. Many a runner has rendered himself excrutiatingly impotent by from a bollard in the bollocks, his attention diverted by a casual sideways glance.

Amid cheering from the crowds that lined the road, the sweaty, wheezing throng tore on past the Musée du Louvre, able to catch only a peek of the huge glass pyramid standing in the central *cour carrée*, the courtyard of this former royal palace. The enormous building – or rather collection of buildings faultlessly grafted together – is the culmination of generations of additions and adaptations. Parts of the original moated medieval fortress still form sturdy foundations beneath the courtyard. Above ground the delicate grandeur of Renaissance and Baroque architecture packages the stunning collections of art and antiquities within for the edification of the millions who visit the museum each year. Behind the elegant windows and graceful façades of the Louvre is stored a bewildering array of Oriental, Egyptian, Greek, Etruscan and Roman antiquities. Here also are priceless works of Islamic, African and Asian arts, and more than six thousand European paintings dating from the thirteenth to the nineteenth century, including Da Vinci's smirking *Mona Lisa*. As I sprinted past the building, I reflected that on my first visit there, after several hours trudging past seemingly endless displays of archaeological finds, I had barely scratched the surface. I had emerged from Chinese-American architect I.M. Pei's controversial glass pyramid – the subterranean entrance to the museum – glassy-eyed and culture-blind.

On we ran parallel with the Seine, although the river was largely hidden from view by the buildings and the mass of onlookers lining the streets. Every five kilometres we ran the gauntlet of the water stations: this was a dangerous stage in any marathon, since some runners took these pitstops as an excuse to stop running, causing those behind to bulldoze into them. Discarded plastic bottles became a serious trip hazard, while the road surface was either slick with water and soggy sponges or sticky with spilt, sugary energy drinks.

Ten kilometres into the race, about forty minutes since the start, we entered the beautiful parkland of the Bois de Vincennes on the western side of the city, and ran along the little intersecting pathways. Created at the behest of Napoléon III during the latter part of the 19th century, this swathe of green was designed by Baron Haussman and inspired by central London's Hyde Park and Regent's Park. The route of the race took us alongside the man-made Daumesnil Lake, popular with canoeists, and through lush woodland. As we ran we could catch a glimpse, on our left, of the *grand rocher*, the artificial rock that towers from the centre of the fifteen-hectare Zoo de Vincennes, and the quaint funfair attractions of the Foire du Trône amusement park.

From about twenty-five kilometres the race followed the northern bank of the Seine. To my left I could see the Ile de la Cité, considered to be the birthplace of Parisian civilisation, and also the geographical centre of France. The small island in the river had been home to the Parisii tribe, who were conquered by the Romans in 52AD. When the Romans were sent packing, the Francs had made the island their capital, and it thrived during the Middle Ages, becoming a religious and cultural centre. Only two buildings remained from that era: the gothic magnificence of Notre-Dame Cathedral and the graceful beauty of Sainte-Chapelle. Ghostly white against the clear blue sky, I could see the twin bell towers of Notre-Dame rising above the tightly packed streets of more modern buildings that surrounded the cathedral. Seeing the lofty towers and the flying buttresses with their hideous gargoyles glowering down, it was hard for me to disassociate the cathedral from Victor Hugo's story of Esmerelda and Quasimodo, the hunchback, a tale so familiar to me as a child.

Sainte Chapelle, if more diminutive than the cathedral, was no less impressive in its gothic architecture. Built by Louis IX in 1248 to contain holy relics, the Crown of Thorns and a fragment of the True Cross, the building's upper chapel is resplendent with fabulous stained glass windows.

Drinking in all this historic beauty helped only marginally in taking my mind from the physical discomfort I was beginning to feel. My shoulders were tense and my hips ached. I was also bursting for a pee but was too stubborn to stop: that would add minutes to my time. The run was taking its toll, not only on me but also on many of my fellow runners. More and more people were walking or had stopped to rest. At thirty kilometres, running adjacent to the Eiffel Tower on the opposite side of the river, the crowds lining the road were thick and noisy. There were whistles blowing and loud cheering spurred on the runners. To my joy, leaning from the throng I could see Al frantically waving, shouting words of encouragement. I reached out and touched her extended hand briefly then had passed by, carried along by this moment. Soon the route curved south-west before leaving the riverside to veer off to the right to enter the Bois de Boulogne, thirty-five kilometres from the start. The park, covering 865 hectares, lies on the western edge of the city, in close proximity to the business sectors of La Défense, Levallois and Boulogne Billancourt. Like the Bois de Vincennes, it was also designed by Haussman. During the daytime it is popular with walkers, cyclists and horse riders, and contains the Auteuil and Longchamp racecourses. At night, the area becomes a haunt for prostitutes, as the city's red light district. Today the pleasant, winding pathways were lined with people waving flags and banners and offering sweets to runners, whose energy levels were on the wane.

I was beginning to flag as we traipsed along the circuitous rout through the parkland but knew that the finish line was there for the taking, if I could only maintain my pace. I would not crack the magical three hours goal, but was happy that I would achieve an admirable time. Suddenly, I was afflicted with a severe pain in my left knee and stumbled badly in an attempt to avoid falling over completely. I limped a few paces. The pain in my knee was excruciating. I was done for. I hobbled on then was obliged to stop. My knee appeared to have locked in a semi-bent position. I could not straighten it or bend it. I whacked my palm hard against the side of the knee and my leg straightened immediately, although with severe pain and a most disconcerting grinding sound from deep within. I tried walking a few paces and, while the knee was still stiff, I was able soon to break into a slow jog. As I ran I quickened my pace, although with a limping gait. Soon I was able to run at a respectable pace, although the left leg was slow to respond. I continued on, wincing with every stride.

At last I was within a few kilometres of the finish and I quickened my pace, determined to finish strongly. I passed under the huge inflated arch that marked the finish line and found myself brought to a sudden halt by a long queue of runners who had just preceded me. Panting heavily, my entire body aching and craving to flop down on the ground, I was instead ushered along at a slow shuffle by the waiting marshals. Slowly we wended our way along the queue to the little ramps we would be obliged to scale – like a steep incline to the tired runners – in order to have the microchip timing devices removed from our shoes by the waiting staff. After that we collected our goody bags, and our precious medals – pausing to have our photographs taken for posterity by a bank of photographers – then on to a line of trestle tables that groaned under the weight of tonnes of bananas, oranges, apples, huge boxes of raisins, bottles of water, energy drinks and fruit juice. Finally, fighting our way through the crowd, we were able to find our friends and family. I emerged from the crowd to meet Al, David, Dennie and Anna and all but fell into their arms.

I had been so concerned about completing the race at all that I had forgotten to look at the digital clock as I passed over the finish line. Now, I gazed back at the digital clock at the apex of the arch and noticed that the time had only just registered three hours and twenty minutes. Given the time it had taken to file through the finishing pens I estimated that I had achieved my own personal goal: I had completed the marathon in under three hours fifteen minutes. Incredibly, despite the problem with my knee, this was the fastest time I had ever run the distance in over one dozen marathons. I was ecstatic, although it was hard to forget the terrible pain in my left knee. The joint clicked with every step, as I was led through the crowds to a relatively clear area, where I flopped down on the pavement with an enormous sigh of relief.

'That's the last time I'm going to run a marathon,' I stated matter-of-factly to my companions.

'You said that last time,' was Al's reply. She was right, and I was sure in my own mind that I would have cause to say it again.

Walking with llamas

Chapter Fifteen

Llama karma

For the occasion of my fiftieth birthday that June, Al and I had decided to hold a celebratory lunch party for our friends. To feed the masses, we had ordered large pizzas, forty-centimetres in diameter from the local *boulanger*, Monsieur Monadiere, whose enterprising establishment provided a nice line in extra-curricular baking. Our own *potager* yielded more than enough green salad and bulging red tomatoes for our needs, plus a copious supply of *haricot verts*. Home-grown spuds would form the basis of potato salad, while others would be boiled complete with their brown jackets then tossed in walnut oil. We cooked several chickens and prepared platefuls of *charcuterie*: thinly sliced Auvergne sausage, slivers of dried beef and slices of ham. In the centre of the *grenier*, we arranged a row of tables to accommodate the twenty guests that we expected, and scrounged chairs from Véronique so that everyone could be seated for lunch. Plastic dustbins full of ice were brought into service as a receptacle for bottles of white and rosé wines, and bottles of beer.

This auspicious occasion was also to be the day when Bernard would deliver Talisman and Thursday to their new home. Al and I had successfully fenced off the large field at the back of the *grange* in advance of their arrival, and had constructed a western-style corral in front of the *maison du pain*, which was to become a stable for the llamas and a tack room to contain all their grooming and training accoutrements. From here the animals would have a fine view over the communal green and the comings and goings of the villagers. Bernard was first to arrive and he and I busied ourselves with coaxing the animals out of the little tin trailer – he pulling on a lead rope from the doorway at the front, while I pushed and shoved the woolly *derrières* from the ramp at the back of the trailer. Contrary creatures that they are, while the llamas had not enjoyed their road trip one iota, they point blank refused to exit the trailer now that they had arrived. A few swift back kicks to the shin made me a little more cautious when approaching the rear end of a llama, for I can vouch that their toenails are extremely sharp. First out was Thursday, who appeared to have received something of a personal makeover since I last saw him. He actually looked quite presentable. Once he had been prised out of the trailer, his companion followed willingly and Bernard and I led the animals to the corral, where we removed their lead ropes and allowed them to investigate their new home.

'Keep the halters on for the first few days,' advised Bernard. 'It will be more easy for you to catch them like this… you are a novice remember!' What a pity I did not heed his words of wisdom.

Guests began to arrive in their droves, and all were eager to view the llamas. The animals took to their newfound celebrity with verve, prancing around the corral to the delight of the onlookers. Véronique came out of her house, shepherding her nephew's three young children. Jérôme, the beefy farmer from whom we had bought the *grange*, was nowhere to be seen, although his wife followed close behind the others.

'Where's Jérôme?' I asked my neighbour.

'He's just coming, Monsieur Richard. He's fetching your present!' she replied. Just then Jérôme's tractor hove into view at the far side of the hamlet. Spiked on its front hydraulic arm was a huge rectangular bale of hay. Behind him came another tractor, driven by Jérôme's right-hand man, Johan. It, too, supported a huge hay bale. The tractors rumbled up to the corral. Jérôme leaned out of the cab.

'*Bonne anniversaire*, Richard!' he hollered above the roar of the engines. 'These bales are part of your present,' he announced. 'And there will be another three, plus five bales of straw. That should see you and your llamas through next winter!' Thanking the farmer for his generous and extremely practical gift, I herded the llamas to one side while we opened the double gates and allowed the tractors to deposit their loads in the barn.

Inside the *grange* our party gathered for pre-prandial drinks. A great Anglo-French cacophony of voices struck up as strangers were introduced, old friends re-established contact and the various children raced around the huge room playing a game of tag, with an enthusiastic Jazz in pursuit. This was just the type of occasion where the vast barn could come into its own. In fact, I often used to lob a ball across the room for Jazz to fetch, a game he adored. Al was dubious about this practice. Apart from the fact that I was continually smashing ornaments and table lamps, the ball had occasionally shot out of the open window, tempting the pup to follow. Thankfully, he seemed to have more sense than to launch himself from a first floor window.

The Yorkshireman and Dennie arrived fashionably late, clutching a huge parcel, which was thrust into my arms. On unwrapping the parcel I found that I had been presented with another extremely practical and unique gift.

'An *épouvantail*,' explained Dennie, as I examined the full-size scarecrow, dressed in sackcloth trousers, checked shirt and sporting a wide-brimmed straw hat.

'Marvellous! Just what we need for the *potager*!' I exclaimed, thrilled with the gift and thanking my friends.

Eventually we all sat around the dining table and delved into the platefuls and bowls of food. Bottles of red, white and rosé wine were deposited at strategic intervals, along with jugs of water. Jérôme, sitting centre of the table, pulled his personal *couteau* from his trouser pocket and, wielding the knife like an expert carver, took it upon himself to dole out portions of chicken, ripping apart the birds with his huge hands and handing wings, legs and great chunks of breast meat to the other diners. Strangely, all of the French guests, without exception, seemed unable to cope with the potatoes we had boiled in their jackets and to a man painstakingly peeled off the brown skins before consuming the contents. Enormous loaves of crusty bread were passed around, while plates of meat and bowls of salad seemed to fly back and forth across and along the lengthy table. In what seemed like a matter of moments it was as if a plague of locusts had passed by, since most of the food was gone, leaving only crumbs. After various fruit flans, cream and ice cream were eaten, a vast selection of cheeses were delivered to the table and glasses of red wine provided to accompany them. At the end of the meal we were all well fed and many of us tipsy on alcohol.

When a serious political discussion broke out between Jérôme, Claude and Jean-Michel, the table began to empty and little groups gathered around the sitting areas to talk of lighter matters.

'Flippin' archetypal Frenchmen!' squeaked Bernard, joining me at the breakfast bar, where I was about to open another bottle of chilled rosé. He apparently did not count himself amongst the breed. 'Why do they 'ave always to talk politics? Crikey, it's your birthday, too! It drive me flippin' crazy! Why can't they talk about music? Or nature?' I gave the matter some thought for a moment, and decided that while I could imagine sensitive Claude Norrin and sophisticated Jean-Michel Regnier conversing on the finer points of a particular counterpoint in classical music, I could certainly not see burly, bull-wrestling farmer Jérôme L'Heureux pondering on the delicate beauty of a daffodil.

Jean-Michel extricated himself from the rather heated discussion, which Jérôme had skilfully and pointedly manipulated towards what he regarded as the shoddy state of the mayoral profession. The mayor was a born entertainer and normally a man loved by all children. He was soon surrounded by a gaggle of kids: Harry and Sue's four delightful horrors, Jérôme's son and two daughters, and Jeff and Amanda's daughter. However, Jean-Michel surpassed himself on this occasion by demonstrating a sleight of hand trick in which he appeared to have pulled off one of his thumbs. While most of the assembled kids howled with raucous laughter as the mayor appeared to twist his thumb through one hundred and eighty degrees, one poor child apparently thought the demonstration was real and burst into a flood of fitful tears. She became quite inconsolable when Jean-Michel, sorely embarrassed that he had upset the child, attempted to set matters straight by offering the girl a close up demonstration of the gory illusion, revealing its innocent secret. It was too late, however: the damage had already been done and the poor child spent the rest of the afternoon cowering behind her mother, fearful of this French ogre and his detachable digits.

By the early evening the party was winding down and guests were starting to depart for home. We exchanged the necessary hugs, kisses and handshakes. Even for the young boys, it was perfectly acceptable – and in fact expected – to provide *bisous* on each cheek: growing up in France had taught them that kissing was the natural way of greeting or saying goodbye to friends and adults, not something only 'soppy' girls did.

'It's been great, darlin',' said Jill, a little tipsy.

'Ah, but first!' said Jean-Michel, raising an index finger as though he had forgotten something. *'J'ai un gros sausisse!'* He promptly departed for the bathroom.

'What did he say?' said policeman Harry's wife, Sue, clearly puzzled by what she took to be the mayor's rather crude comment about the condition of his bowels.

'Sounded like he said he needed to take a dump,' said Harry, a person who also did not mince his words. The boys giggled. Jill looked highly embarrassed. After a few minutes Jean-Michel reappeared, wringing his damp hands. He beamed at his partner, who merely frowned back at him.

'What iz ze matter, *mon coeur*?' he said in his finest franglais, sensing something was amiss.

'Oh, nothing Jean-Michel,' she snapped. 'But sometimes I just do not understand you Frenchmen at all!'

'What 'ave I done? What 'ave I said?' said the mayor, flabbergasted. Jill stomped off towards the car and climbed into the passenger seat. Jean-Michel shrugged. '*Ben*! I theenk it iz me who does not understand ze English women.'

I escaped for a while to the corral and released the llamas through the little back gate into their field. At first the animals appeared wary of their partial freedom, but then, tempted by the lush grass they soon began to canter away, twisting their heads on their long necks as they ran and emitting loud shrieks of delight. I watched them for some minutes as they began their early evening leap-dance, sproinging gaily in the warmth of the setting sun. I felt a warm glow inside me, and a spreading feeling of contentment. Al approached me quietly from behind and slipped an affectionate arm around my waist.

'Happy birthday, darling,' she said, planting a kiss on my cheek. 'Are you happy?'

'Ecstatic,' I replied, pecking my wife back on the cheek. Together we watched Talisman and Thursday at play, savouring the delights of their new territory, then returned to the *grange*, where the last of our guests were preparing to depart. It had been a good day. We had enjoyed the company of our friends and the future looked rosy. For the first time in many years I felt I belonged somewhere. I had come home. Life was sweet.

Although my initial attempts at capturing the llamas resulted in utter failure and my unfortunate deposit in their communal toilet, I soon developed a kind of uneasy trust with the beasts. Although they would come running whenever I whistled, it appeared to be with deep suspicion as to my motives. If they saw that I clutched a halter and lead rope, they would invariably keep their distance. I had, in fact, spent many hours trying to perfect a suitable whistle. At first the whistle had been identical to that used to summon Jazz, who had rightly been miffed that he was continually being woken from his slumbers and called to heel for no apparent reason. Various other mangy mutts would also appear from far-flung corners of the commune, called forth by my practice warbling. Eventually I latched onto a sound that seemed appropriate – and which would not act as the Pied Piper's call to all the sundry beasts of the neighbourhood – and used the whistle in conjunction with a discreet rattle of the tin of sheep pellets I had taken to carrying in my jacket pocket.

Bribed with pellets, the llamas would allow me to slip their halters on and tie them to the fence post. I could then start work on grooming their thick fibre. Although I had notions of collecting the fibre for spinning, I had read that the process was also beneficial in promoting healthy skin and circulation. The wool of a llama is, strictly speaking, hair because the individual fibres have a hollow core; the wool of a sheep, by contrast, is composed of solid fibres. The outer layer of fairly straight guard hairs provide an extremely efficient moisture barrier that is able to repel rain and snow and protects the downy, insulating undercoat. The undercoat, which has more crimp, or waviness, and therefore more elasticity, is the only part of the fleece that is harvested for spinning.

Taking into account the teachings of Bernard, I at first concentrated on surface brushing, using a wire-toothed comb. This had the effect of removing mats and tangles from the fleece, although the hairs I gathered would be of no practical value. I started with the neck, brushing downwards and taking care not to scratch the animal's skin with the teeth of the brush. Working to the shoulder, I continued down the legs. This was difficult, since llamas do not appreciate their legs being fondled, and usually caused them to perform a jittery dance in an attempt to avoid the ticklish sensation. Working along the back of the animal, I made sure to avoid creating a centre parting along the spine, as this could allow debris to collect on the skin. Next the torso could be groomed, working downwards towards the underbelly. Finally the bobble of a tail could be tackled – understandably a delicate area, concealing the genitals – followed by the back legs. This was the trickiest area and it was necessary to stand to one side of the llama to avoid a painful kick.

A final groom with a bristle brush left the llama's coat looking sleek and shiny. When I became more confident that I would not hurt or upset the animals with a poor grooming technique, I would part the layer of guard hairs for access to the downy undercoat. Using a wire, wide-toothed comb, I would gently brush the fleece to remove the fine down. After several sessions I had filled a carrier bag.

While I found grooming to be enjoyable and relaxing, feeling as if I was communing with the animals, the experience was one that the llamas appeared to detest, particularly the irritable Thursday. He would stamp his feet angrily when I approached him wielding a comb, wriggling on his tether so that I could not grab hold of him. If all else failed he would simply flop down onto the ground and roll onto his back. Talisman was more co-operative, generally standing motionless during this terrible *toilettage*, and emitting a low, throaty and sorrowful moan. Invariably, when released after a grooming session, both llamas would trot off to the area of bare earth they had grubbed out in a dry corner of their field, where they would take turns rolling over in the dust bath. They would emerge filthier than when they started.

My confidence around the animals grew rapidly. They grew used to my presence and would even trail along behind me whenever I embarked upon the periodic collection of their excrement in a wheelbarrow. Happily, their constitutions had returned to normal and the healthy pellets they deposited, which resemble those of goats or deer, could be put to good use in the vegetable and flower garden as an excellent source of slow-release manure. High in nitrogen, the pellets could be used without risk of burning the plants and did not require composting first.

I was soon able to start training the llamas to walk on the lead. Al and I, each leading a llama, would set off from the corral, passing through the hamlet to the consternation of the neighbours, then heading off along the dusty *chemin d'exploitation* that provided the various local farmers with access to their distant fields. Jazz, whose presence was now tolerated by the llamas, would follow along at our heels, occasionally tempting providence by scuttling between the animal's legs. Along the way, the llamas would pause to sample the different treats that nature presented them with. It was amazing to witness just how tough their mouths – and their constitutions – were, for they would think nothing of chomping through spiny bramble or rose stems or devouring rose hips. The sweet, stinging growing tips of nettles would be nibbled off and swallowed without the batting of an eyelid, while long, sinuous tufts of grass were encircled by the llama's long tongues then torn off with a sideways twitch of the head, and chewed to pulp.

I was concerned about the quality of the forage available in the field, particularly the presence of plants regarded in some llama literature as poisonous. One meaty tome I had been studying on raising llamas had brought to light the dangerous nature of the common buttercup. 'The entire plant is toxic,' warned the book. 'It affects the central nervous system and can result in paralysis (in advanced cases), colic, blindness, and diarrhoea.' Areas of the llamas' field were carpeted with the dainty yellow flowers and I became paranoid that Talisman and Thursday would succumb to the quoted ailments. I telephoned my guru, Bernard, for his wise advice.

'Buttercups?' he said. 'Blimey, but I 'ave never 'eard of this before! My fields are full of buttercups and none of my llamas 'ave ever suffered.'

'So you think it will be OK?' I sought his confirmation.

'I think you will find the llama will simply not eat plants that are poisonous,' Bernard said. 'You are like the mother 'en, Richard! You fuss too much over these boys. The llama, 'e is very 'ardy.'

Nevertheless, armed with my trusty guide to poisonous plants, I would scour the field for signs of black locust, black mustard, deadly nightshade, boxwood, ragwort, poison hemlock and other plants considered to be deadly. Even oak – which was abundant on the property – was reckoned to be toxic: the immature acorns and wilted leaves were cited as the cause of kidney failure. But the llamas continued to prosper. Even the previously scrawny Thursday seemed to thicken up and to exude a healthy glow, although his fleece was continually tangled with dried twigs, straw and bramble stems. I had grown quite attached to the cantankerous creature, whose comical behaviour never ceased to amaze me. Outwardly, he possessed a rather feeble demeanour, which I suspected was a front: a cunning ploy to persuade Talisman to do his bidding. Thursday, in fact, was the boss of their little herd. He would incite his companion to chase him by biting his legs, then would scamper off with a shrill scream. Talisman, falling for the bait, would then give hot pursuit, galloping after Thursday at full pelt, his neck stretched out in front of him, his head low to the ground as he snapped at the retreating back legs of his companion. Thursday would then appear to surrender and flop onto the ground, leaving Talisman to pounce on top of his prone body. They would then roll over, kicking wildly. With their long necks entwined, the two llamas would playfully nibble each other's ears, then collapse exhausted to the ground before jumping to their feet again and haring off in another game of catch.

Hunters in France enjoy the right to roam freely over the countryside shooting whichever permitted prey comes within their sights. Highly organised groups of hunters would, during the killing season – which depends on the *département* and the species, but is generally from September until February – traipse across the landscape from early morning onwards, dogs at their heel, shotguns and rifles slung over their shoulders. At various points along the highways, signs placed at the verges would warn motorists: '*Prudence! Chasse en Cours!*' Groups of hunters wearing orange fluorescent vests and hats, shotguns draped in the crook of their arms, barrels cracked, would stand guard at entrances to fields. Their vans would be parked haphazardly at the verges, rear doors open revealing dog cages. The more organised groups would be in radio contact with the pack of hunters, who would advise them of their progress, and they would be prepared to hold back the traffic in order to to allow the hunt to cross freely in pursuit of its quarry.

Hunters clearly relished the adventure afforded by our unkempt fields and woodland. When strolling with Jazz in the undergrowth, Al and I would frequently discover mysterious passageways – 'bunny holes' Al called them – no wider than would permit a man to pass. These tunnels appeared to have been freshly hacked by the hunters with a machete, leaving roughly cut stalks protruding from the ground. Winding their way across our more remote fields and through choked copses, they led to improvised wooden stiles that had been erected to permit access over the barbed wire fencing into adjoining properties.

We would often be awoken early on weekend mornings by the tinny sound of the brass horns the hunters used to summon their dogs. Their progress could be followed by the frequent cracks of gunfire and the sight of flocks of birds breaking cover and ascending above the treetops. At other times we would see deer fleeing for their lives across our fields with lithe dogs snapping at their cloven hooves.

While not interested in partaking in hunting ourselves, we were content to allow the hunters to follow their ancient tradition, provided they did not cause any damage to our property. So when I happened to glance from the window of the *grange* one morning, after preparing Al and me coffee and intending to return to bed, I was incensed to see two men clad in hunting gear strolling through the field at the back of the building. This field was the llamas' paddock and protected by high fencing that would be impossible for a man to clamber over. How had the men entered the enclosure without damaging the fencing, I wondered? And why should they be parading, bold as brass, with loaded weapons in what was effectively our back garden, a mere twenty metres from our house?

I recognised the duo as Pierre and Jean-Luc, two brothers who lived in the hamlet. The youngest of four brothers who lived with their ancient mother in a tiny cottage and tended a small herd of cows, these two were the smarter element of a family for whom brain cells had been shared out unequally. The hunters had four dogs, themselves of dubious parentage; two long-legged hounds and two short-legged animals resembling hairy sausage dogs. I grabbed the binoculars that I used to spot interesting birds and homed in on the interlopers: as I watched, Jean-Luc tossed the two sausage dogs he had been carrying under his arms over the high fence then brazenly leaned his full weight on the fence, squashed the wire and, along with his brother, clambered over, leaving the grille crumpled.

Llamas are intensely nosey animals and it was not long before Talisman and Thursday appeared, alerted by the presence of the intruders and intrigued by the damaged fence. I dressed quickly and ran across the field to where the llamas appeared to be contemplating a joint bid for freedom. Shooing them away, I quickly hauled the fence back up. The staples had been ripped out of the posts, leaving the fence sagging and loose. With Al's assistance, I repaired the damage, by which time the hunters had long gone, swallowed by the woodland beyond the fence line.

Later that day, when out running, I chanced upon the duo, emerging from a rickety gateway onto the lane that led back to the hamlet. The two hounds circled around me barking. Jean-Luc, bronze-faced with a large hooked nose, black full moustache and lank, greasy black hair, had a sausage dog tucked under each arm. His brother Pierre, round-faced with a high forehead, ruddy complexion and receding grey hair, sported a shotgun at each shoulder. The canvas satchels they each carried were stuffed with an assortment of small birds. I skidded to a halt intending to tackle the smiling duo.

'*Ecoutez*,' Listen, I said. 'I have no problem at all with *la chasse*, but please not enter the field with the llamas…'

The brothers just stared at me, displaying identical gap-toothed smiles, but no sign of inner comprehension. How on earth could these guys be granted a licence to walk around in public with a loaded weapon, I mused?

'And the fence, *messieurs*…' Blank looks. 'My *grillage*… you damaged my fence…' The men continued to smile. The hounds continued to circle, barking and growling menacingly at me, unchecked by their owners. But I wasn't going to submit to intimidation. '*Vous comprenez?*' I said sternly in French, hoping to reinforce my point. 'The fence is there to keep the llamas in. *C'est clair?* It's clear?'

'*Oui, monsieur! Oui oui oui, nous avons bien compris!*' Yes, we have understood well, said Pierre. He looked at his brother and they both nodded extravagantly, grinning broadly.

'So it won't happen again?' I clarified. They simply continued to nod and smile. Am I speaking French or Martian, I asked myself? '*Ecoutez*,' I said, calming my tone, attempting a tack these men might follow. 'For the sake of your dogs… *les lamas détestent les chiens*. Stay out of the field or the llamas will attack the dogs and kill them!'

Puzzled expressions appeared on the faces of both men. They turned to look at each other like Tweedle-dum and Tweedle-dee, and then one by one at their dogs. Had my veiled threat struck home? Suddenly, as if the centime had just dropped, clink! into the single tiny brain cell they apparently shared, both men reached out their hands and clasped mine in firm handshakes, laughing heartily and nodding their stupid heads as if I had just cracked the funniest joke of all time. The dark-haired brother actually managed this feat without dropping one of his sausage dogs. Now they were shaking their heads and I could swear that tears of mirth were welling up in their eyes.

'*Oh, monsieur!*' giggled Pierre, dabbing his shiny forehead with a filthy handkerchief he pulled from his pocket. 'The big *mouton* will kill our dogs?'

'Llamas,' I stressed. 'Not big *mouton*…'

'*Merci monsieur…*', said Jean-Luc, shaking my hand again.

I parted from the duo and continued with my run, not at all convinced that they had the slightest inkling of what I had said.

The following day the sound of a hunting horn roused me from my sleep. Racing to the window, I saw Pierre and Jean-Luc in the field again. This time they were heading for the marshy area flanking the little stream that divided the llama paddock from the adjoining, unfenced field. I was just about to throw on some clothes and make after the pair with a big stick when I was rooted to the spot by the sight of Talisman, poor placid Talisman, standing in the centre of the field surrounded by two mongrel hounds and a pair of sausage dogs. The canines, creeping inextricably forward in a well-conceived pincer movement, were closing in on the hapless llama. Talisman hung his head, his banana ears folded flat against his neck. The dogs were almost upon him and I watched, helpless. In one swift movement any kung-fu fighter would be proud of, the llama bucked, catching each of the hounds a nasty kick with each back leg. At the same time his long neck reached out and he swept both sausage dogs aside with his bony head.

The hounds, regaining their feet, pelted off across the field towards the safety of their astonished masters, while the sausage dogs were left to the mercy of one enraged llama. Talisman made chase after the short-legged canines, soon catching up with them. One received a swift kick and was sent sprawling, while the other finally reached the waiting arms of Jean-Luc, who scooped up the little animal just in time. Talisman shuddered to a halt in front of the trespassers, raised his regal head and then delivered a monumental spray of green spit that doused the two brothers and their shivering mutts. Backing off, clutching their animals to them, the brothers made for the gate, swung it open, politely shut it behind them and scarpered along the lane to their mean cottage. Talisman, satisfied to have trounced the interlopers, swaggered off to receive adoring praise from his stablemate, who had been watching the show from the wings. The hunters and their dogs never again entered the field.

Bernard had received his replacement hip and was more mobile than he had been in many years, and so he was able to complete the preparatory handling of my second llama, the sweet, innocent yearling Uriel: angel by name and angel by nature. And a real little scallywag. Short in stature and outwardly quiet in nature, Uriel was, deep down, a conniving creature who soon after his introduction to my small herd, made his presence known in no uncertain terms.

I had also agreed to buy another llama from my friend, but Bernard was worried about the animal's propensity to leap over extremely high fences, and considered that he needed more hands-on treatment before he could be passed on to a mere novice like me.

'Listen, Richard,' said the Frenchman. 'I will make you a deal, *non*? I will give you this Thursday…'

'I can't accept that, Bernard!' I exclaimed.

'But you will do me a favour! I have more boys than I can sell at the moment. Everybody wants girls! He is settled here now, part of the 'erd. And when the other llama is ready I will give you him half price. Blimey, it's not a bad deal! And you must admit Thursday has improved, eh?' I had to admit that the previously scrawny Thursday had become a fine specimen, despite the fact that he was a filthy wretch at the best of times. But I had become quite attached to the beast and he appeared to enjoy my company, tagging along closely whenever I was about my farmerly business in the field. And so it was agreed that Thursday would remain at Le Mas Mauvis.

By permitting the amorous advances of his randy companions, Uriel's submissive behaviour softened up Talisman and Thursday until they were butter between his toes. Thursday had considered himself the leader of the herd, but soon realised that he had been demoted. He and the older, wiser Talisman became nothing more than the little brute's bodyguards. This meant ensuring that I was not able not get within a fleece's whisker of the youngster. All of Bernard's preparatory work was to no avail, since it proved impossible to collar the animal without incurring the attentions of his guardians.

I resorted to cunning to try to catch Uriel. Laying a trail of sheep pellets from the field and into the corral, I would entice all three animals into this secure area and bolt the gate. Once they were trapped, I would usher the older llamas into the little lean-to that was their stable and barricade the doorway. With Uriel confined alone to the corral, I would attempt the technique I had perfected in order to hem him in and slip the head collar on. So far so good. After receiving few swift kicks to the shins, I had succeeded in apprehending the llama. But once he had been attached to the long line of rope I was still in trouble, since he would invariably commence bounding around the corral, dragging me along with him, or else would simply *kush* down onto the ground and refuse to budge. The animal was uncontrollable.

Chapelle St. Aurélien, Limoges

Chapter Sixteen

Gypsy's kiss

L iving in the depths of the countryside, surrounded by an abundance of green, we occasionally felt cut off from the real world and yearned for an injection of culture – or, rather, a bit of hustle and bustle. It was on these occasions that we clambered into our car and headed off for the city of Limoges. Battling with traffic jams of cars and trolley buses – if only for a brief interlude – kept our wits sharp. One had to be on the alert, also, to avoid knocking down pedestrians. While the streets of French towns and villages are interlaced by numerous striped pedestrian crossings – similar to the zebra crossings of England – motorists rarely stop to allow waiting pedestrians to cross. Foreigners who do pull politely to a halt, oblivious to motoring etiquette, are generally greeted with a look of total disbelief by those paused on the pavement. Jaywalkers, however, are likely to step into the path of oncoming traffic with little regard for their own, or anybody else's safety. It was always something of a lottery driving in Limoges.

The city, however, had much to offer us country bumpkins in search of a little urban relief. We parked the car in one of the multi-storey car parks and headed off for a tour of the city. Compact and accessible, it was possible to visit the major parts of Limoges in one relaxed day, stopping for lunch in one of the restaurants along the way.

Renowned for its medieval *champlevé* enamels and fine porcelain, Limoges was a city with a colourful and somewhat chequered history. Founded as Augustoritum by Caesar Augustus in 10BC, the city lay at a strategic crossroads. It had boasted spectacular arenas and sumptuous thermal baths. In the fourth century the Roman Empire acceded to pressure from barbarian hordes and Limoges was born. Saint-Martial Abbey was constructed and became a spiritual and cultural centre for pilgrims. The enamels on copper produced by the monks were exported throughout the Christian world. During the Middle Ages the city was divided into two fortified strongholds, the site of bitter feuds between the Viscount of Limoges and the Cathedral and Bishop's Residence, each struggling for control. When a source of the soft clay, kaolin was discovered in nearby Saint-Yrieix-la-Perche, the city reunited and became a prosperous centre for the manufacture of fine white porcelain. The city flared into renewed life as kilns and factories were constructed. There are several porcelain factories and retail outlets dotted around the city: Al and I loved to visit these in search of bargains in plain white crockery marked down in price due to some insignificant flaw.

The modern city sits on seven low hills overlooking the Vienne river. Graced with a micro-climate, the city often enjoys fine weather when that of the surrounding area is less than clement, or conversely can be a snowy haven in winter encircled by green countryside. Dominating the skyline is the gothic bell tower and flamboyant north portal of Saint-Etienne cathedral. This massive stone building looms over Les Jardins de l'Evêché. The botanical gardens are arranged in a series of terraces stepping down towards the river frontage. Also housing an orangery, the gardens are planted with more than one thousand specimens from across the world, and there is also a fascinating thematic garden of melliferous, honey-producing plants, medicinal plants, aromatic plants and those used in dyeing. Al and I would wander around the gardens, making mental notes of some of the interesting plants we would like to incorporate in our own garden: when we had the opportunity to create it.

Vying for attention on the skyline is the sixty-metre art deco campanile of Bénédictins railway station, which resembles a mosque. The station's limestone-clad ticket hall, adorned with sculptures and pierced with stained-glass windows, is capped by a magnificent copper dome of pale green patina.

The Château neighbourhood, originally a feudal *motte* or mound on which once stood the viscount's keep, was our favourite sector, and one we loved to stroll in. It is a lively quarter of medieval buildings with complex, chocolate-coloured half-timbering. The quaint buildings are set along narrow streets that open onto sunny squares where there were bars and restaurants to tempt us from window-shopping. In the *quartier des bouchers*, nineteenth-century shop fronts are still home to meat traders, some of whom are said to be descendants of the core of half a dozen families who originally set up business there. The road opens onto a square containing the Chapelle St. Aurélien. This tiny chapel, built in 1471 by the Guild of Butchers to worship the relics of their patron saint, which are preserved in its vault, is crammed between pretty half-timbered buildings with a grotesque block of flats as its backdrop. Inside this miniature gem, however, lies an impressive, candlelit collection of statues and paintings dating from the fifteen to the eighteenth centuries.

In Les Halles market square we visted the covered market that was designed after a machine gallery originally built for the World Exhibition in 1878. Beneath its roofline, a porcelain frieze runs around the exterior façade, depicting all the foodstuffs that can be found within. Nearby there is a mural painted by Limoges native Auguste Renoir.

Most of the inner city's tree-lined riverbanks are accessible by pathways for the enjoyment of fishermen, walkers and runners. This was a fitting end to our brief tour of the more frenetic parts of the city. Saint-Martial Bridge, a graceful sweep of arches, was built during the eighteenth century on the original Roman foundations, which are still visible above the waterline. We sat on a large rock on the riverbank and watched the fish jumping in the fast flowing water. Further afield along the river frontage lay porcelain factories and the Naveix harbour area, where raftwood was originally brought upstream for the construction of buildings and to fire the porcelain kilns.

Later, we retrieved our car and headed for Le Mas Mauvis, satisfied with our brief reconnection with civilisation. On the drive back up the autoroute, I reflected that while Limoges was indeed a fascinating cultural and commercial heart of the Limousin, I loved the surrounding region for its rural charm and solitude. It reminded me of my childhood in 1950s England, with its old-fashioned, unsophisticated simplicity. And this quaintness gave me the comforting feel that I had found my home.

It is often the case that, just when life seems to be going swimmingly well, something unforeseen happens to put *le chat* amongst *les pigeons*. I am not pessimistic or prone to bad omens, by contrast believing in the happy chance of serendipity. Yet my resolve was sorely tested by certain events that came to pass, which threatened to upset not only the applecart but also the *bonne chance* that had graced my life thus far. These sinister occurrences began with the incident of the gypsy and the motor car.

Since moving to France Al and I had managed, as many strangers in a strange land do, to drive our right-hand drive vehicle on the right-handed roads of France. It was dicey in the extreme, since hugging the grass verge was not entirely conducive to safely negotiating the highways and byways. On our infrequent trips to Limoges, we had come to realise how dangerous it could be driving in amongst the bustle of the city's traffic. Overtaking was, understandably, a tricky manoeuvre because it called for the driver to rely on advice from the passenger as to the presence of oncoming traffic. When one was driving alone, overtaking slow-moving vehicles became even more risky. The car, an ancient Peugeot I had owned for over a decade, was coming to the end of its useful life, despite the fact that the bodywork was in perfectly good order. When the engine was pronounced gravely ill and we had been quoted an outlandish fee for having a new one fitted – more than the Peugeot was worth – we decided that it was time to bid the car a fond farewell and invest in a left-hand drive vehicle of French nationality. That was until my wife crossed paths with the gypsy mechanic.

Limping back from a fact-finding mission to car showrooms down in Limoges, Al had by some mysterious force been drawn to knock on the door of a local mechanic, whose acquaintance we had briefly made at a birthday celebration at the home of our policeman friend, Harry. Not that I was at all biased towards gypsies, but I had not liked the look of this shifty character at that time, and nor had Al. So I was more than a little surprised when she came home with the news that she had decided on the spur of the moment, on our behalf, to place the Peugeot in the hands of Gérard the Gypsy, who went by the name of Bo-Bo. The man owned a ramshackle garage on the outskirts of a nearby village, which consisted of two huge, decrepit workshops flanking a little pent-roofed shack where he, his wife and three children lived. Bo-Bo had a reputation for being a bit of a loveable rogue, although apparently, we had been assured by previous customers, he was an extremely good mechanic. He seemed to have a problem with deadlines, however, and his forecourt and the adjoining field were littered with cars, vans and tractors in various stages of reparation. Hand-scrawled notices leaning against oil drums announced that he also sold chain saws, tyres and other mechanical items of dubious provenance.

'So why on earth did you decide that we were keeping the car?' I demanded crossly of my wife. 'We'd agreed that it was time to get rid of it. The engine is completely knackered.'

'I don't know,' admitted Al. 'I just had a feeling. But coincidentally Bo-Bo says he has a replacement engine in stock right now. He can fit it within the next three days.'

'He just happens to have the right engine lying in the back of his workshop, does he?'

'So he says, Rich.'

'But the car's not worth anything. You know that. Why prolong the agony? And how much is the new engine anyway?'

'Five hundred euros,' she revealed. 'He's given me a *devis*…' She handed me a scrap of paper torn from an exercise book, with the figure scrawled on, plus his name, address and signature.

Three days later there was an ominous silence about the status of the repair. Al telephoned. Bo-Bo's wife explained that her husband had been obliged to go away on business and would be back in a week. Two weeks later he still had not reappeared and the car languished with its engine removed in his workshop. After three weeks Al carried out a surprise raid on the Bo-Bo household and found the mechanic hiding in his kitchen. She returned to the *grange* with an update on the situation.

'He needs to get some parts from England. Because it's a right-hand drive car, he can't connect up the new engine without them.'

'And how long will this take?' I demanded gruffly.

'Another few weeks. He needed some money on account,' she revealed shyly.

'On account of what?'

'On account of the fact he hasn't got any. So I gave him some.'

'How much?' I was getting rather worried.

'Half the total cost of the new engine.'

'What? Are you mad?'

'But Rich, if you'd have seen the state of his house. They have no money. His poor wife was in tears, Rich.'

'And clutching her poor, starving babe to her withered breast, no doubt?' I said sarcastically. Al did not appreciate sarcasm. She frowned. 'We're not a bleeding charity, Al!' I said, raising my voice angrily. 'Don't give the bastard any more money! Do you understand?'

'Yes Rich,' Al said wanly.

I was convinced that the gypsy had ensnared my wife with a mysterious spell. She was not behaving rationally. After six weeks the car had still not been repaired and Bo-Bo had gone into hiding again. Having no other transport, we were obliged to borrow a spare car donated by our friend, the Yorkshireman. Whenever we arrived at Bo-Bo's door to demand an explanation for the delay, there was a deathly silence within the shack, although the mechanic's own car was parked outside. Managing to get through on the phone one day, Al was told by the sobbing wife of Bo-Bo that her husband had suffered a hernia, and after an operation was not able to work on heavy equipment for the next fortnight.

I returned to France from a short working trip to England surprised to find that the car had been returned to the fold, looking spic and span. Opening the bonnet, I gazed into the engine compartment.

'It looks like the same engine to me,' I said, although I had to admit that one engine looked pretty much like any other in my mind. 'But what's that hole there?' I indicated a space through which the offside wheel was visible.

'Oh, that,' said Al nervously. 'Bo-Bo told me that the bit that fits there – a metal plate that protects the hoses and things – was never there in the first place. I took the car to the Peugeot garage in Magnac and they told me that it wasn't possible to remove the engine without taking out the plate…'

'And what did Bo-Bo say about that?'

'He told me that was rubbish, that he had managed to take the engine out without removing the plate. But he said that he just happened to have an identical plate in stock and would sell it to us for fifty euros.'

'And?'

'I refused. I thought it might be our plate anyway.'

'Good move. We won't be crossing his greasy palms with silver any more!' The car behaved itself for the next few weeks, although it was necessary to continually top up its cooling system with water prior to every trip. The gypsy's curse finally got the better of the poor vehicle after a month of use and a reputable garage pronounced it well and truly *mort*. Shouldering our losses, we arranged for its removal and destruction and invested in a second-hand, left-hand drive vehicle. On passing Bo-Bo's establishment some weeks later we were amazed to see the old Peugeot sitting on the forecourt, stripped of engine, its wheels and its exhaust system. Peering out from the empty engine compartment, the swarthy gypsy smiled broadly, revealing a mouthful of gold teeth, and winked.

Ever since she was a small child, Al had adored all things American. At ten years old she had confidently announced to her father:

'Daddy, when I grow up I'm going to marry a cowboy and live on a ranch in America.'

'Well, jolly good for you, darling,' the Doctor had replied, not realising how his daughter's resolve would have considerable longevity. A decade later Al was living and working in the States during a seven-year, round-the-world trip. Her childhood dream had partly come true: but well-heeled cowboys, it seemed, were rather thin on the ground in bustling San Francisco and Beverley Hills, where she had ended up.

She had returned to England during her elder sister's illness and subsequent death and had put her dream on the back burner. Having by chance met and fallen in love with me – not a cowboy by any stretch of the imagination – her life's ambition had receded further into the recesses of her memory. She had neatly compartmentalised this dream, had locked the door and misplaced the key. But one day Al confided in me a wish that had never come true. Her admission came while we were watching the seminal mid-life crisis movie *City Slickers!*. In the movie, the character played by the actor Billy Crystal rediscovers his smile and the focus of his life during an eventful cattle drive in Missouri.

'I've always wanted to bring the cattle in,' admitted Al, as the credits rolled at the end of the film.

'Then why don't you?' I asked.

'It's a silly idea.'

'Why silly? It would do you some good. So they really do this… I mean for real?'

'Yes, of course. Some are purely commercial – a kind of activity holiday. But there are real cattle drives that you can join. They take the herd back and forth to the seasonal grazing land.' It seemed that Al had already done her homework. She showed me a leaflet her mother had sent to her. The International League for the Protection of the Horse organised annual charity events, whereby participants collecting a specific amount of money for the cause won the right to attend a real-life cattle drive in Montana.

'Why don't you do it, then?' I suggested, after reading the leaflet. 'Two weeks in Montana, sleeping under the stars, singing around the campfire and eating beans! You'd be in your element!'

'It's selfish, Rich. I'm not working, remember, but you are… you're the one who needs a break. And anyway we should be going on vacation together.'

'We have all the time in the world for holidays together. Life with you is one long holiday anyway! So why don't you indulge yourself this once and go on the cattle drive? You deserve it.'

'I'll think about it.'

It took a fair amount of cajoling from me before my wife finally took the plunge and signed up with the ILPH to attend the next Montana cattle drive. A number of fund-raising events, ably assisted by Al's mother, soon brought in the requisite amount of money for the charity. But although she had been a professional rider, Al had not seriously ridden a horse for many months.

'I'll need to get a bit more fit if I'm going to survive five hours a day for a week in a western saddle,' she announced. 'I'll need to toughen up my inner thighs and bum or I'll be a mass of blisters from day one!'

A horse-riding establishment located not far from our French home offered her the chance to re-familiarise herself with life in the saddle, western style. Bizarrely, this French-run establishment preached the Mongolian form of riding, and even ran theme holidays whereby guests would ride the leafy trails during the day and at night sleep in *yourtes*, circular tents common in Mongolia. At *Le Domaine de Gauchoux* in nearby Peyrat-de-Bellac, Al reawakened her dormant interest in equine matters, and was able to fuel her passion for riding long in the saddle.

'Listen,' she said one day out of the blue. 'This isn't fair on you. Why don't you come with me to Montana?'

'What? Me on a horse. Come off it, darling. You know me and horses…' Although I had been around horses most of my adult life – my first wife and children all rode – I had what I considered to be a healthy respect for the animals. I enjoyed watching them but I had absolutely no desire ever to clamber onto the back of one. 'No, Al. Thanks for the thought, but no.'

'Then I'll only go on the cattle drive if you do something for yourself…'

'Like what, for instance?'

'An adventure race. Ever since you ran the London to Brighton race you've talked about going on another endurance run.' True, fifty-five miles on the open tarmac had whetted my appetite for ultra-distance running. I had been tempted by the challenge of such epic events as the notorious Marathon des Sables, in which runners take on vast desert wastes in a gruelling six-day, self-sufficiency race.

'Well, maybe I'd be interested in the desert race…' I replied, sorely tempted.

'Desert? Yuk, Rich. Sand, sand and more sand… Bit boring don't you think? Aren't there any races in the jungle, for example?' She had a point. Research on the Internet revealed that there was, indeed, a jungle race. The Jungle Marathon took place deep in the Amazon rain forest. Runners would cover two hundred kilometres in a self-sufficiency event that took place in ever-lengthening stages over seven days. Entrants would be required to carry all their own food, water, clothing and equipment for the duration and would sleep in hammocks strung up in the trees. The threat of being eaten by a jaguar, bitten by a deadly poisonous snake, or trampled to death by marauding herds of wild pigs seemed to offer just the thrill I needed to enhance my running. I was hooked.

So that is how my wife was to participate in her own personal dream, helping to bring in a herd of some two hundred head of cattle, while the following month I would journey to Brazil and pit myself against the numerous dangers that lurked in the jungle. Little did I know how these events would be responsible for changing my life utterly and profoundly.

As part of my training for the Jungle Marathon I would condition myself to the expected heat and humidity of Brazil by running in the full summer sun of France's Limousin, where midday temperatures were climbing into the late thirties. Smeared with high factor sun lotion and wearing 'technical' running clothes designed to wick moisture away from the body, I would haul the ten-kilogram rucksack onto my back. A chest-mounted pouch contained energy gels and isotonic capsules to keep me hydrated, and I carried two bottles of water mounted on the rucksack's shoulder straps and a five-litre bladder containing energy drink in the sack itself, fed by a tube. Thus attired, I would head off for my brother's house seventeen miles away then, after a rest, set off for home again.

An ideal way to train for the long distances of the jungle run was to participate in races in France. For me running provided the ideal means of exploring new regions, discovering the wealth of architectural and natural gems that were hidden from view of the motorist. In this way I felt that I was absorbing the culture surrounding my chosen new home rather than just looking without seeing. I was greedy to participate in French races in the same way I had been in England, when exploring new vistas. After becoming enervated with surroundings that had become too familiar, I was once again refreshed.

Kitted for the jungle, I was a curiosity to the French runners. I tackled *Les Gendarmes et les Voleurs du Temps*, a twenty-kilometre race set in the wooded hills of Ambazac. Despite the hardship I suffered in negotiating the steep, rutty trails I found the trek a magnificent way to experience the beauty of the area. Another race saw me sprinting around Lac de Vassivière in a twenty-three kilometre road race that circuited the enormous body of water.

Most spectacular in breathtaking natural beauty were the views afforded by four well-established *sentiers de promenade*, a network of pathways that stem from the heart of the Corrèzien village of Ségur-le-Château. This was the venue for *Les Trails des Brigands*, a forty-kilometre race that connected the pathways before returning to the heart of the village, where a meal awaited contestants. Setting off early in the morning, Al, Jazz and I arrived at the village and parked in the main square under the shade of some lofty *platane* trees, between the river frontage and a tented registration post.

The centre of Ségur – its name taken from the latin *securus*, signifying a 'safe place' – certainly had the feeling of enveloping one in its embrace. A quaint jumble of medieval stone-built and half-timbered, or *colombage* houses clustered at the foot of a craggy, jutting rock. Perched high on the rock is the ruin of a twelfth century feudal château. The village was built within a loop of the broad, shallow waters of the river Auvézère, which trickle over rounded, half-exposed stones.

Renowned for its beauty by the non-profit-making association Le Plus Beaux Villages de France, Ségur-le-Château is steeped in history. Home of the Viscounts of Limoges since 875AD, and loyal to the King of France, it was held under siege and the château all but destroyed by Richard Coeur de Lion. During the Lionheart's third crusade, the overlords strengthened their defences against him with a line of fortified towns and chateaux, of which Ségur was one. The route of the Lionheart also passes

Châlus (where he died), Nexon, Rochechouart, Pompadour and Montbrun.

Later Ségur became the seat of the Cour des Appeaux, a court of appeal that pronounced judgement over the Limousin and Périgordin regions. Today the noble houses of the magistrates and men of law are now comfortable homes for the citizens of the village; here are houses with steeply pitched roofs in slate and stone, façades with elaborate turrets and jutting bartizans, and stone mullioned windows. Stone spiral staircases adorn the exteriors of the houses in the quaint alleyways of the village.

Taking my place at the start line along with the fifty or so runners that were to attempt the race, I waved to Al as she and Jazz prepared to venture out on one of the *sentiers*, then set off at a slow trot in the hot sunshine. Climbing out of the village we soon veered off under the welcome cover of the trees and headed along well-trodden stony pathways, passing through lush meadows and along quiet lanes, following the red ribbons that marked the course. It was one of the most beautiful routes I have ever run and I was determined, despite the discomfort of my heavy sack, to savour the experience. After over two hours of running it was with enormous relief that I found myself re-entering the village, running along the riverbank to finally cross the shallows of the river itself and pass through the finish line to rapturous applause from the crowd gathered there.

The *repas* that followed – a delicious paella and fresh salad – was a welcome end to a memorable day. Al and I lounged on the grass under the shade of the trees to watch as the slower runners staggered across the line, some three hours after commencing the race. A noble effort by all, and one I vowed to return to another year.

Ségur-le-Château, Corrèze

Chapter Seventeen

Winds of change

In August, Al departed from Poitiers airport on the start of her journey to Montana in a strangely melancholic mood that I could not account for. When questioned about this, she merely explained that she was sad to be leaving me, her home and little Jazz, yet I could sense apprehension in her tone. Putting it down to an understandable bout of nerves, a fear of the unknown, I confined the matter to the back of my mind, as I waved her goodbye from the departures hall.

During the following fortnight I occupied my time, when not busy with work or the constant attention required by the vegetable plot, with jungle training runs. Amidst reports of worldwide changes in weather patterns, Limousin sweltered under abnormally hot, dry conditions for the second year running. There was no escape from the intense heat, for even inside the cavernous *grange* the air hung heavy and still, despite having all six double windows wide open day and night. Sleep was difficult and working at my computer became an uncomfortable chore: my hands were constantly bathed in perspiration, making it difficult to manipulate the mouse. My fingers simply slipped off the keys, making my normally accurate touch-typing a hotch-potch of typographical errors.

On one particularly hot day, I accepted an invitation by Jill and Jean-Michel to attend a lunchtime barbecue at the home of their English friends, Elaine and Paul. We had taken refuge from the baking sun in a pleasantly shady area beneath the apple trees in their orchard. After a delicious meal, we sat chatting and sipping wine while the children of the family cavorted in the swimming pool. Suddenly we all became aware that the air had become intensely hot and deathly still. An eerie silence fell over the proceedings.

'Something's brewing!' remarked Jill out of the blue, somewhat ominously. I felt a distinct feeling of disquiet in the pit of my stomach and found myself suddenly, inexplicably worried about Al. I could sense my heart beating faster than normal. Time seemed to stand still and I could sense a rush of air, although there was no wind.

'Mummy!' cried the youngest child all of a sudden. We all snapped to attention and looked around. 'Mummy! The grass is flying!' The young girl was pointing towards the adjacent field from the swimming pool. We all gazed in the direction of her outstretched arm just in time to see the recently cut grass swirling into the air. Before our very eyes the grass took the form of a revolving column almost three metres in diameter. Rising up into the sky, the tornado formed rapidly, drawing the dry strands into a tightly packed mass that was perfectly circular. Decreasing in diameter, the column of grass was carried hundreds of feet into the air in mere seconds, and still it ascended, veering over our heads.

We all stood and marvelled at the sight, but were relieved that the phenomenon had occurred in the adjacent field rather than in the orchard, when we might have all been scooped up by the tornado. After a few minutes the intense heat seemed to dissipate and a light breeze began to waft over us. We watched as the mass of hay began to descend, spreading out as it did over a wide area. Soon we were being showered with strands of dried grass and great clumps of straw, and we imagined the scene miles away, where people sat in their gardens taking aperitifs, as the grass descended from on high.

I still had an uneasy, queasy feeling without knowing quite why, although I knew that it was not just the passing of the tornado. Something else was troubling me.

'What's the matter, love?' said Jill, touching my arm and snapping me back from my reverie. 'Missing Al, I expect?' I smiled wanly, nodding. Yes. That was it. I was missing my wife.

'Anyone for pud?' asked the jovial Elaine, appearing from the kitchen with bowls of fresh fruit salad.

When it was time to leave, Jill, Jean-Michel and I said our farewells to our hosts and headed for our cars.

'First,' said Jill brightly and ever so proudly. *'J'ai un gros saucisse!'* and headed for the bathroom. The mayor's face fell and he shuffled in embarrassment. Elaine, Paul, Jean-Michel and I stood around waiting for Jill's return, not knowing what to say. She soon reappeared, smiling. Jean-Michel drew her aside and tactfully whispered something in her ear. Her eyes widened as a sudden realisation struck her.

'What?' Jill shrieked. 'You're kidding, Jean-Michel?' The mayor shook his head mournfully. 'You mean…?' The mayor nodded. 'Bloody hell! All this time I've thought you were being really crude, saying you had a big sausage and you were really saying…'

'*J'ai un gros souci…*' said Jean-Michel. 'A worry, *mon coeur*, a concern, a preoccupation. Not a fat sausage. It is perfectly polite to say one has a worry if one requires the bathroom before setting off on a trip.'

'Bloody hell,' lamented Jill. 'I thought it sounded a bit crude, but you seemed to use it all the time. So I started to. I've been attending all your mayoral functions and excusing myself by saying…'

'*Oui, mon coeur,*' said the mayor solemnly. 'It has been, shall we say, a leetle indelicate, embarrassing.'

'Oh Jesus! Jean-Michel, I'm so sorry!'

'*C'est pas grave,*' said the mayor, pouting. 'People know you are English. They make allowances…'

Jazz and I waited eagerly at Poitiers airport for the flight from the UK that would bring our beloved Al back into our arms. I had missed her terribly during her trip to Montana, and hoped that the trip had been all she had dreamed of. But I had been confused and a little worried by her minimal contact with me during the trip. I knew that she would be *incommunicado* while out on the trail, but had expected a phone call once she had reached the ranch and civilisation. I received no such call. She had booked an extension to the main trip, which included a visit to Yellowstone National Park. But when she finally did put through a very brief call, three days later, it was to mysteriously inform me that she had remained at the ranch while the other cattle drivers had left without her. She had sounded solemn, at low ebb.

The plane landed and there followed a typically long wait while the bags were taken from the aircraft and fed onto the conveyor belt. Finally, the passengers, having retrieved their luggage, began to filter through the customs and into the arrivals hall, to be met by friends or family. Jazz and I waited just outside the door until eventually Al appeared, looking a little sombre, I thought. She was wearing jeans, cowboy boots, a western-style shirt and a straw cowboy hat.

Jazz was ecstatic to see Al, and promptly jumped up and knocked her to the ground, whereby he began to lick her furiously. Parting the two, I helped her to her feet and hugged her. On the way home in the car, she was effusive about the trip. It had been all that she had hoped for and more, she claimed.

'But why didn't you go on the extension you'd booked?' I asked.

'I needed to think,' she revealed.

'About what?'

'About how I felt.'

'Felt about what?' I was confused. She smiled wanly at me.

'About America,' she said. I snatched fleeting glances at my wife while I guided the car to our home and I was aware that her mind was troubled with conflicting notions.

'So I imagine you want to go back to the States?' I ventured. She nodded. 'To live?' I suggested. She nodded again. I took a deep breath. This was not exactly what I had imagined would be the result of her two weeks in America.

'Then we have to talk this through,' I stated the obvious.

'I guess…' We said nothing more for the rest of the journey. At home, however, she described her adventure in fine detail and it was apparent to me that the experience had touched her so deeply.

'Rich, when I stepped off the plane onto the tarmac I knew that I belonged there…' she announced.

'…at the airport?'

'No, you fool. America. I belonged there. All my life I've thought that I belonged in America. And now I'm convinced of it.' She thought for a moment, then said: 'Rich, would you come back with me next spring… Just to see if you like it?'

'Next spring? Why next spring?'

'Look, I have the chance of running some horse clinics. I've met people there who tell me that my talents as a trainer with British disciplines would be much sought-after by western riders. Even while I was there I managed to help the ranch owner to cure a riding problem she'd had for years.'

'So you've been considering this seriously, I see. OK, we're together through thick and thin. Of course I'll come with you. But you must realise: if we should decide to give up everything here, for one it's not going to be easy to get into the US; two, it wouldn't be possible for me to carry on my work from the States; and three, basically – I might not like it there!'

Al excused herself, saying that she needed to get out of the house, into the fresh air and walk on her own for a while. She headed out across the fields at the back of the *grange* with little Jazz in tow. She was gone for almost three hours. On her return, it was clear that she had been giving serious thought to her notion of returning to the States. She asked me to accompany her along the little *chemin* that ran behind our property. Hand-in-hand we strolled down the dusty path, saying nothing. Little could have prepared me for the bomb-blast that she then delivered.

'Rich, I've been thinking,' she stated. 'This is hard, very hard. But I've worked out that I need to go back to the States to live.'

'Yeah, we'd established that… I said I'd give it a go, didn't I?'

'Yes Rich, but the thing is I need to go back alone.'

'Alone?' This made no sense.

'Rich, this is something I need to do on my own. I belong there. It's my dream. But it's not your dream. I need to go on my own.'

'For how long?'

'For good.'

'So what are you saying, Al? Spell it out.' Was I being pathetically stupid?

'I guess I'm saying that I don't want to be married any more. I don't want to live here in France any more. I guess I don't think of you as a husband any more, but as a friend.'

The following day, Al packed a bag and went to stay with Jill, leaving me with the remnants of a life that I had thought was perfect. As the days wore on, amidst countless telephone discussions, it became clear that my wife's resolve was unshaken. It was not that she approached the situation heartlessly, for I knew that she was suffering with the repercussions of her momentous decision. For me, I had to face up to the bald fact that my life was suddenly in tatters, the dream of our perfect life at Le Mas Mauvis suddenly nothing more than a sour taste in my mouth.

Friends and family rallied around – to both Al and me – but frankly there was little anyone could do. Al's mind was made up. I, however, could not think straight, could not sleep and took to drinking too much red wine and even reverted to my old habit of smoking cigarettes. The situation was reaching boiling point and I felt that I was about to explode.

'Why don't you get away,' suggested Harry. 'Take yourself out of the picture for a while. Take time out to think. Go to the jungle, Rich…' The concept of carrying on with my plans to participate in the Jungle Marathon had eluded me since Al's admission. But now that I thought about it, why not? Perhaps, as my friend had said, taking myself out of the equation for two weeks might help me to reconcile matters in my troubled mind. After all, I had studiously followed a rigorous training programme and felt physically fit and healthy to face the rigours of the event. I left for England the following week to meet up with fellow runners at Heathrow airport, from where we would catch a flight to Brazil and transfer to the campsite in the jungle, where the race would start.

Al had agreed to return to Le Mas Mauvis in order to look after Jazz and the llamas in my absence. It was to be a temporary stay, for she had arranged for our friend Roy to come from England in order to take her back. She intended to move back with her parents in the short term, before returning to the States and her new life. Bizarrely, she wanted nothing of our joint possessions and intended merely to take her clothes. On the day I was due to return from Brazil, my wife Al would leave for England and our marriage and our charmed life together would be finally over.

Swamp, Amazon rainforest

Chapter Eighteen

Call of the jungle

Swaying in my hammock, suspended between two of the slender trees that were dotted around the rough clearing in the dense jungle, I dangled my bruised and blistered feet over the side. I was physically exhausted and mentally numbed by culture shock, unable to ponder the events that had led to the break up of my marriage. This was somewhat a relief, a respite from my torment of the previous weeks. The all-encompassing canopy of the rain forest was a totally alien and hostile environment for a human to find himself in, although it was a staggeringly beautiful place. The oppressive heat – with temperatures well into the forties Celsius – plus sixty per cent humidity, meant that the body was bathed in perspiration constantly. It was impossible to dry oneself. I slugged back more of my water allowance, probably the eighth or ninth litre I had consumed that day. Taking on so much liquid, however, meant that one was obliged to urinate with irritating frequency. All around the campsite men stood against trees relieving themselves, while in the bushes female runners squatted. The jungle was alive with the sound of running water, drowning out the calls of the monkeys, parrots and the thrum of the insects.

The first stage of the Jungle Marathon had been utter hell, and without exception all of the entrants – even the fittest of the one hundred runners who had come to Brazil from all over the world for the event – were thoroughly exhausted. Around me, other hammocks swayed gently, their occupants silent and introspective, arms and legs lolling from the sides. Other runners had zipped themselves into their army-issue, camouflage-patterned hammocks, which had a mesh mosquito screen and a separate waterproof awning in case of the predicted rain. At the centre of the clearing was a large fire contained within huge stones, monitored by a small group of local indians, who were acting as forest guides and ancillary crew. A huge metal cauldron hung suspended over the flames, containing the boiling water with which we runners were to prepare our evening meal: invariably pre-packaged, freeze-dried survival rations. Elsewhere, little gaggles of runners sat around eating, drinking their water supply, and chatting casually about the day's events.

After a gruelling twelve-hour flight from London to São Paulo, on the south-eastern coast of Brazil, the contingent of competitors had been separated into two groups. Half were to fly north to the city of Manaus, then on to Santarém in Pará state; while the others, of which I was one, were to fly via the capital, Brasília, before continuing on to Belém on the northern coast. There, a smaller plane would then carry us to Santarém to be reunited with the other competitors. After one night in a hotel in the beautiful village of Alter-do-Chão, all pretences to comfort would be forgotten as the party boarded two typical Amazon river boats and set off along the Rio Tapajos on a ten hour, one hundred kilometre journey to the base camp at the community of Itapuama, deep within the Floresta Nacional de Tapajos. We would be running back this distance and more to the finish line.

The river trip was itself a truly memorable experience. Although not as well known as the Rio Amazonas itself, the Tapajos is a vast body of water, some nineteen kilometres across in some areas. Where it meets the Amazon River, close to Alter-do-Chão, there is a clearly visible division between the almost blue water of the Tapajos and the brown of the Amazon. As the boats chugged along the riverbank, they were trailed by schools of pink dolphins.

The two days we were to spend at base camp before the race were meant as a means of acclimatising to the heat and humidity, but this was laughably insufficient preparation. All runners had trained long and hard for this event, and most were extremely fit, but the reality of pitting oneself against the hostile environment was quite another matter. The first stage of the race was, at fifteen and a half kilometres long, the shortest of the seven stages that we would cover each day for the next week, but it was perhaps one of the most treacherous and gruelling the organisers could have imposed so early in the event. It began with a fast pelt along a stretch of the sandy beach that skirted the river, followed by a ten-metre swim across a fast-flowing creek, our rucksacks removed and stowed into bin bags to keep them dry. Our shoes, however, were drenched at the outset and would remain that way for the rest of the week. After the river we had a five metre high slope to ascend, followed by kilometres of shockingly steep gradients and dizzying ravines enclosed within the tree canopy. Only a single trail, cut by machete by the indigenous guides, was our means of progress through the jungle. The level of light under the canopy was akin to a constant dusk and it was impossible to fully appreciate the beauty of the surroundings since we had to constantly watch our footing. There were many branches, fallen trees to climb over or crawl under, deep, ankle-twisting holes and twining roots to trip us or slow our progress. We had also to be constantly alert to the presence of poisonous snakes, spiders, scorpions and other creatures of the jungle. Some parts of the trail swarmed with millions of fire ants, while we were frequently assailed by bees and wasps. Nothing seemed safe in the jungle, as most plants, trees and other flora seem to possess razor sharp spines and vicious stings.

Running was impossible, as was walking in some cases: it involved hiking to the top of the inclines only to slither and slide down the other side into shallow creeks of crystal clear water that criss-crossed the terrain. We were warned that there were piranha in the waters, although contrary to popular belief, they were unlikely to attack us and strip our flesh to the bone.

Since this was a self-sufficiency race, each runner was expected to carry all his food, clothing, water and equipment in a rucksack. My sack weighed some ten kilograms at the outset: my only consolation was that each day it would become lighter as I ate through my supply of rations.

The following day, after a sleepless night, kept awake by the screams of the howler monkeys in the trees above our heads, we were roused at six o'clock, breakfasted then prepared our kit for the second stage of the race. When the starting pistol was fired, we lumbered off into the trees in single file, managing only a brisk walk. The faster competitors, including barefoot Brazilian runners, soon passed the slower ones and I eventually found myself staggering along in the company of Simon Hutchings, a RAF engineer in his early thirties. The two of us were similarly paced, so agreed to stick together. It was unwise to run alone in the dangerous jungle, although we knew that a team of 'sweepers' were following at the rear of the field of runners. It was their task to collect anyone forced to drop out of the race, or who might be injured after a fall, or more likely to be suffering the debilitating effects of dehydration.

At pre-race briefings we had been warned of the presence of herds of wild pigs in the undergrowth. These marauding creatures could easily fell a grown man and we were advised, if we should encounter them, to climb a tree or get to high ground. More worrying was the possibility of encountering a jaguar, the most dangerous of predators. Apparently several of these big cats had been released in the jungle by the army, whose job it was to protect and preserve the forest environment. There was little that we mere humans could do to protect ourselves against a jaguar: we would be nothing more than a snack.

'Remember,' the race director had told us. 'Jaguars do not like the smell of humans, so they will probably stay well clear of you.' A comforting thought, although several runners had been convinced that they were being stalked during the first stage and Simon and I had been aware of the distinctive stench of the animals lingering in the foetid air as we shambled along through the trees. On one occasion Simon and I became aware of rustling in the bushes alongside our trail, appearing to keep pace with us. We stood stock still, not really knowing what we should do.

'Simon,' I whispered. 'What the hell is it? What should we do?'

'We're supposed to make ourselves look bigger, mate,' hissed Simon. 'Discourage it from attacking.'

'How the hell do we make ourselves look bigger?'

My companion adopted an aggressive pose, wielding the stick he had been using to assist his ascents and descents as if it were a samurai sword. Shivers of fear ran down my spine. Whatever the creature was, it was approaching. The bushes a few feet away from us parted and the animal stepped onto the trail.

'Holy shit!' murmured Simon, as the animal slowly turned its fearsome head to regard us. 'We're done for, mate!'

'It's a sodding puppy dog!' I said. The little brown mongrel, about the size of a terrier, turned its beguiling gaze away from us as if we were an everyday occurrence in the jungle and continued on its way through the undergrowth. We both broke into peels of laughter, somewhat relieved that the beast had spared us from a severe licking. Although the jungle is dense, we reasoned, our trail probably took us close to habitation, where the puppy apparently lived. He was simply out for an afternoon stroll.

When we reached the campsite at the end of the stage the other runners were excitedly chattering about the creatures they had seen in the jungle, which ranged from huge boa constrictors dangling from the trees, jumping spiders the size of dinner plates, wild pigs with fearsome tusks, capybaras that resembled giant guinea pigs, scorpions and fire ants.

'The bloody jungle is alive!' said Martin, a seasoned ultra runner who went by the name The Little Fat Welshman. 'Did you lads see anything out there, did you?' I looked at Simon and he looked at me. Keep schtum, seemed to be our joint decision: don't mention the puppy.

'Wild dog, mate...' said Simon casually, unclipping his rucksack. 'Bloody ferocious, rabid wild dog. We were damn lucky to get away alive.'

The third stage of the race took us deeper into the jungle and we were obliged to cross vast areas of swamp, up to our thighs in black silt filled with leeches. Clambering over the exposed roots of the vast trees that grew in the swamp, we frequently slipped and fell into the murky water, emerging filthy and stinking. A welcome break came when we reached a river crossing. The fast-flowing and extremely deep water was to be traversed by a rope suspended between trees on opposite banks.

'Take your packs off, guys,' suggested the race marshal stationed at the crossing. 'Grab onto the rope and let yourself relax in the river for ten minutes. It will cool you down.' We did as recommended and the sensation of cold water rushing past our bodies was pure bliss. 'You'll need that,' shouted the marshal. 'Because there's a really disgusting swamp coming up next!'

It was at the end of the third stage of the race that I began to feel unwell. In the middle of the night I was afflicted with stomach cramps, diarrhoea and sickness. While I knew that lariam, the malaria tablets I was taking, had a reputation for disagreeing with the metabolism of some sensitive souls, including the likelihood of severe psychological disturbances, my symptoms were more like a bout of food poisoning. How could the tablets affect my mental state, I reasoned, when I was on the brink of psychosis at the best of times? I went to the medical tent, where I was examined by a doctor, who himself collapsed while taking my temperature as a result of lack of sleep and dehydration. Assigned another medic, I was subsequently given medication and a hammock under the scrutiny of a particularly attractive nurse, who during the night came to check my condition and mop my fevered brow. Being ill had its benefits. But as the night wore on it was clear that I would be unable to start the fourth stage of the race. I was weak, vomiting frequently and had barely slept a wink. Many other runners had been forced to drop out of the race, so I was not alone.

Once the field of runners had set off on the fourth stage, we drop-outs boarded the river boat that would take us to the next campsite in time to greet the first runners. While I had recovered sufficiently to rejoin the race on the fifth stage, I decided not to. I was satisfied with my performance in this intolerable environment and vowed to return another year. My partner Simon had also been forced to drop out of the race at the fourth stage due to painful shin splints in both legs. For the rest of the race, we enjoyed a leisurely river trip, relaxing in our hammocks strung above the deck, as the boat chugged along the course from campsite to campsite. Occasionally we would stop, moor the boat, jump over the side and swim in the cool waters of the Tapajos. The area through which the river flows is known as the 'Caribbean of the Amazon' for its beautiful stretches of sandy beaches.

When I boarded the plane to fly back to London, in order to catch my connection back to France, I began to feel a change within me. Having been displaced for two weeks in the beautiful and intriguing environment of the rain forest, I had been unable to consider what life had recently flung at me. But now I felt somehow stronger, more capable of facing what lay ahead of me. I was physically wasted, but mentally energised. This feeling was not to last long.

I arrived back in the UK from Brazil with a day to kill before returning to France. I was staying the night in the London flat owned by a publisher friend. My mind had become troubled about my imminent return home, for I new that Al would by then have left for good. When she telephoned my mobile later that day, I instinctively knew that it was because she had some untimely news to impart.

'Rich, I'm sorry but Uriel has been taken ill,' she blurted out.

'What happened?' I had not expected this.

'We don't know. I just found him yesterday lying in the field, breathing heavily, very weak. Roy and I managed to get him to the house, then he collapsed.'

'To the house?' I said.

'Well, I thought it best to be near to him, so he's in the hallway downstairs…'

'You put the sick llama in the hall?'

'Yes, Rich. So the vet thinks Uriel's eaten a poisonous plant,' she went on. 'I'm afraid it doesn't look good, Rich. He's been pumped full of drugs but he's in a sort of coma. I'm so sorry. Roy and I have been taking good care of him and, well,' she paused. 'Harry said he'll come over tomorrow and take over…'

'Because you'll be leaving in the morning.'

'Yes,' she said, sounding sad but resigned to the fact. I hung up the phone and strolled down to the Fitzroy Tavern on Charlotte Street, where I consumed several pints of bitter before returning to the flat to pass out and blank out this terrible day.

The following day, hungover and jet-lagged, I headed for Stansted airport to catch my flight back to France. My mobile buzzed in my pocket. It was Al.

'Rich, I'm so sorry. But Uriel didn't pull through…' she said suddenly. Although I knew that the llama was sick, I was nevertheless stunned into silence by the news that he had died. I felt that I could not properly absorb the information I was being given. 'Are you there, Rich?'

'Yes,' I murmured. 'I don't know quite what to say. The llama's dead. And you're leaving.'

'Sorry,' she said sadly. 'I've arranged for a man to come and collect the body. The vet wants to carry out an autopsy to find out the cause. The other two llamas are fine, Rich. Absolutely no problem with them.'

'Great,' I said half-heartedly, mumbled a brief goodbye and hung up. Several hours later, after an uneventful flight and drive back from Poitiers airport, I inserted the key in the lock of the *grange* with a shaky hand. Swinging open the door my nostrils were immediately assailed by the acrid odour of llama urine. At the back of the hallway was a large pile of wet straw, which still bore the imprint of Uriel's small body. My emotions were mixed. I knew that I had plenty to weep for but I could not summon up a single bitter tear. I climbed the stairs to the *grenier* with weary legs. The vast, open-plan room seemed even more voluminous than usual.

Little Jazz, who was obviously confused by the events of the last few days, sat shivering in his bed, as if petrified to move. Ordinarily the exuberant pup would have come bounding over to greet me. I slumped down next to him in his bed and held him in my arms. Eventually, he started licking my hands.

'Just you and me now, Jazzou,' I said. I sat there for a very long time, as the pup nuzzled into my body. From this vantage, gazing around the room, I could detect no outward signs that any of my wife's possessions were missing. She had taken only her clothes, abandoning everything else that had been part of our joint life together. I reflected that she would be in England by now, returned to the bosom of her family and ready to start the next chapter of her life. In a strange way, I wished her well.

'These last seven years with you have been the best years of my life,' I recalled her recent words. 'But it was a stage in both our lives, which is now over.' A stage our marriage might have been for Al, but for me it had not quite come to an end. Al simply felt she needed to be in America. I still lived surrounded by the trappings of our partnership. I would need time to reconcile this situation.

The next months passed in a blur as I attempted to keep pace with my workload, attend to the needs of Jazz and my two surviving llamas, and maintain the house and property. I was unsure whether I wanted to remain at Le Mas Mauvis. My instincts told me that the dream was over, that I should sell up and move away. The memories here were too strong of the life Al and I had created. But where would I go?

'Don't make any decisions yet,' advised Harry when I suggested that I might leave the hamlet. 'Leave it for at least a year. Be sure of making the right decision.' It was wise advice. Meanwhile, I knew that I was beginning to lose enthusiasm for my surroundings. I was less meticulous with the grass-cutting and constant strimming necessary to keep the property looking neat and well cared-for. I could not even bring myself to clean the house properly and tended to walk around the vast *grenier* blind to the mounds of dust that were accumulating, and the cobwebs that dangled from the beams. While I had adored cooking for both of us, now that I was alone I existed on a diet of frozen pizzas and quick-cook pasta, drank far more red wine than was good for me, and smoked cigarettes like they were going out of fashion. I even abandoned my beloved running, content instead to slouch on the sofa in front of a blaring television set.

Our marriage was irretrievable, this much was made abundantly apparent. Al's resolve was unshaken, as our numerous telephone conversations confirmed, and I knew that I would have to take the next onerous step. I would be unable to move on with my life unless I took legal action to divorce my wife. Severing the legal bond between us was just a part of relinquishing the emotional bond. It was a painful process, but at least one that promised to be relatively straightforward. We would not have to undergo a lengthy two-year legal separation, as can be the requirement in some divorce proceedings. Unlike my previous divorce, which had dragged on for years because of my former wife's recalcitrance, I would be able to file a petition that cited Al's unreasonable behaviour. She agreed wholeheartedly with this definition and promptly signed and returned the relevant papers. It was necessary for me to sign an affidavit that would have to be witnessed either by an English-registered solicitor or court official. Enquiries proved that finding an English solicitor living in France was problematic. A call to the British Embassy in Bordeaux, the city under whose jurisdiction my French home fell, revealed that it would be possible to visit the embassy and have my affidavit witnessed. Reluctant to make the long trip to Bordeaux for a process that would take approximately two minutes, I opted instead to fly to England. Combining the trip with a short working trip to London, I took the opportunity to visit the court in Tunbridge Wells, the district in which we were married. Taking the train from London – which brought back old memories of my previous life as a commuter on that very line – I was able to have my affidavit witnessed and submitted to the court in less than five minutes, catching the next train back to the city.

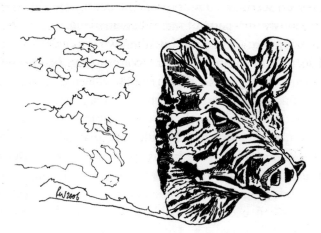

Boar's head detail, hunting knife by Phillip Wiles

Chapter Nineteen

Ties that bind us

My loneliness and despair were somewhat alleviated by an unlikely friendship that developed between me and an ebullient Belgian named Patrick Vandevivere. I had first encountered the Flemish fellow at a barbecue to which Al and I had been invited by our English neighbours, Jeff the builder and his wife Amanda, some months previously. My initial impressions had been far from favourable. I considered the man to be overpoweringly loud, overbearingly opinionated, blatantly bigoted and an outrageously unrepentant male chauvinist pig.

Breezing into the soirée clutching two bottles of vodka, he had seen fit to commandeer any conversation that followed, espousing the biggest load of drivel I had heard in a long time. With him was his partner of three years, the attractive and comparatively placid Sarah. How she could have put up with this bombastic individual I could not imagine. In his early forties, I guessed, he was in my eyes an archetypal Belgian. Tall and large framed, he had blue-eyes with long blonde lashes and straight, fine, blonde hair cut in a kind of pageboy style that had been fashionable at one time, but rarely by men of his advanced age. He had a high forehead and quite delicate features that belied his overblown personality. In fact, he looked rather like an overgrown schoolboy.

'Obnoxious bastard,' I had commented to Al, when we had managed to extricate ourselves from the drunken melée, which had resulted from the Belgian braggart and poor, gullible Jeff quaffing both bottles of vodka, followed by a bottle of gin. Jeff, who led a relatively quite life and didn't get out much, was chastised by poor Amanda, who did not drink. She abandoned the disastrous evening early, escaping to her bed under the pretext of a headache.

Although the Belgian had bought a barn for conversion in a nearby hamlet – suitably distant that his booming voice could not be heard from our own village – it had been Sarah who had purchased the large detached house just round the corner from us in Le Mas Mauvis. A teacher, she planned to visit the house during the long school holidays. But it was this house that the dreaded Patrick had chosen to occupy, while directing renovation works at the same time as, bizarrely, completing studies for an English law degree. Soon villagers were agog at the sight of a large pink Belgian wearing nothing but too-tight, white tennis shorts disporting himself on a plastic patio lounger on the patch of concrete in front of the house. Not only this, but he was also apt to shower naked in the garden using only a hosepipe, there being no plumbing facilities at the property at that time.

So how could I possibly have warmed to the dubious charms of this loud-mouthed Flem? This phenomenon had occurred in the wake of my failed relationship with Al, and his with Sarah. Each evening it had become the norm for the Belgian to be witnessed standing by the *poubelle* in the centre of the hamlet, shouting into his mobile phone. The location of the wheelie bin was the only hot spot where a signal could be received. On this evening, however, he had turned up at my door looking very down in the mouth.

'I just thought dat you might want a bit of company,' he said in an oddly muted tone. His accent was a blend of neat Belgian with a dash of Yorkshire relish. The northern influence had been gleaned from the many years he had spent living in England. 'My point is, we're both in de same bleeming boat, you and me, isn't it? Trouble wit women.'

While I had no intention of sharing my woes with the man, against my better judgement I invited him in. During our subsequent conversation – by necessity fuelled by a bottle of red wine – I came to realise that Patrick was, in fact, a sensitive soul. He was distraught at the demise of his relationship. This person was, if not an entirely different man to our previous encounter, a much subdued one. His outward brashness, I realised, was not merely idle boasting, for he was much travelled, widely read, intelligent. Once one had penetrated the flamboyant outer shell of the man, the nut that lay within was, in fact, hugely entertaining.

While I could not bring myself to agree with his extravagant opinions on the inner workings of the fairer sex, I realised that Patrick spoke a lot of common sense. He was a man who had studied psychology and was apt to psychoanalyse himself as a means of better understanding his motives, his failings and his successes. In the weeks that followed I learned more about my new acquaintance and his colourful history and found myself growing strangely fond of this outrageous character.

My brother and I had taken to frequenting a bar, *Au Cochon Fidèle*, situated midway between my brother's house and Le Mas Mauvis, and a handy place for meeting up with him and Stephanie. Locally known as the Pink Pig, the establishment – run by a jovial Parisian called Olivier – not only offered a praiseworthy selection of hundreds of strong Belgian beers, but also was occasional host to live music or played an admirable selection of blues and jazz. We could dine handsomely for only five euros on *la pitance*, a wooden platter in the shape of a pig, piled high with bread, a selection of cheeses, cured ham, grated carrot and sublime potato salad. If there was no live band playing on a particular night, no matter: Patrick would hold the floor and regale us with tales of his eventful and wholly unbelievable life.

'I'm quite funny, I am,' he was oft to remark, quite immodestly. And it was true: the Belgian never ceased to amuse us, although it was always difficult to make one's own voice heard above his monologues.

'So why the English law degree?' interjected the Count one evening, bravely butting into one of Patrick's tales.

'Well, Phill, let me just tell you. I just thought dat it might come in handy,' replied the Belgian. 'It was quite fricking difficult really, because I don't read English very well.'

'Oh, and what did you do before the degree?' ventured Phill, while he was onto a winning streak.

'I used to export VW Beetles from Belgium to England. Dat's after I sold de pub in Antwerp…'

'You owned a pub in Antwerp?' I asked.

'Yes, and a night club. I bought dem when I left de Belgian police force.' The thought of our friend as staunch upholder of the law, and particularly the vision of him dressed in a uniform, was just too much to seriously contemplate.

'So why are you here in France, then, Patrick?' asked Stephanie.

'Well, Stephanie, my point is this. Opportunity.'

'Opportunity in what?' continued my sister-in-law.

'I don't know. But I've got plenty of ideas. I can tell you about dem…'

'You know, Patrick,' I announced before the Belgian could begin, my mood softened by a bottle of a local brew, Lemovice. 'I've amended my initial opinion of you.'

'What's dat den, Richard?' said Patrick, momentarily sidetracked from another lengthy discourse. It would only be a brief respite, I was certain.

'First I thought you were an obnoxious bastard…'

'Dat's nice, Richard.'

'Not at all, Patrick. But I've grown used to you and I've realised I made a gross error of judgement. I've come to realise that you're not a bastard at all.'

'Thank you, Richard. But dat just leaves obnoxious…'

'It does.' There was a brief pause as Patrick contemplated my words.

'So what exactly does dat mean? Obnoxious? Does dat mean I'm difficult?'

'Not exactly, my friend,' I replied. 'Not exactly.'

Bonne Chance!

The Yorkshireman David Wrightam and his partner Dennie Hands had been an item for five years and had lived together for more than two of those years in a state of unmarried bliss. They had displayed no outward signs of joining together in wedlock, although they were clearly besotted with each other. Both had been married previously. The Yorkshireman had divorced his wife many years ago, when his daughters Kate and Anna were quite young, and had done an admirable job of bringing them up alone, while holding down a full-time and responsible job. He had become used to his own company and had never considered the fact that he might one day meet someone with whom he would want to share his life. Dennie had been married twice before and had three children, Alex by her first husband and Anne-Marie and Tom by her second. All their joint offspring were now grown up and living their own lives, and so the pair had settled into their own happy existence together in France.

The dour Yorkshireman had once confessed to me that, although he loved Dennie to distraction, he could never see himself wanting to get married again: 'No, lad,' he had said, drawing thoughtfully on his ever-present cigarette. 'Once is quite enough for me. I can't see it 'appening again, lad. Won't make same mistake twice. And any 'ow, I'm fifty-six and she's fifty-five. We've both been through't mill, lad…'

He had seemed ineffably adamant about the matter, so it was something of a surprise when he paid me a visit one afternoon with a coy confession. Caught in a romantic moment while walking with his *amante* by the sea at La Rochelle, the sentimental old fool had seen fit to metaphorically drop to one knee and pop the pertinent question. To his overwhelming joy, tinged with a certain degree of trepidation verging on blind fear, the gorgeous Dennie had agreed to be his blushing bride. A summer wedding beckoned. But that was just the start of their problems.

French law recognises only the civil marriage. Religious ceremonies are an optional extra, but have no legal status, and can only be held after the civil ceremony has taken place, although this can be on the same day. The civil marriage must be performed by an *officier de l'état civil*, a French civil authority. This may be the *maire*, the *adjoint*, or deputy mayor, or a *conseiller municipal*, a city councillor. The happy couple planned to marry in the local Mairie at St. Lèger Magnazeix, where civil ceremonies such as this – occurring, as they did, rather infrequently – are generally presided over by none other than the mayor himself, Monsieur Rouaux. This honour does not carry the same kudos as it perhaps would in England, since in France the mayoral office is frequently held on a part-time basis. Therefore, the mayor himself – the man reading the wedding vows and pronouncing the union legally binding – might in fact, when not adorned with his mayoral sash, be an abattoir attendant, a used car salesman, or a pig farmer.

The wedding was to be a quiet, intimate occasion with just immediate family and a few close friends in attendance. 'Nothing brash or flashy, lad,' explained the Yorkshireman. 'And we're certainly not 'aving a grand bash, that's for bloody certain!' The joint offspring, however, had other plans, when the news of the impending marriage was revealed. No way would they permit their parents to marry without marking the occasion with at least a modest soirée. Soon, almost one hundred guests had been invited to the rapidly expanding occasion: a lunch party was planned as a reception in Le Mas Mauvis, where the Yorkshireman and his bride-to-be currently lived, with a candlelit evening barbecue, music and dancing. 'I think the wedding's been hijacked, lad!' confessed poor David, who had taken to escaping to the sanctuary of the *grange* for a few beers and countless cigarettes while arrangements mushroomed around him.

To enable the marriage by foreign nationals in France, one of the parties must have been resident in the commune where the service was to take place for a minimum of forty consecutive days prior to the marriage (or for thirty days if both parties were resident in different communes). Before the marriage could be countenanced by the authorities, however, numerous documents would have to be produced: an Affidavit of Law, the *certificat de coutume*, and an Affidavit of Marital Status, which certify that the parties are free to marry under the law of their country; the *extrait d'acte de naissance*, or birth certificate; certified copies of any previous marriage certificates or divorce certificates; and an *attestation tenant lieu de déclaration en vue de mariage ou de non-remariage*, which is effectively a certificate of celibacy.

Additionally, it would be necessary to provide *justicatifs de domicile*, proof of ownership of a French property, valid passports or *cartes de séjour*. In the case where pre-nuptial agreements were made, a certificate must be submitted to the Mairie via notary. Where no pre-nuptial contacts exist, the marriage would be carried out under the *communauté réduite aux acquets*, which means that whatever the parties owned before the marriage, or whatever they may inherit in the future from other sources, would remain theirs if the marriage should end. Anything that the couple should acquire during the marriage would be considered jointly owned.

The Mairie seemed to be ruled over by a bumptious, officious clerk with an often aggressive manner. At the numerous interviews the couple were obliged to attend, the clerk seemed determined to adhere strictly to the letter of the law, scouring ancient legal statutes for long-forgotten clauses that might forbid the union. On these occasions, the mayor himself sat at his desk, hands clasped in front of him, grinning inanely, nodding his head and barely uttering a word. To cap it all, since David and Dennie had the audacity to be English, all the required documentation would by necessity have to be translated into French by a sworn translator, the *traducteur assermenté*. The formidable notary, Mâitre Marsolet, was such an *agréée*, but her services would come at a hefty price. The simple affair was on the verge of turning into an expensive and complicated extravaganza.

Not only that, but it seemed that the Mairie would require other undertakings that would prove that there was no just cause why the happy couple should not be bound together in the chains of wedlock. Some of these requests were utterly ridiculous and often hugely and embarrassingly intrusive. One day, when the marriage plans were still rumbling on and David and Dennie's patience was beginning to wear thin, the Yorkshireman telephoned me with an update, and some revealing and relieving news.

'Well lad, you'll be pleased t'know that I don't have AIDS, and Dennie's not pregnant!'

'A comforting thought indeed,' I said. 'But why are you telling me this?' David explained. The couple had been asked to provide evidence that they were not the personal carriers of a range of ailments. A *certificat d'examen médical prénuptial*, less than two months old, would be issued by a doctor *en vue de mariage*. Serological tests were required for syphilis and blood typing, and for a woman rubella and toxoplasma. A woman would not be allowed to marry again until three hundred days after a divorce. Presumably this time lapse (approximately nine months) was intended to prove that the woman could not have fallen pregnant by her previous spouse, and thus be seen to be cuckolding her new lover. Because Dennie's last divorce had only recently been made absolute by the English courts, she would have to suffer the indignity of having to undergo a pregnancy test. Her complaint was met with a shrug by her doctor. '*Oui, je comprends, madame*. But it is the law,' he said, before packing her off for an appointment at a local clinic.

Once all of this documentary evidence had been compiled and submitted to the Mairie, the banns could be posted, no less than ten days preceding the date of the marriage. After the marriage ceremony itself, the *livret de famille* would be issued to the couple. This official document serves not only as a record of the union but would also note subsequent events, such as births, deaths, divorce or changes of name.

If all this seemed too much red tape, a couple could opt for France's legal alternative to marriage, the *Pacte Civil de Solidarité*, which also recognises same-sex couples. Although France did not allow same-sex marriage, a domestic partnership law was passed by the National Assembly in 1999, which included gay partnerships. The PaCS, as it is known, bestowed some of the legal benefits of a traditional marriage, including claims to inheritance, tax relief, housing rights, social security, and some financial allowances. Partners hitched under PaCS are considered liable for each other's debts and contracts, although they do not receive adoption, lineage or custody rights.

The occasion of the wedding itself was blessed with a glorious day, as the threatened thunderstorms tactfully kept their distance and allowed the summer sunshine to beat down unfailing on Le Mas Mauvis. The civil ceremony, held in the austere surroundings of the Mairie at St. Lèger Magnazeix, was witnessed by almost one hundred guests, crammed into every conceivable nook and cranny within the building. Outside, many more who could not squeeze in were content to cluster around the windows and doors. Monsieur Le Maire, wearing his red, white and blue sash of office, greased-down hair, a lopsided smile and a twinkle in his eyes, dictated the official decree from a crib sheet, while his officious assistant hung on his every word as if waiting for him to make an error. Apart from difficulty in pronouncing the happy couple's surnames, Wrightam and Hands – a terrible set of tongue twisters for a hapless Frenchman – his recitation was faultless. David and Dennie, looking a mite nervous, fulfilled their part of the proceedings by saying '*oui*' when prompted.

After group photographs were taken on the Mairie forecourt, a long motorcade sped its way along the rod-straight road back to Le Mas Mauvis, tailing the happy couple in their chauffeur-driven vehicle, horns blaring loudly in the typical post-wedding style dictated by French custom, little fluttering bows tied to the roof aerials. Back at the hamlet, a bountiful lunchtime spread was laid out for the guests on the perfectly manicured lawns. Several open-sided pergolas had been pitched around the garden, while other tables and chairs were clustered under the shade of the trees. In the evening, as darkness descended, candlelight and solar-powered garden lamps flickered into life and the smoky aroma of a splendid barbecue filled the air.

Heading back to the *grange* around midnight, just as the rain started to fall, I stood at the gate and congratulated a tired-looking David, dapper as ever in his newly-purchased grey linen suit.

'Eeh, well, kid,' he said, drawing contemplatively on an illicit cigarette (for the Yorkshireman had promised his new bride that his smoking days were over). 'I suppose all this were a bit close to 'ome for you… Divorce looming and all.' I considered his thoughtful words, but shook my head.

'No, David,' I said. 'I'm very happy for you both. And I still believe in the institution of marriage. I'd do it again without question. If I could find the right person. I thought I had, but it seems not. I don't hold it against Al. It's obviously best for her, and I guess best for me in the long run. We always said that if either one of us thought it wasn't working, we should say so.'

I returned to the *grange*, undressed and climbed into bed, feeling for the first time that the vast room had become somewhat inhospitable. What was I doing here, alone in the middle of France? My previous, well-signposted direction in life had turned out to be a blind alley. I fell asleep wondering whether the good luck I had been blessed with so far – my *bonne chance* – had finally run dry.

Le Menhir de Cinturat

Chapter Twenty

Allegory and acronym

Your bathroom stinks!' remarked the Count, emerging from the room after relieving himself, with a look of utter distaste on his face.

I felt a surge of embarrassment. What had I eaten the previous night, I struggled to remember? Nothing too noxious, I thought. But my brother's words were disturbingly true. Despite Jeff Dedman's costly installation of the grease trap, which had seen the lake of grey sludge in the field dissipate, the bathroom still emitted a horribly foul odour.

'There's a damp patch on the back wall, too,' continued my brother, not one to leave a subject well alone. He indicated the bloom of salts leeching out of the exposed stonework on the wall against which the WC and shower were set. Outside, a huge semi-circular tidemark could be clearly seen on the stonework.

'It's always been there,' I admitted. 'It just never seems to dry out.' Even after we had cured the previous problems we'd had with a pipe that leaked unnoticed for months, resulting in our household wasting half the water supply of the entire hamlet, the damp patch still remained. But I had had my fill of do-it-yourself. 'Never mind, leave it.' I said. But the Count, determined to buck up my ideas, had other plans. The following day he returned to the *grange* clutching a large plastic suitcase, which he opened to reveal an enormous power hammer.

'Come on,' he prompted. 'We'll dig up the floor and take a look. Something is definitely not right under there.' A few hours later he had dug a considerable hole in the six-inch thick concrete floor, which I had cast years previously during the initial stages of renovation. The disgusting smell worsened the deeper he dug and the sub-base was found to be soaking wet and quite slimy. The source of the dampness seemed to come from beneath the shower tray itself, which had been laid on the concrete slab.

'We'll have to take the shower tray up,' said my brother. It took us another hour to free the ceramic tray from the concrete that bound it to the floor. We hauled the heavy tray out of the way, having disconnected the rudimentary and laughably inefficient waste trap. Phill set to work again with the power hammer and very soon the entire floor of the bathroom was littered with a pile of concrete rubble.

More dampness was evident. Eventually we managed to clear enough of the concrete to expose the grey plastic drainpipe that carried the waste water away and into the septic tank. It was then that we discovered the root of the problem, a last laugh on behalf of poor, dearly departed Monsieur Laborde, the plumber-electrician. His methods of 'finishing' a job had been slipshod to say the least, but this installation was possibly his finest hour of ineptness. Instead of being connected to the drainpipe with a conventional socket, the branch pipe leading from the shower tray was simply shoved into a roughly sawn hole cut in the side of the pipe. Needless to say, the joint was wholly ineffective, sporting a wide gap around its perimeter.

'What else is connected to this pipe?' demanded the Count, quite grumpily.

'The shower, the washing machine, the dishwasher upstairs, the drainage system for the *chauffe-eau*...' I said, counting off the appliances on my fingers, mentally tracing the route of each waste outlet to this pipe. 'Oh, and the kitchen sink. And the bathroom basin.'

'When was this installed?' asked the Count.

'Must be, ooh, seven years ago...' I calculated roughly. It seemed that for seven years we had been discharging our entire 'grey' water waste system underneath the bathroom floor. This foul water had, unable to drain away efficiently, festered and fermented ever since Al and I had owned the property. This accounted for the foetid aroma that had become an embarrassing trademark of our bathroom.

A few days later, having made good this appallingly shoddy legacy from Monseiur Laborde, I travelled down to Limoges with the intention of treating myself to something extremely costly and unnecessary. I came away from Mr. Bricolage's fine do-it-yourself warehouse the proud owner of a spanking new, and spankingly expensive, all-in-one, state-of-the-art shower unit, with luxurious bath-sized tray, overhead shower rose and wall-mounted pressure jets designed to blast away worries and invigorate the body. It was quite the most ugly, modern and ill-fitting accoutrement I could have chosen for my rustic barn conversion, but I had been feeling in a perverse mood.

Was my world crumbling? What sins had I committed to warrant my current spate of bad luck? What other horrors would come to light, I contemplated, as I stood naked in the shower with purifying needles of scalding water peppering my humble body? I emerged, red and blotchy – it was quite painful, actually – but thoroughly cleansed of my sins. Despite the refreshing and curative qualities of my new shower appliance, however, nothing seemed to wash away the bald fact that my home and my life felt somehow tainted.

'That damned gypsy Bo-Bo has put a curse on me!' I moaned. 'My *bonne chance* has been sucked from my body...' My brother regarded me through the rear-view mirror of his car with an expression of pity on his face. He always looked at me that way, but somehow it was different this time. Sitting next to him on the passenger seat, my sister-in-law exchanged a subtle, knowing glance with her spouse. I could swear that the old Count raised his eyes to the heavens. I was being treated with kid gloves, I knew. My nearest and dearest obviously felt sorry for me because they had offered to take me on an outing. Sitting in the back seat of the car I felt like a demented granddad, who would soon have to be delivered back to the home for the mentally challenged.

'So where is it we're going?' I said, changing the subject, since neither of my companions had responded to my claim of mystical intervention from the gypsy mechanic. I peered through the misted-up side window as Phill steered the car through the traffic-choked centre of Bellac.

'I told you already,' said the Count, his patience worn a tad thin. 'We're going to see some big boulders and have a nice walk. And if you're good we'll buy you an ice-cream.' He laughed at his own smart-arse comment, goading gullible Stephanie to laugh at my expense as well. I sneered at my brother's reflection.

'Huh!' I grunted petulantly. I did not appreciate the Count's sarcasm. I left them to their jibes and pretended to drink in the beauty of the surrounding countryside. We passed through the town and took a left turn along a straight road that led towards the villages of Blond and Mortemart.

Forty kilometres north west of Limoges, Mortemart is the only village in the Haute-Vienne to be classified as one of the most beautiful in France. Built around a tenth-century fortified *château* of which the keep, guard's room and *salle de justice* still remain, the *bourg* was also the site of a Carmelite monastery built in 1330. At the centre of the village is a fine seventeenth century *halle*, an open-sided, roofed marketplace that still hosts sales of farm produce on Sunday mornings in July and August.

Leaving Mortemart, we headed off towards the village of Blond, then on the way to Villerajouze, took the winding road as it climbed into the hills of the Monts de Blond, reaching an altitude of five hundred metres. We marvelled as breathtaking, panoramic views unfolded, although the steep drops at the side of the road made Phill quake with fear. The slopes of the Monts are strewn with remnants of prehistory: sacrificial stones, *dolmen* and *menhirs* from the Neolithic and Gallo-Roman periods. One such site that has drawn the curious for generations was to be our first goal, *le Rocher de Puychard*, not far from the village of Montrol-Sénard.

Set in the heart of the mountains, most of this village has been styled as an open-air artisanal museum. Visitors arriving between May and mid-November can stroll around various restored stone buildings for an insight into what life was like in a traditional Limousin village at the beginning of the twentieth century. The various restorations include an elementary school, a bakehouse and a laundry. There is also an accurate reconstruction of a typical Limousin house, a *chabatz d'entrar*, with an integral cattle shed and storeroom. Fascinating too is the workshop of a *sabotier*, where traditional wooden clogs were crafted. The imposing cemetery contains a daunting funerary vault, the *lanterne des morts*, in which reside ancient granite tombs with upright *stèles*, or stones bearing plaques.

Leaving the village, we presently entered a stretch of road flanked by dense woodland, and came upon a small, deserted parking space. A sign pointed up a slope into the woods. We parked the car and headed off up the little stony path, soon entering a clearing in the trees. Huge boulders twice or three times the height of a man were scattered erratically around the clearing. The site, dimly lit through the sunlight filtering through the leaves of the trees, was awesome and somewhat disconcerting; a shiver ran down my spine. Some boulders, craggy and pitted with mysterious holes and scored with furrows, appeared to protrude from the hard earth. Others, like giant, rounded beach stones, green with moss, were stacked one on top of the other, somewhat precariously. Trees, self-seeded generations ago, had grown so close to some of the rocks that their trunks had moulded around the stone. What was stunning was that the positions of the boulders were no accident of nature: they had been arranged deliberately by ancient druids, in what was regarded as a symbolic site. The rock pile marked the boundary between the *langue d'Oc* and the *langue d'Oil*, or the Occitan and Old French languages.

A slate plaque fixed to one of the boulders bore a dedication to Frédéric Mistral, poet and winner of the Nobel Prize in Literature in 1904. Mistral, born in the Rhone Valley town of Maillaine in southern France, was a lifelong champion of the Provençal language, also known as Occitan. The plaque itself was written in this intriguing tongue. The language, strictly speaking a dialect, bears a close relationship to French, Italian and Catalan. Occitan was the language disseminated by wandering troubadours and men of culture in the South, which fell into decline with the spread of dialects from the north of the country.

One of the largest boulders had been inset with iron handgrips, well worn by many years of intrigued visitors. Phill and I scaled the rock, the top of which was broad, gently curved and pierced with large, basin-sized holes that were filled with brackish water. On one side we gazed down at Stephanie, some three metres below, while at the opposite side the ground fell sharply away towards the road and beyond into a deep, forested valley. The sensation was quite giddying, and we quickly scrambled back down to earth again.

Back at the car, we consulted our map. The area was veritable trove of megaliths. *Dolmen*, the flat stones set atop vertical supports, believed to be ancient burial chambers, fairly littered the area, and there was a large count of *menhirs*, or standing stones. The *Roc Tremblant de Boscartus* was a massive boulder weighing around one hundred and twenty tonnes. Perched nervously on its plinth, the stone was subject to frequent attempts to dislodge it: the landowner supplied stout poles with which visitors could prod the rock. The *Pierre à Sacrifices*, a knobbly chunk of stone in a nondescript site off a long public footpath, was less impressive; its many indents and gashes were rumoured to have been the result of its violent history, but the legends were more than likely a creative interpretation of natural erosion.

We found our bearings once more and headed off to the site of what was billed as a truly remarkable stone, *Le Menhir de Cinturat*. Remarkable it certainly was. Concealed in a small clearing, the standing stone, over five metres tall above ground, juts into the overhanging branches of the trees like an accusatory finger. Roughly arrow-shaped, and leaning slightly to one side, the *menhir* – which sound tests have revealed is buried over two metres beneath the ground – has a narrow, horizontal ledge cut about half way up. Legend has it that a person wishing to marry in the following year should lob a stone onto the ledge: should the projectile remain there, the wish would be granted. I wondered bleakly whether performing this mystical slam-dunk would breathe new life into one's failed marriage. Somehow, I doubted this. Nevertheless, I tossed a chunk of granite onto the ledge. The stone rolled along the ledge, then tottered before descending to earth, narrowly missing the head of the Count, who had appeared from an inspection of the *menhir's* rear façade.

'You always were a useless tosser,' he remarked. My brother always did have an uncanny knack of quashing a poignant moment.

Despite my marital and plumbing problems, life had to go on. I had to work. I had to maintain a semblance of being able to cope with the practicalities of day to day living, although inwardly I felt that I could not. Since I had become a permanent resident in France it had become necessary for me to regularise my situation in the eyes of the law and to join the system. Foreigners are obliged to do this within three months of moving to the country, and the authorities regard any individual to be resident if they spend over one hundred and eighty three days in France during a calendar year. Although concerned friends and acquaintances had warned us about the costly implications of joining the French system, particularly when it came to paying income taxes, there was no denying that we would be living and working in the country and I had no intention of searching for loopholes in order to avoid paying what was legally due – even though it might turn out to be expensive. Moving to France had been our choice and we had to live with the consequences. Too many Britons arrive in France with the express intention of milking the numerous benefits while not paying for the privilege.

Al had commenced the process of applying for our residency approval, the *Carte de Séjour*. She obtained the necessary forms from the *préfecture de police*, the police station, and started to collect together the various documents and certificates that would need to accompany our applications. In addition to certified copies of our passports, we required four recent passport photographs, full birth certificates, marriage and, in my case, a divorce certificate. An enquiry at the Mairie revealed that all documents would need to be translated into French by a person approved by the French Consulate. Several copies of each would need to be submitted. Furthermore, we would need to provide proof of the purchase of our property and details of our employment. We were warned that the process of obtaining the *Cartes de Séjour* could take anything from a few weeks to several months.

I had sorely neglected my responsibilities in regularising my working situation in France and I now determined to set matters straight. First of all I needed to establish whether I would be required to pay French or English income taxes. After countless enquiries to the tax offices in both the UK and France, the results had still been inconclusive. Both countries appeared to be squabbling over who would get their sticky hands on a portion of my loot. The Inland Revenue in England said I must continue to pay UK taxes because my work was carried out exclusively for UK companies and that I was paid in sterling, while the French authorities insisted that, since I was resident in France, I must pay into the French system. Eventually, we managed to fight our way through the morass and determined that residents in France – whether English or foreign nationals – are obliged to be taxed in France on their global earnings.

Taxes in France are calculated annually according to an individual's earnings from the previous calendar year, commencing on the first of January. Calculations are based on information that the individual must provide on a form called *la déclaration des impôts*. The form must be completed and sent to the local tax office by the twenty-eighth of February each year, although the deadline is frequently extended. Taxes may be paid in three instalments spread over the year, or by a monthly direct debit system. In order to prevent people who still have tax liabilities in the UK from being taxed twice on the same element of income, there exists a double taxation agreement between the UK and France. This agreement, formulated in 1969 and amended by four protocols since then, goes by the snappy title of The Convention for the Avoidance of Double Taxation and the Prevention of Fiscal Evasion with respect to Taxes on Income.

Although my sister-in-law Stephanie was going to act as my bookkeeper, I would need to find a French *expert-comptable*, a certified public accountant, to prepare my annual accounts and submit them to the tax authorities. We were recommended an accountant and made an appointment to visit her office in Ambazac, midway between Le Mas Mauvis and Limoges, set in the forested hillsides of the Monts d'Ambazac. Madame Routet's office was a tiny single room – previously a shop on the high street – not much bigger than a broom cupboard. Stephanie and I wedged ourselves in front of her desk, between mounds of official-looking accountancy tomes. The accountant had kindly agreed to assist in the completion of the complicated form I had received, which would enable me to register my business. The definition of recognised professions was complex and confusing in the extreme and Stephanie and I had been mystified by some of the questions the form asked. Madame Routet, a pleasant, smiling lady with curly blonde hair and wearing a fetchingly semi-casual denim trouser suit, prepared to take details of exactly what it was that I did.

'*Alors*, monsieur, what exactly do you do?' she said.

'I am a self-employed editor and author,' I volunteered. She looked somewhat bemused. 'I write books and magazine articles, edit books and magazines and develop new magazines.' She looked even more puzzled.

'*Rédacteur et auteur?*' she mused, stressing the '*et*'. She began leafing through an extremely thick, flimsy-paged book with minuscule writing. She flipped to another fat tome, mouthing the entries to herself slowly and deliberately, then shaking her head. '*Non. Il n'existe pas!*'

'What do you mean, madame? It doesn't exist?' interjected Stephanie.

'Monsieur Wheels cannot be both editor and author. *Il n'existe pas en France.* Can you not use another description?'

'No I can't, actually. That's what I do. Both.' I said, slightly miffed. Madame Routet sighed, then grabbed another book and began riffling through the pages again. After what seemed like an eternity, she looked up, smiling.

'I suppose you could just say that I am a journalist,' I suggested.

'Ah, you work for the newspapers!'

'No. Never. Not newspapers at all. Just magazines and books.' I always preferred not to label myself a journalist, although strictly speaking that is what I was. Most people assume that you work in the world of newspapers.

'Oh,' she said, and began leafing through the book again. 'Ah, I have it!' she suddenly exclaimed. 'You fit in the category *profession libérale, activitiés artistiques*. This is how you will be registered with the CFE...'

'The CFE?' I asked.

'The *Centre de Formalités des Entreprises*. This is a department at the local chamber of commerce. They deal with all the administration in registering a business. You will then be issued with a SIREN and a SIRET number by INSEE.' My eyes had already begun to glaze over at the mere mention of the forest of acronyms beloved of the French bureaucracy. This type of officious claptrap left me cold. Madame Routet could see that she had almost lost me as I started to slip into catatonia. 'Monsieur, the SIREN identifies you as a person, while the SIRET identifies your establishment,' she elaborated. It was no good, I was sinking fast. 'INSEE is the *Institut National de la Statistique et des Etudes Economiques*,' she went on. It was sheer torture. I had lost the will to live. 'After that, your details will be forwarded to URSSAF.'

'Please stop,' I murmured in English.

'*Pardon?*'

'Sorry,' I said, snapping from my trance. 'URSSAF is?'

'URSSAF is the *Union de Recouvrement des cotisations de Sécurité Sociale et d'Allocations Familiales*.'

'That's your social security payments,' clarified Stephanie.

'Families in France benefit from *le quotient familial*,' continued the accountant.

'But I'm not a family,' I explained. 'There's just one of me.'

'*Alors*, taxable income is divided into units,' explained Madame Routet. 'A married couple are considered two units and their joint income divided by two. A single person is regarded as one unit and you would be taxed on the whole of your income. You are a single person, *non*?' I thought about that bald pronouncement. It seemed that I was, indeed, a single person once again. The thought saddened me.

I left Stephanie and the accountant to discuss the practicalities of presenting my accounts for calculation and drifted off into a world free of acronyms. Snapped from my reverie, I thanked the lady, and we shook hands and departed for home. In the weeks that followed the submission of my registration form to the authorities, my *boîte à lettres* received more mail than it was accustomed to as official certificates, information circulars and a bewildering array of documents flooded in. Along with them came bills from the dreaded URSSAF, demanding immediate payment of social security payments. Failure to pay on time would result in a hefty fine with little recourse to appeal. It seemed that I had joined the system, for better or for worse. The only light at the end of the tunnel was that the *Carte de Séjour* had been abandoned and our application deemed unnecessary.

Oddly for a man who had transplanted himself into the depths of rural France, the Belgian Patrick Vandevivere abhorred solitude. But he had a master plan. He considered that the area was rife for development. All he needed to do was to work out what to develop. He had an inkling that the demographics in the area were changing, that perhaps newcomers, particularly from England, were no longer just looking for cheap houses to renovate but that they might now want completed properties that were ready to move in to. While he was evolving a means of tapping into this resource, he bought and installed himself in a spacious apartment in Magnac Laval, with a large shop premises below. Since he had parted ways with Sarah, he had needed to move out of her house in Le Mas Mauvis. Persuading bank managers to lend him money, he began to purchase other properties with the intention of converting them to apartments to rent out. As a native Flemish speaker, his command of French was faltering, but his bluff attitude had nevertheless managed to secure him a job with a major real estate franchise. Soon he was regularly playing tennis with work colleagues, had joined a local football club for Sunday matches, and had woven a social life around him populated by a broad collection of acquaintances and friends.

Although Patrick admitted that his previous life as rake, libertine and seducer was over and he was in search of his soulmate, he kept a healthy eye open for members of the opposite sex. Some of his ideas for attracting women were laudable, others laughable.

'Can you drive a speedboat?' he asked me out of the blue on the telephone one day.

'No. Why?'

'Well, I've just had dis speedboat brought over from England. But I don't have a licence.'

'Speedboat, Patrick? *Pourquoi?*'

'I thought we could take it to de lake for water-skiing. Girls are attracted by men which water-ski. Do you water-ski?'

'No.'

'Oh. Well, I don't have a bleeming licence any way...' he sounded disconsolate, his girl-baiting plans thwarted by French bureaucracy.

'But you don't have to actually ski, Patrick,' I suggested. 'Just moor the boat at the jetty, strip down to your shorts, oil your lithe body and pretend to be swabbing the deck. Tall, blonde-haired guy like you: girls will flock around you, I'm sure.'

'You think dat will work?' he sounded a little brighter.

'Perhaps...'

'Actually, Richard, I was thinking of buying a bleeming motorbike as well...'

'I see where you're heading with this. But they're too fast, Patrick. Motorbikes are too fast. By the time the women have clocked you, you've already gone!'

'Oh, I see your point,' he mused, momentarily downhearted. Then his boyish face lit up. 'Well, it would have to be a slow motorbike, then. Perhaps a Harley Davidson. Something you can pose on.'

While my new friend Patrick had embraced his new life in France, I was becoming increasingly disillusioned with mine. During the times I spent with my friends and family I was able to laugh through my considerable sorrow, but when alone in the vast coldness of the *grange*, I felt crushed and alone.

A cruel and savage winter fell upon Limousin and in an attempt to keep warm I bought and installed a second wood burning stove in the *grange* at the opposite end to the original. The sight of licking flames through the window of the stove helped to thaw out my misery only partially, since even with two means of heating the vast room I still struggled to keep comfortably warm. My stock of wood depleted rapidly as the stoves consumed an enormous amount of the fuel. It was difficult in the depths of winter to buy good, seasoned oak for a reasonable price and I was forced to pay for poor quality cherry wood, which burned furiously and rapidly.

A severe cold snap gripped the region, with temperatures falling to minus twenty degrees Celsius. One morning I rose from my chilly bed, reignited the stove, which had been snuffed out during the night, and went to fill the kettle. I turned on the tap. Nothing. I crouched down under the sink and felt the pipes. They were icy to the touch. I tried the bathroom plumbing: the pipes feeding the shower, the washbasin and the WC were similarly frozen and the water in the toilet pan was a block of ice. Further investigations revealed that the entire plumbing system had frozen up, despite being well lagged with insulation. Unable to light the original wood burning stove because its internal water tank was connected to a pair of radiators in the *grenier*, I soon found that my new stove was unable to warm the vast room. The need to keep warm and my pressing work deadlines meant that I and my laptop computer were forced to abandon ship and head for the warmth of my brother's home. Shutting down the plumbing system at the water main, I left the llamas to their own devices and drove away from the hamlet feeling frustrated and angry.

A few days later a thaw set in and the Count and I hurried back to Le Mas Mauvis in time to see water spewing from copper pipes that had been rent in two by the expanding ice within. We made hurried repairs to the plumbing, mopped up the flooding that had ensued, then began the process of trying to restore some warmth to the *grange*. I knew that I was fighting a losing battle. There was no earthly way that my stoves could heat the interior of the *grenier* to a comfortable temperature. Without back-up central heating the enormous cavern would constantly be subject to draughts as the hot air that was produced simply rose to the apex of the roof, cooled and fell. Phill implored me to return to his house to sit out the cold weather, but I was insistent that I would stay at Le Mas Mauvis. Waving goodbye as my brother headed for home, I donned extra clothing and, sitting at my desk wrapped in a duvet, tried to concentrate on my workload. Although the temperature did not fall to its previous low levels, snow began to fall heavily and soon blanketed the fields.

The llamas, despite the availability of a relatively warm stable with a cosy bed of straw, chose instead to lie out in the middle of their field in the deep snow. Even during the frequent blizzards, the animals remained outdoors, their bodies thick with a covering of white. From the windows of the *grange* I watched with fascination how they would lie there until the warmth of their bodies melted the snow beneath them. They would then rise, eat the grass they had exposed, then move to another spot, lie down again and repeat the process.

When the snow had melted, I ventured out to attend to the animals. One morning Jazz and I discovered Talisman sitting in the field with his long neck low. As we approached, the animal remained in his prone state. This was unusual, since llamas will generally stand immediately when approached. I monitored his condition over the next few hours and it became clear that he was ill. He had managed to clamber to his feet, but stood, head bowed, back hunched. The classic signs of a llama suffering. I led him slowly to the corral whereby he immediately fell to his knees, then flattened onto the ground.

The vet came immediately and examined the animal. Talisman was unresponsive, breathing laboured, and his eyes had glazed over. Examining the animal's rear end, the vet shook his head at the sign of an unpleasant discharge. 'This is part of the intestine,' he said.

'What is the cause of this?' I asked, worried.

'I do not know, monsieur. But I would imagine he has eaten a *mauvaise herbe*, a poisonous plant.' Rain began to teem down.

'Should we try to move him into the barn, where he will be out of the rain?' I asked. The vet shook his head.

'No. We cannot risk moving him. He is in great pain. You have straw?' he said. I nodded and pointed to the huge bales in the barn. 'Then take this straw and pack it around the body, to keep the warmth in; leave just the head of the animal exposed. This is all you can do, monsieur.'

While the vet administered several doses of drugs via syringe, I collected armfuls of straw and piled it around and over Talisman's stricken body. The vet wrote out a prescription for other medicines and handed it to me. 'These *médicaments* you must give to this animal three times daily. You must administer it with three litres of water per dose.'

'Three litres of water?' I exclaimed. 'Monsieur, llamas drink very little water. The two animals will not even drink one bucketful between them each day.' Although I had religiously adopted a policy of changing the llamas' drinking water each morning, invariably more or less the same amount would be left the following day. Llamas appeared to take in sufficient water for their needs from the dewy grass alone. How could I possibly entice Talisman to drink such a vast quantity?

'No, all animals must drink more than that,' said the vet starkly. It struck me that this was perhaps the first llama the man had ever had cause to treat. 'This must be done. You will have to force-feed the llama with this mixture. It is vital.'

'What are his chances of survival?' I asked.

'Very slim, monsieur. Very slim.'

That day and the following day I attempted to administer the medicine to the sick animal, by pouring the liquid down his throat from a plastic water bottle. It was extremely distressing, both for me and the animal, for it was necessary for me to sit on the sodden bed of straw with Talisman's heavy head cradled in one arm, as I forced the neck of the bottle into his mouth. Although he would drink a very small quantity, most of the liquid was simply spewed out of his mouth as I poured.

'This is a fucking impossible task,' I cursed to myself. 'Please Talisman, drink. Drink it boy, please…' The llama merely groaned, a low, throaty sound that seemed like an expression of his pain and fear. I knew that this was a pointless exercise.

Thursday appeared ill at ease and spent his time loitering close to his companion. Jazz had assumed the role of Talisman's guardian and seldom left the llama's side either, crouching in the straw alongside the big animal's body and occasionally licking the llama's cold nose and ears. Even Thursday did not attempt to oust the dog, perhaps realising that, after all, he meant no harm and represented no threat to his companion.

On the third day, it was little Jazz who alerted me that the llama's condition had worsened. Sitting with me in the *grange*, he suddenly began to sniff the air and to whimper. He ran to the stairs and looked back at me, encouraging me to follow. We descended and I opened the front door, grabbing my head torch. The dog ran at full pelt towards the corral. I followed. It was a dark, cold night and a steady rain was falling. In the light of the head torch I could see that Talisman had somehow climbed from his straw bed, walked a few paces then had fallen to the damp earth. He lay stretched out on his side, his legs splayed out at odd angles. I climbed through the fence and ran to his side. His breathing was laboured and he wheezed as his abdomen rose and fell fitfully. I sank to my knees on the wet, muddy grass and lifted the llama's head onto my lap. His long tongue was lolling out of the side of his mouth. He groaned.

'Please don't die,' I murmured. 'Please don't die, Talisman.'

Suddenly the wheezing stopped. Talisman's body became motionless. His head became heavy in my arms. Although his big eyes still appeared to be glaring up at me, I knew that the creature could see nothing. Life had expired from his poor body. My own eyes filled with tears and I wept for some time.

The next morning I telephoned the vet to explain that the treatment had not worked and that Talisman had died.

'Ok. We must carry out an autopsy,' announced the vet, rather bluntly. 'It is obligatory on the death of farm animals. First you must telephone the *équarissage*…'

'The *équarissage*?' I said. The word was unfamiliar to me. 'What is that, monsieur?'

'The *chantier d'équarissage*, monsieur,' he elaborated. Then, sensing my lack of understanding, he switched to heavily accented English. 'How do you say eet? Zee knacker's yard, Monsieur Wheels. You must ask zee knacker to collect zee corpse and bring him to me. Zen I will cut open zee carcass and take a look inside… you understand?'

'Yes. I do. *J'ai bien compris*. Thank you.'

The knacker-man arrived later that day in a rattling old truck with slatted sides, through which poked the limbs of various dead animals. The stench of rotting carcasses that was emitted from the vehicle made me want to gag. A man jumped from the cab. He did not offer, so we did not shake hands. His legs were encased in long plastic gaiters like a fisherman's waders. He wore a grubby string vest and the remnants of a hand-rolled cigarette dangled from his lips. Tossing the cigarette butt into the grass, he began to whistle jovially as he lowered the ramp at the back of the truck to reveal a mass of some twenty or more tangled and stinking bodies: sheep, calves, goats, pigs. A pitiful melange of death. Swarms of flies buzzed around the corpses. The knacker-man jumped onto the ramp and clambered over the pile of stiff corpses, returning clutching a long cable with a large hook attached to the end. He unreeled the cable, dragged it into the corral and wound it around Talisman's neck, then locked the hook back onto the cable.

'Llama, heuh?' he muttered. 'Don't get many of these around here…' Still whistling, he moved to the front of the truck and operated the winch motor. With a jerk, Talisman's corpse, stiff with rigormortis, was spun around and dragged towards the open door of the truck. I wanted to look away, for this seemed such an ignominious end for what had been such a proud creature. But I was somehow transfixed on the gory operation, compelled to see my llama friend hauled disrespectfully over the corpses of other farm animals that had suffered similar fates.

'Ça va,' said the knacker-man, slamming the ramp back into place and lighting another roll-up. 'C'est tout, monsieur! Au revoir!' With that, he jumped back into his cab and departed with a screech of tyres on the gravel track. From the other side of the fence in the field that adjoined the corral, Thursday watched, ears cocked forwards, as the truck sped off, carrying his companion away to be cut up and quartered. He emitted a low, mournful *hmmm* as if saying a final goodbye.

Chestnut, staple of the feuillardier

Chapter Twenty-one

Moving on

I've decided to sell up and go,' I repeated into the mouthpiece of the telephone. There was a brief silence on the other end, then Bernard's voice came back at me.

'You 'ave decided to go? But Richard, after so long? After all the work you 'ave done?'

I had telephoned to explain the circumstances regarding Talisman's death and the momentous decision that had been prompted by his demise, that of Uriel, and the parting of the ways between Al and me. Bernard was stunned at my news.

There was an embarrassed silence on the line. How, after all, could anyone offer sympathy on hearing such a tale of woe?

'No. My mind's made up, Bernard. Things are not the same anymore. Two dead llamas. I'm here on my own rattling around in this huge house with five hectares of land I can't maintain… no, I can't do this any more, my friend. I've had enough. I'm beaten.'

'But where will you go?'

'Hmm, good question,' I mused. I had given this much thought over the last few months and had weighed up my options.

'Back to England perhaps?' asked Bernard. I had considered this option, but only briefly. That decision had been easy to make. What would I gain by returning to England with my tail between my legs? My children still refused to see me, or even contact me. I would find it difficult back in the country where memories of a previous life came thick and fast. France was my home now and, while I felt that I could no longer stay on at Le Mas Mauvis, I was still unclear where exactly I would want to move to.

When I had broken the news to my brother, the wise old Count had suggested the option of selling up and buying a smaller place in the same region, with less land and property to maintain. It was a sensible, logical solution to my predicament, but not one I was happy with. I had made a list of the things I wanted out of a home – and out of life – and had come to the conclusion that I hankered after seeing some hills. For all its beauty, the Haute-Vienne was predominantly flat, agricultural land and I yearned to see some more dramatic vistas that might reignite a spark of enthusiasm in me. The climate was a huge factor in my choice of a new location. The last winter had been bitter in Limousin and I simply did not function well in such cold extremes of temperature. By a process of elimination, therefore, I had arrived at what seemed to be a logical step. I should, like a migrating bird, head for a region where the summers promised to be warmer and the winters less severe and perhaps shorter in duration.

'I think I will move down south, perhaps towards the Dordogne.' I revealed.

'The Dordogne?' puzzled Bernard. 'But it's full of the flippin' English! Pubs and fish and chip shops! That's not France!' I had to admit that he had a point. But one reason for considering this more populated region was that there *was* more life there, more chances for a social life that did not mean driving for miles.

'So anyway,' I said to Bernard. 'My reason for phoning is; will you take back Thursday? I'm afraid that my llama rearing days are over, Bernard.'

'Oh Richard, I am so sorry about this! But of course I will take Thursday, if this ees your decision.'

'And one other thing,' I added.

'What?'

'As you're also an *agent immobilier*, will you sell my house for me?'

'But of course, Richard! I will be only too pleased to sell your 'ouse!'

And with this, we agreed that my llama-breeding friend, who had first introduced me to the fascinating world of the *petites camelides*, would come along with his trailer and return Thursday to the herd, while at the same time taking down the details of the property and putting it on the market.

One thought that was clear in my cluttered mind was that I did not want to be on my own for the rest of my life. While I was at ease with my own company in small doses, I yearned for the closeness of another person. But how was a fifty-year-old twice-divorced man expected to go about searching for his *âme soeur*, his soulmate? The enterprising Patrick had some very definite ideas about how we relatively aged men should drag ourselves off the scrap heap. I was not so sure.

'Why don't we go down to Limoges one evening, Richard?' The Belgian had breezily suggested one day, when we had been bemoaning the dismal choices life had tossed us, and quaffing hard spirits in the cavernous *grange*. This mutual whinging had become our wont of late. 'We can check out a few bars and night clubs,' he went on. 'Meet up wit some women... have a bit of fricking fun, isn't it? What do you say about dat?'

'Basically, Patrick, no.'

'Why not, man? My point is, you're never gonna meet dem just by staying here at home feeling sorry for yourself is it? And we both know dis, my friend, dat there isn't any bleeming women locally!' He slugged back his vodka, ice and all, and stared contemplatively into the empty glass.

I was at pains to stress to my wildly over-enthusiastic friend that trawling seedy bars in order to prey upon vulnerable members of the opposite sex had never been a favoured pastime of mine, and nor would it ever be. A misspent youth working as a barman in south London night clubs had soured those noisy, crowded venues for me once and for all. On top of this, in practical terms, my decrepit old hearing did not seem to function successfully in such hubbub. Not only this, but I failed to see the romance in shouting until I was hoarse at some girl I could barely see clearly in the flashing of strobe lights. The life of a barfly had little appeal either, as I am generally quite reserved. I could never imagine an occasion when I would have the balls enough to approach a table of giggling females and come out with the immortal line: '*Bonsoir*, gorgeous. Can I buy you a drink?' Or whatever the equivalent in colloquial French might be.

Clearly, Patrick could not understand my reservations. 'Den you are going to end up to be a bleeming sad, lonely old man, my friend,' he said, rather brutally. I poured him another vodka, resisting the urge to spit surreptitiously into his glass.

The stark reality of the Belgian's pronouncement sank in over the next few weeks, and I began to wonder just how my situation would ever change, unless I became more proactive. Loitering with intent on the sidewalks of the information superhighway one evening I chanced upon a link to an Internet dating agency. How exactly did these things work, anyway, I mused? With one click of the mouse I had entered the site.

'No, silly idea,' I said out loud to no one in particular. Jazz looked up drowsily from his bed and yawned. 'Silly idea...' Click. I entered the sign-up screen. Ten minutes and many mouse clicks later I had, against my better judgement, signed myself up to encounter the hundreds of thousands of eager women who, the agency's blurb assured me, were simply longing to meet me, fall in love and live happily ever after.

After checking the boxes that would highlight the special qualities I sought in a perfect mate, I had written a lengthy set of paragraphs in French, highlighting the main points of my personal profile, which I hoped would reveal my scintillating character and sparkling wit.

Was this true or just utter flannel, I asked myself? Even though I am a writer, I'd never before written anything about my innermost feelings, let alone in French. The French, I was certain, must be absolute crap. But my old spontaneity had crept back in. I'd written far more than I needed too, far more than anybody else's profiles, I noticed. Was I the caring, passionate, honest, gentle, yet determined and supportive individual the first part of my message claimed? Whatever. I was gagging for a drink, that's for sure. I broke away from the computer briefly and fetched a glass of red wine. And the bottle.

'Spontaneous, romantic and demonstrative, with a sparkling wit,' I read. Yes, I considered that was true. I loved to laugh. Fair enough. OK, on with the next section: *'I'm a writer/editor. I've owned a house in France for seven years; have lived here three years.'* Hhmm, yes, that sounds good, I mused. Professional, home-owner. *'I love to stroll in the country, run long distance.'* Fit, in other words. Excellent selling point, I considered. *'I adore fiction with a historical context; movies. Musical tastes are eclectic but I'm passionate about jazz and play saxophone.'* Hah! I was sure I'd come across as cultured, artistic, intelligent. A splendid touch. I quaffed a little more wine.

'I'm an intuitive, adventurous cook. Travel, new cultures, enthrall me.' Brilliant! The picture of a domesticated man who is also adventurous for new challenges. *'I have a hot-air balloon and adore to fly where the wind takes me.'* Very romantic, but does that sound like bragging? Oh, what the hell! I slugged back the glass of wine rather too quickly and poured another.

The *dénouement* pleased me: *'Home renovation, interior design, gardening are my enthusiasms. But it's a hollow place without a soulmate to share it.'* Oh, a wonderful touch to tug the heartstrings, I felt. Homely but lonely. Playing on sympathy maybe?

I slurped another mouthful of wine, feeling somewhat mellow. Now down to who I'm looking for:

'She is affectionate, intimate, considerate, intelligent, committed to a lasting relationship, loves to chat about everything and nothing, to cook together, to play chess while sipping champagne, or to savour the warmth of togetherness.'

Sheer poetry! Another slug of Bordeaux and without thinking any more about what I had just written, click! I had uploaded the profile to the site, along with a fairly recent photograph of myself looking suave and debonair, perched above the capital city of England in the London Eye. Click. It was like a secret chamber being opened at the entry of a password. In no time at all there I was browsing through the profiles of dozens of smiling and available ladies, who had been filtered through the system as potentially matching my criteria.

Click. Click. Click. It was rather like browsing through an estate agent's shop window. In the same way that photographs of houses are skilfully shot in order to present their best features, I suspected that many of the ladies' portraits I viewed concealed certain attributes that might be considered to put off potential suitors. I became quite blasé when reading the profiles, cruelly discounting certain ladies simply because the colour of their eyes or the length of their hair did not fit into the perfect image I had conjured up for myself.

'Blonde? *Non!*' Click. 'Brunette? Ah, better… oh, hair's too short. *Non!*' Click. Here, also, was a veritable feast of physiques to choose from, described by such terms as 'petite', 'average', 'athletic', 'well-padded'. I felt a momentary flush of guilt. This was rather like the cattle market at Magnac Laval, where the rumps of shapely cows were admired by those who appreciated such attributes. Was I really that shallow as to go by looks alone?

'Am I really that shallow?' I said out loud. Jazz sighed. He was used to me talking to myself by then. I considered my own question for a few minutes. 'No, I'm not! Actually, I happen to think that physical attraction is an important first impression of a potential partner. Yes. Definitely.' No one argued with me, least of all the sleepy pooch. At least I was convinced.

'And anyway, I happen to be very attracted to slim brunettes with green eyes. Mind you, I don't think I've ever met one...' I argued the toss with myself for about an hour, as I scoured the profiles, forming a shortlist in my mind. Then I started again at the top of the menu.

All of a sudden an infectious smile leaped from the screen and caught my eye, a delicate, beguilingly impish face framed by a mass of wavy, brunette hair. According to her stance, the lady appeared to be perched on a motorbike and a pair of cool shades concealed her eyes. Click. Her full profile sprang up, a relatively short entry when compared to others I had seen, written in French:

'Bienvenue à la complicité, aux fous rire, au partage, à tolerance et respect d'autrui... Je viens sur ce site pour faire des nouvelles connaissances. Se recontrer pour bavarder, échanger, partager, voilà ce qui serait sympa. Je te souhaite libre, équilibré, vif, à l'écoute...'

I pondered the words. She said nothing of actively searching for a life partner, but nevertheless I read the profile again. I was intrigued. Click. I summoned up other photographs that accompanied the profile: a picture of the young lady standing on a beach looking simply radiant; and another picture of her smiling face caught on camera as she crossed a darkened room in what appeared to be a restaurant.

Click. I had registered my interest in this attractive individual, without really comprehending what that registration would do in practical terms. As usual, my spontaneity had ruled my decision-making process. I continued to browse the lady's details, which were arranged on the system in terms of life goals, ideal partner, personal style. I was increasingly entranced by the image of this person, but it was only when I flicked back to the first page of her profile that I realised that I had overlooked one fairly crucial factor: her location. My eyes lit upon the listing under *Pays*, or country. My jaw dropped and I felt suddenly deflated. *Hongrie*, I read. Not even France, but Hungary.

I thought no more of the matter until the next day I received an email from the dating agency, which revealed that the Hungarian lady in question had apparently also registered her interest in me, virtually at the same time I had selected her. In order to chat with her, however, it would be necessary for me to upgrade my current free membership and pay for the privilege. I tussled with myself for some minutes, then gave up and entered my credit card details. What harm could it do, I asked myself?

The first messages that I exchanged with the young lady, whose name was Ildikó, were structured attempts to determine just how compatible we really were, although of course I was well aware that perhaps our goals were at odds. According to her profile, Ildikó was simply searching for new friends to chat to. We used the dating agency's integral email facility at first but, when this became restrictive because of the word limit imposed, swapped to an instant messaging software that enabled us to 'chat' in real time.

At the outset we seemed to have much in common. Ildikó adored France and the French, having previously worked in Paris for a French company. She had also travelled extensively throughout France. It was a country she was keen to maintain links with, despite the fact that she now resided in Budapest, her birthplace, after three years and a failed marriage in Florida, USA. Ildi, as she liked to be known, spoke and wrote fluent French, and her command of the English language was admirable, although she refused to accept this fact. She had also learnt Russian at school and could still read the language, although professing to have lost the ability to speak it; she also possessed a good grasp of German. We tended to write emails to each other in French, but I preferred to use my mother tongue when conversing on the instant messenger: typing live in a language I was still trying to get to grips with taxed my ability to express myself fully. I was aware, however, that Ildi was constantly writing in a foreign language, since I had not an inkling of Hungarian.

I had been shy to tell the Count that I had been chatting online through a dating agency because it was my considered opinion that he thought me a raving lunatic at the best of times, for my impulsive behaviour. But after a few weeks of chatting to Ildikó, I decided to break the news to him. Over dinner one evening chez lui, I revealed my well-kept secret.

'Good for you,' he said without pause. I was quite taken aback. 'Perhaps you could supply me with the web address of this dating site? I've been thinking of trading in the very-temporary-Mrs. Wiles for some time in any case.' Stephanie clouted the insolent Count across the back of the head.

'That's excellent news, Richard,' said Stephanie, recovering her composure. 'Tell us all about her, then.' So I did. The pair listened intently, smiling and nodding their approval as I ran through Ildikó's list of credentials.

'Ildikó. It's not a French name, though, is it?'

'Not exactly.'

'And where exactly does she live?' asked the Count, raising his wine glass to his lips.

'In Hungary,' I blurted. Phill spluttered into his glass, sending a shower of full-bodied *bordeaux rouge* across the table. Stephanie choked on a mouthful of chicken and dropped her cutlery with a clatter onto the plate.

'Where?'

'Budapest,' I elaborated.

'You're a raving lunatic,' said my brother. 'How on earth will that work? Why can't you find a nice local French girl?'

'I don't know,' I admitted. 'But it's not that far away, really. Only two thousand kilometres. And…'

'And what?'

'I'm going to meet her next weekend.'

Jazz was invited to stay with Phill and Stephanie during my temporary absence in Hungary, so we arrived for dinner the night before. Worryingly, a light scattering of snow had started to fall, and we consulted the Count's digital weather station; as usual the device seemed to be fixated on forecasting sunshine. By late evening the snow was falling heavily. When I arose at five o'clock in the morning, intending to make an early start on the four hundred and fifty kilometre journey to Beauvais-Tillé airport, north-east of Paris, there was at least fifteen centimetres of snow covering the ground and large flakes were still falling. The weather station still depicted a little sun icon.

'So I expect you'll be calling it off,' said the Count, peering into the blizzard from the kitchen window.

'Bugger that!' I replied. 'The roads will be clear, I'm sure. It should take me about five hours to drive to Beauvais, and I've allowed eight hours until I catch the plane.' I loaded up the car with my weekend suitcase, bid a fond goodbye to my brother and sister-in-law, and young Jazz, and headed off gingerly up the lane that led to the main road and to the motorway system beyond.

I clicked on the car radio just in time to hear the tail end of a report announcing that France had awoken to the heaviest snowfall in over thirty years. Even the Mediterranean beaches of the Côte d'Azur were rumoured to have received a dusting of snow, and I was heading north to what promised to be colder climes. I clicked the radio off. Enough of that scaremongering! None of the roads, of course, had been cleared at all and it took me nearly an hour to reach the motorway, a distance of only ten kilometres. There were very few cars on the road, despite this being a Friday morning: most sensible people were still tucked up in their beds, with a good excuse for not being able to get to work.

Once on the motorway, the driving conditions became treacherous. Three lanes had been reduced to a single, slippery track. To make matters worse, the windscreen washer froze, so my screen became constantly grimy, unable to clear the snowflakes that settled on the glass. While common sense niggled at me to turn back, stubbornly I ignored it and persevered with my mission. As I slithered warily past a line of some two hundred trucks that had become marooned in the snow on the motorway's slow lane, I was filled with a determination to succeed. I was not going to let a little flurry of snow stand between me and the route to potential future happiness. What I would find when finally I reached my destination would remain to be seen. I had an open mind. But for now, despite the crushing blows I had received of late – the departure of my wife, the death of my llamas, the floundering of my dream at Le Mas Mauvis – despite the blizzard, I clung to a single grain of optimism. At least now I was moving forward.

Richard Wiles

Bon Courage!

A French renovation in rural Limousin

Bon Courage!
A French renovation in rural Limousin

Richard Wiles

£7.99 Paperback

ISBN: 1 84024 360 0

A dilapidated, rat-infested stone barn set amidst thirteen acres of unkempt pasture and overgrown woodland might not be many people's vision of a potential dream home. But for Englishman Richard and his wife Al, the cavernous, oak-beamed building in a sleepy hamlet in the Limousin region of France is perfect.

'This boo██████████████████ ███████ humorously highlights the obstacles they had to overcome to fulfil their dream'

Country H

'Covers the pitfalls and successes of the ambitious █████

French Pr████ ████

'From the first chapter […] you will be hooked. In turns hilarious, farcical, frustrating and poignant, the writing of the ever-optimistic Richard captures all that is French'

Lucy Watson, The Book Place

www.summersdale.com